Small Business, Big Society

Rupert Hodder

Small Business, Big Society

 Springer

Rupert Hodder
School of Economics and Management
Harbin Institute of Technology Shenzhen
Shenzhen, Guangdong
China

ISBN 978-981-10-8874-2   ISBN 978-981-10-8875-9   (eBook)
https://doi.org/10.1007/978-981-10-8875-9

Library of Congress Control Number: 2018937702

Printed on acid-free paper

This Springer imprint is published by the registered company Springer Nature Singapore Pte Ltd.
part of Springer Nature
The registered company address is: 152 Beach Road, #21-01/04 Gateway East, Singapore 189721,
Singapore

for
苏珊

Preface

A book about how social relationships come to form small businesses and what this means for societies and their development might be thought unusual on two counts. The first is its accent on relationships: meat and drink to the novelist; matters of occasional interest to the academic (especially the historian and the anthropologist); and for each of us the bread and butter of daily life; but not the means to uncover, comprehend, or explain the great shifts and movements across societies that development entails. The second is its emphasis on small businesses and their use as an entrée into the matter of development. After all, development is more generally understood to be about the growing maturity of government and administration, strengthening civil society, and more ambitious infrastructure and health programs, as well as about economic growth. It is about interventions by foreign governments and international organizations (such as the World Bank); the actions of large corporations and the extractive industries; the bargains struck through international trade agreements; investment in manufacturing for export; advances in agriculture and technology; and the impact of global climate change. It is about transforming attitudes to gender. It involves the efforts of international aid organizations, charities, development workers, non-governmental organizations. It is about these and countless other issues. In all of this, small businesses have only a passing influence and only a very modest role in development practice. On both these counts, the reader is quite likely to wonder just how this book might fit into existing discussions on development?

My response is simply that the angle of debate is best determined by the problem at hand. In this case, the problem is a widespread tendency across geography and over time to separate conceptually everyday social relationships from business. This problem, which I take to be a reflection of emotional change, points to an understanding of society in which relationships *themselves* bring regularity and stability. This in turn enables their arrangement (though in a somewhat haphazard way) into patterns of all kinds, including even the largest and most complex commercial, industrial, and modern societies.

In this view, everyday relationships are the stuff of big society whittled into shape through emotion. All organizations, including large bureaucracies, give expression to these changes as I have tried to show in the case of Philippines (Hodder 2014, 2017). Small businesses, though, have a particular role. So often family affairs and, collectively, involving large numbers of people, they reach into every corner of society. The emotional shifts they encourage sweep throughout society as waves, laying the groundwork for subsequent changes in aspects of life—from, say, science and the arts, to government, education, and welfare—in which small businesses might otherwise seem to have no part.

One general implication of these arguments is the possibility of setting aside what are, in the social sciences, often called 'structure' and 'agency'. (Structure, and similar terms like 'structuration' or 'structural functionalism,' describes variations in the strength and direction of influence that practice and phenomena—such as values, norms, representations, meanings, rules, or institutions which are held to constrain and mold practice—have on each other. Agency describes free or less constrained actions which are performed by individuals and introduce a wild card, a degree of uncertainty and change, into structured life. Relationships also introduce a measure of spontaneity because they rarely coincide with structural arrangements. For many writers, organizations are not so different from individuals in that they interpret and modify the rules of the game just as those rules alter and constrain the organization.) My contention is that by focusing on relationships, a way around structure and agency is opened up. The spontaneous ordering of relationships derives from their two central qualities. From the first—and the psychological sleights of hand it occasions—arises firmness, directional alignment, and the drive to cohere. From the second—an indissociable interdependence between mental states and practice—arise unbidden highly effective representations of world, others, and self.

What people say is said and done, and observations of what they do, provide the only access to relationships. But relationships, not the individual, remain the focus. The individual, like structure, society, and culture, is a representation, not a means for explanation. This is not to say that individual or society are in some way residual matters. To the contrary, this emphasis on relationships makes clear that the moral and practical significance of individual and society obtains not from their elevation into corporeal absolutes, but from their treatment *as if* absolute or, in other words, *as if* significant in their own right. Indeed, the reification of individual, society, and structure (and their use in what is now often described as 'virtue signaling') is one illustration of a broad emotional shift (or what I call Puritanism) that is especially prevalent in the West today.

If readers are tempted to see in this discussion a restatement of methodological individualism or the influence of Confucianism or Taoism or some 'eastern' philosophy or 'relationship-based' culture, then I hope to disabuse them of that view and steer them in quite another direction. Having said that, the fact that this book has been written in China (and at a Chinese university established nearly a century ago) has undoubtedly had its effects, though in ways that audiences outside China might find surprising. It is in this connexion that I wish to thank the Harbin Institute of Technology at Shenzhen and most especially Professors Zhang Sumei, Huang Cheng, and Tang Jie for their help and support, for their patience, and for their openness. These qualities, I should add, pervade the university. I do not think that it would occur to anyone here to question interdisciplinary or experimental work or departures from popular trends and expectations. This atmosphere is invaluable and, in China, it is not unusual. But it is extraordinarily delicate. It quickly thins and risks being lost altogether unless protected and cultivated, as universities in England and throughout much of the English-speaking world have discovered over the last forty years.

Shenzhen, China   Rupert Hodder

References

Hodder, R. (2014). Merit versus kinship: A category mistake? The case of the Philippine civil service. *Public Administration and Development, 34*, 370–388.
Hodder, R. (2017). *Emotional Bureaucracy*. Routledge: New York.

Contents

List of Figures

List of Plates

Chapter 1
Introduction

1.1 Questions and Answers

This book started with a question: why are different people in different places and at different times behaving in ways similar enough to allow the groups they form to be called organizations? The question arose from observations of families, friendships, associations, businesses, government, and bureaucracy in the Philippines and China. 'To protect social relationships' is the answer I came to. By this is meant that, to preserve their social quality, relationships are transformed psychologically into 'the organization'.

The answer is straightforward, but at odds with an emphasis on transaction costs found in so many accounts of the origins of the firms. The answer also infers a kind of social monism—that relationships (how people think about, treat, and behave towards each other, self, the wider world, and their place in that world) are the sole substance of society. This runs against swathes of social theory bound to the supposition that structure shapes and reshapes thought and behavior. Clearly, if sense is to be made of that answer—that through a kind of psychological *legerdemain*, relationships are arranged into organizations to protect those relationships' social dimensions—then it needs to be set within a broader understanding of society in which it coheres rather than grates. But what understanding of society might that be?

The most obvious place to look is social theory. This leans heavily towards structural accounts of society, but not always. A continuum might be imagined, one formed in response to an obvious question: how far can anyone rely on their own interpretation of what is happening and why? At one end of that continuum are those who believe that each person depends on that sense of 'me', their 'essential self', to perceive and understand faithfully. Husserl wanted to uncover an individual's inner mental states by "bracketing" more and more of the physical world (and, eventually, even the empirical self) until the pure essence of consciousness was left exposed. At the other end are those who believe that social phenomena are

© Springer Nature Singapore Pte Ltd. 2018
R. Hodder, *Small Business, Big Society*,
https://doi.org/10.1007/978-981-10-8875-9_1

independent of everyone such that there is no need to worry about interpretation at all. To Parsons' (1949, 1951, 1951 [with Shils], 1956), for instance, the individual is merely the product of complex social structures which the very existence of society presumes. Between one end of this continuum and the other are differing shades of opinion on the strength and significance of structure.

Precisely where along that continuum to set up stall is not an easy decision to make. The greater the dependency on 'self', the likelier it is that a study will be thought to teeter on the fringes of serious debate. It will be read 'not [as] an attempt to increase explanation and predictive power', but as a 'personal project for the observer', one that may, at best, help individuals to 'understand themselves ... increasing the depth of their self-knowledge and enabling them to improve the quality of their lives' (Johnson 1992, p. 94). Guelke (1974), on the other hand, argues that order is already present in rational action and only needs to be uncovered. An explanation of rational behavior does not require the investigator to 'impose order on data by inventing theories and laws' (op. cit., p. 193) many of which are in any case 'nothing more than rational explanation sketches of limited applicability' (op. cit., p. 200).

Tension generated by uncertainty over whether individuals make up a larger thing, and puzzlement over the connections between individual and a larger whole, is probably at least as old as written thought. From Aristotle (d.322 BC), Plato (d.347 BC), and Porphyry (fourth century AD) to Abelard (d.1142), Bernard of Clairvaux (d.1153) Aquinas (d.1274), Duns Scotus (d.1308), Ockham (d.1347), and the early Lutherans and Calvinists, writers were kept interested in the links between genus and species, between individual, kind, polity, man, mankind, community, and God. In the seventeenth century, Descartes (d.1650) supposed that the separation of mind (or soul) and body unites individuals. It is through certainty of God's existence that the mind sees the universe clearly and distinctly, and through the pineal gland that the body (which belongs to the mechanical world) is worked by the mind. Spinoza (d.1677) took quite another view: there is only one substance. There is no distinction between mind and matter or creator and created. In his writing also lies the implication that mathematical and mechanical truths, and works of poetry and art, literature and music, though created by individuals, become common property, greater than the individual minds who created them and upon which still greater things are built. The Great Crisis of the seventeenth century, and the Enlightenment which stretched far into the eighteenth century, allowed a secular 'whole' (such as polity, state, economy, society) and its relationships with individuals to replace God as the focus of inquiry. Biological science, too, had moved on, working its influence through ideas about the evolving complexity of mutually dependent parts (structures). To nineteenth century writers, society resembled an organism. Its structures had specific functions. The growth and differentiation of these interdependent parts described society's increasing sophistication. Spencer (d.1903) believed that competition amongst societies drove structural differentiation; and this, in turn, led to changes in the form of cooperation. Spontaneous or individual cooperation (which operates in a market economy) gradually replaces compulsory or militant cooperation (terms which describe how individual wills are constrained and directed by the group and its regulatory agencies). Change in the form of cooperation takes place because it is not possible to coordinate increasingly complex interactions through coercion. Instead, a flexible trading system is required.

In his understanding of social evolution, Durkheim (d.1917) envisaged two kinds of society: a simple, undifferentiated, and segmented entity (described as mechanical solidarity); and a more complex entity (described as organic solidarity). The shift from the former to latter kind is encouraged by growth in the volume and density of population. At the heart of this distinction lies two forms of consciousness. *'The one comprises only states that are personal to each of us, characteristic of us as individuals, while the other comprises states that are common to the whole of society. The former represents only our individual personality, which it constitutes; the latter represents the collective type and ... the society without which it would not exist'* (Durkheim 1984, p. 61). 'Collective representations' emerge from groups, take on an autonomous existence, and hold together segmented societies. Organic societies are held together largely by the practical demands which attend the sharpening division of labor, and by justifications for their domination by individual consciousness. As the various fissures deepen, and individuals become isolated, society is characterized by anomie—a condition of moral de-regulation.

Structural views of society and social change are also characteristic of those who studied non-western societies. Firth (1951) had few doubts about the connection between culture and structure. Culture, he believed, was socially acquired behavior. It formed the content of structure, and structure described: *'the set of relationships which make for firmness of expectation, for validation of past experience in terms of similar experiences in the future. Members of society look for a reliable guide to action, and the structure of society gives them this—through its family and kinship system, class relations, occupational distribution, and so on'* (p. 40). Change is described by social organization, by which he meant 'getting things done by planned action' or 'the systematic ordering of social relations by acts of choice and decision' (Firth, op. cit. p. 36 and p. 40). Put another way, social organization is 'variations from what has happened in similar circumstances in the past' (ibid.). Structure, then, sets the precedent and provides a range of alternative possibilities, while in social organization 'is to be found the variation or change principle—by allowing evaluations of situation and the entry of individual choice' (ibid.).

Twenty years earlier, Radcliffe-Brown (1930) had reached a similar view of structure. Stable society comprises networks of social relationships which necessarily form cohesive and integrated patterns, each part which is dependent upon every other. Change is understood as the process of integration and disintegration. When this involves the disappearance of simple and narrow systems of integration (comprising only hundreds or a few thousands of people) and the emergence of more complex and wider systems (comprising millions of people), then social evolution is said to have taken place. But change is not always effective; nor, even if successful, does evolution necessarily avoid the problems that attend disintegration and ineffective re-integration. An insufficiently integrated society (a society in a state of dysnomia) suffers from moral unrest—a condition which manifests itself through, say, neuroses, revolutionary political movements, new religious sects (characterized by emotionalism and hysteria), forms of criminality, and increases in the rate of suicide.

For the Wilsons (1945), too, the movement of society from full integration—or, to use Radcliffe-Brown's term, a state of eunomia—to one of disequilibrium, produces circumstances in which people become unsure of their responses. Each person now begins to act in their own way, such that their behavior is, from the point of view of every other person, illegal, illogical, or unconventional: this is the root of social change.

By 1952 Radcliffe-Brown (who, in his previous writings, had often seemed to equate culture with structure) had come to view culture as little more than an abstraction, while the networks of social relationships—or structure—which connected human beings remained the center of the social anthropologists' interests. Leach (1954), who shared these doubts about culture, was also uncertain about the reality of structure. He preferred to understand social systems as a model of reality, a model that *'represents in effect the anthropologist's hypothesis about "how the social system works". The different parts of the model system therefore necessarily form a coherent whole—it is a system in equilibrium. But this does not imply that the social reality forms a coherent whole; on the contrary, the reality system is full of inconsistencies; and it is precisely these inconsistencies which can provide us with an understanding of social change ... Every individual of a society, each in his own interest, endeavors to exploit the situation as he perceives it and in so doing the collectivity of individuals alters the structures of society itself* (p. 8).

Foucault (d.1984), meanwhile, declared that power through its apparatus (such as intellectual debate, scientific reason, or legal statutes) turns human beings into 'individuals' and assigns them a place in society. If a way can be found to escape that apparatus, then the individual can extract some happiness from life; but, for the most part, the individual is both the effect of power and its vehicle (Foucault 1980, p. 46).

For Bourdieu (1980, 1990) as well, structures guide and constrain individuals, and determine their access to different forms of social capital (such as mastery of cultural practices or formal qualifications). Individuals have some room to choose, but only about which form of control they eventually submit to. They are inured to their place in structure through *habitus—'principles which generate and organize practices and representations that can be objectively adapted ... without presupposing a conscious aim at ends ... Objectively "regulated" and "regular" without being in anyway the product of obedience to rules, they can be collectively orchestrated without being the product of the organized act of a conductor'* (Bourdieu 1980, p. 53).

Derrida (1976, 1978), on the other hand, throws the burden of explanation on to a dialectic between narcissistic individuals and 'discourses'. Discourses are, for Derrida, structure. Texts constitute the social world in a very real way. But texts mean only what people want them to mean: all is interpretation. Change, while partly about chance and contingency, is mainly about 'me': individuals have the authority to undermine, to overturn, or simply to ignore whatever they want in the world around them.

Structures for Giddens exist in rather different forms in different places and at different times. The role of the individual also varies with time and place. For instance, structure is to be found deep inside the preconscious mind; or in 'external' influences stabilized as taken-for-granted phenomena (at least in pre-modern societies) (1984, p. 174); while in modern societies there exist opportunities for individuals to exert some control through reflexivity—the incorporation of ideas about social life into social action such that those ideas now begin to influence practice and transform social life.

The emphasis on structure in these debates, and the unfavorable light in which theory-less studies are often cast, is understandable. The creativity which a dialectic between the individual and structure allows is one reason. Another is the sense that scholarship is a collective effort. It is not to 'self', but to what has been established and largely agreed upon collectively that one must look and build upon. This is the only way that idiosyncrasies can be ironed out, cul-de-sacs avoided, and something approaching objective knowledge and objective explanation revealed. Perhaps, then, it is inevitable that pockets of thought in which 'self' is given more room will, sooner or later, yield to structural analysis. Husserl might be the phenomenologists' figurehead, but they prefer to look outside themselves and into the social world. Schutz (1932), for example, rather than cycle down into consciousness, was determined: to examine how subjects build up typical constructs—types—of things (objects and knowledge) and people; and to build a second-order model of that world so that he might understand how real people might act in the real world. In this task, he argued, sociologists must identify, separate and examine representations scientifically. Berger and Luckman (1966) went even further: representations are not only open to scientific scrutiny, but also possess their own independent and objective quality. In other words, representations are real structures.

This understanding was to all intents and purposes taken up social psychologists: representations are by definition 'social'. To Moscovici they are systems of values, ideas and practices with two functions: to establish consensual order among phenomena, and to provide a code for social exchange and so enable communication among members of a community. They exist, argued Duveen and Lloyd (1993), prior to the individual: they are internalized by individuals and used as a framework through which they may interpret the world and place themselves within a community. They are produced socially: that is, they are produced collectively and remain the property of groups. The belief that individual thought exists in isolation and that the individual can be considered as the basic unit of analysis is, therefore, entirely misconceived.

Even Weber (1997) gives way to doubt and impenetrable structures. To him, social phenomena *can* be reduced to the behavior of individual human beings, and that social world (for whom the proper subject of study was the social action of one or more individuals) *cannot* be analyzed with methods and concepts applicable to the natural world. Rational bureaucracy is, in its ideal form, both technically superior over any other kind of organization (Weber, op. cit., p. 214), and the most highly developed means of power (Weber, op. cit., p. 232). These qualities, Weber believed, owe much to a type of rational action described as instrumental or end-rational. This refers to an interest in means, rather than in the given ends or wants to which those means are directed. In contrast, value-rational action refers to the primacy of an interest and belief in values for their own sake rather than how they may be lived out. Both these types of rational action are contrasted with less rational or irrational types of motivated action—'affectual' action (motivated by sentiment or emotion) and 'traditional' action (motivated by unreflective habit). Understood in this way, rational bureaucracy possesses other important and related features. First, it separates the bureaucrats' private life from their official life. Secondly, the bureaucracy, as it develops, becomes increasingly mechanistic and depersonalized. Business is discharged according to calculable rules and without regard to persons. And the more it is dehumanized—and the more completely it succeeds in eliminating from official business 'love, hatred, and all purely personal, irrational, and emotional elements which escape calculation'—the closer it moves towards perfection (Weber, op. cit., p. 216). Thirdly, the bureaucracy is based upon the leveling of economic and social differences, and, once established, works to level those differences still further. Indeed, bureaucracy inevitably accompanies mass democracy. 'This results from the characteristic principle of democracy: the abstract regularity of the execution of authority which is the result of the demand for "equality before the law" in the personal and functional sense—hence, of the horror of "privilege" and the principled rejection of doing business "from case to case"' (Weber, op. cit., p. 224). Fourthly, the bureaucracy takes on a permanent character. It is 'the means of carrying "community action" over into rationally ordered "societal action"'[1] which, if methodically ordered and led, 'is superior to every resistance of "mass" or even of "communal action". And once the bureau-cratization of administration has been completely carried through, a form of power relation is established that is practically unshatterable' (Weber, op. cit., p. 228). Rational bureaucracy, then, destroys those structures of domination (such as patrimonialism and patriarchy) which have no rational characteristics (Weber, op. cit., p. 244). Its march is relentless: the individual bureaucrat 'cannot squirm out of the apparatus in which he is harnessed … the professional bureaucrat is chained to his activity by his entire material and ideal existence. In the great majority of cases, he is only a single cog in an ever-moving mechanism which prescribes to him as essentially fixed route …' (Weber, op. cit., p. 228). As the bureaucracy expands, as the fate of the masses is made dependent upon it and—as all are ushered into the machine—creativity, honor, charisma and the individual are eroded; and humanity is condemned to a dull, repetitive existence.

Symbolic interactionism also eschews a ready acceptance of structure. Practice bears the load: from practice emerge meanings and 'self' and complex and unstable situations, beneath which lie generic social patterns and processes. Subsequently,

---

[1]'Society', 'association' and 'community' correspond clearly with types of action—the rationally expedient (instrumental), 'affective' (the affectual or emotional) and traditional (or habitual).

however, the cultural and structural qualities of practice were brought to the fore, primarily in reaction to criticism that this school of thought was too concerned with instances and with the here and now. Perinbanayagam (1985, p. 58) makes the case for this *volte-face* (if that is what it is). Practice, he wrote, reflects the deep structures of the mind *and* has its own independent significance. *"The structures of languages ... are viewed as features shared, wholly or partly by a community, that enable humans to create ongoing communicative relationships. These shared structures allow actors to take the role of the other insofar as the other articulates signifying acts that are subject to the logic of the structures and equally allow the other to take the role of the self insofar as he is able to articulate gestures arranged in the same logic. Such a structural logic may be founded on language itself, but when translated into other instruments of communication (nonverbal items) they too become ways in which interactions and selves are created and sustained. In this way, by interpreting the gestures around us according to a discipline and articulating our gestures according to the same discipline, it is possible to acquire, if not the "knowledge of other minds" (Malcolm 1966), at least what it is that the "other mind" wants us to take to be in his mind at the moment and to proceed to the next step ... One does not really have to know all that is in the other mind, only enough to be able to respond to the other mind and continue lines of action ... or initiate lines of action that will continue into at least the immediate future. The structures submit communication to a discipline and enable interactions, relationships, and social organizations to emerge and be sustained. Hence one must concede that interactions are not only symbolic but also structural..."*. Structures of the mind and the structure of practice reflect one another.

Very similar criticisms are also levelled at idealism. Foisting the burden of explanation onto an interpretation of other people's understandings of the world, no matter how rigorous the method, is too personal, too dependent upon imagination and intuition, and leaves behind only a collection of case studies. Even according to its own terms there is no need to search for commonalities or for a general understanding of human behavior and society. There is nothing going on which needs a generalized explanation. Perhaps it is for this reason more than any other that, despite Guelke's robust defense, idealism does not exercise greater influence; and that Cooley's vision of individual and society as one and the same (and which is often thought to give too much weight to the individual) is marked out as 'eccentric'.

One further pocket of thought which deserves mention centers its efforts on the question of human universals. Human nature, it is argued, comprises universal features that have an important bearing on society and its explanation. One feature is knowledge—a knowledge of the world as it is (Bloch 1977). People deal with the world as they find it and will do so in ways that are necessarily similar. People must eat; but culture influences diet, preparation, cooking, and the kinds of implements used. The origins of these features are human biology, evolution, and the diffusion of ideas and practice. Biology encompasses the idea of a cognitive niche—a mental world which, though rooted in and physically dependent upon brain and body, operates free of biological, genetic, and evolutionary pressures and determinants.

Here again, though, however important these ideas they may be, they often receive more attention and are given far more credibility outside social theory than within it. This is because they are seen to be deterministic and challenge the view human nature is socially constructed if, indeed, it exists at all.

Within social theory, then, there are accounts that seem to be entirely compatible with the notion of a society comprising social relationships and *only* social relationships. Leach's uncertainty over the reality of culture and structure; a willingness on the part of some anthropologists to align structure and relationships; the social psychologists' vision of the individual as an idea; the symbolic interactionists' contention that self originates in practice; and the idealists' determination to comprehend actors' understanding of their world: all seem to 'fit' with the notion of a monistic society. Yet these accounts often turn out to be fastened either to structural and cultural visions of society, or to an atomistic and individualistic one. A further example of some interest is Homans' (1950) argument that the organization is initiated, at least in part, by a desire to mitigate isolation. The suggestion is predicated on the belief that social phenomena are the product of rational choices which individuals make about costs and benefits (or rewards); and that, in turn, these choices derive from covering laws revealed through behavioral psychology. Though influential, this vision of society, criticized as reductionist, later gave way to Blau's structural version of rational choice.

Much the same can be said of development studies. Here, too, are found accounts of social phenomena that seem at ease with the idea of a society comprising relationships only. Informality, for instance, is not necessarily inimical to organizations and economies and may even help to explain why they are highly effective; relationships described as patronage can be entirely sympathetic to democracy and business organization; marketplaces can be understood as streams of people and things. And yet so often these accounts are fixed in two dominant themes both of which are heavily dependent on structural understandings of society. One theme is that development *is* westernization: raising income levels requires not just technical changes in the production and marketing of goods and services, but also social and cultural changes, such that developing societies follow a very similar path and become very much like the developed west. The other is that developing societies are essentially different and must either find their own path (and even reject development as it is usually understood today) or suffer exploitation and accept the imposition of the West's values and cultural mores.

Both themes, and variations on them, are intertwined, each seeming to eclipse the other at different times and places. Immediately after the Second World War the goal of development was to raise incomes through modernization. Developed societies, it was believed, are distinguished by their economic, social, cultural and political modernity, which contrasts markedly with traditional values in developing societies. Here, markets and government have social foundations; effective contracts and economic transactions depend on trust; profit and capital are cultural notions; and the economic sphere is not separate from social life: all were reason enough to school populations in values and behavior conducive to development.

By the end of the 1960s, modernization gave way to 'dependency' which became *de rigeuer* during the 1970s. This new movement was centered in Marxist theory and in the fact that large swathes of the developing world had long been part of European empires. These territories (the periphery) and their peoples, minerals, and agriculture had been—and, even after independence, continued to be—exploited by the metropolitan centers of America and Europe (the core). Dependency theory, then, focusses not on the process of development but on the origins of underdevelopment, and on the apparently endless ambition of the West to develop the world in its own image (Corbridge 1995: 8).

At the same time, 'alternative' and 'bottom-up' approaches emerged, strongly colored by dependency and socialist thought. Self-reliance and self-sufficiency—favored by Gandhi's *swadeshi* movement even before the Great War, and by Mao in the 1950s—reappeared along with an emphasis on local industry, local production, and local employment. Only by avoiding unequal exchange with the first world can ordinary people hope to raise their incomes and better themselves materially. A concomitant of these beliefs is a very different set of priorities: what really matters is not economic growth but poverty alleviation and a willingness to satisfy a people's basic needs—needs defined by whatever it was that enabled them to fulfill their potential (Sen 1983; Seers 1969; Streeten and Burki 1978)

Thinking on development changed again in the 1980s, this time in favor of a new liberalism. Its outlook was very like one that had evolved more than a decade earlier amongst multinationals as they shaped themselves into 'global corporations'. In thinking and as far as possible in practice their intention was to eliminate 'the domestic-international dichotomy and pay no more attention to national boundaries than the reality of time and place require ... no single national market draws greater interest or attention than its contribution to overall corporate objectives dictate ...' (Schollhammer 1971, p. 349).

The terms neo-liberal and globalization were soon interchangeable. Development is about taking part in global flows of capital, goods, services, and labor. There is a debate to be had about national governments and the role they could or should play in managing these flows and distributing the wealth they generated (see, for instance, Wade 1990; Siddiqui 2016; Krugman 1987; Siwach 2016; Sachs and Warner 1995). To some writers, the market is anarchic; to others, the state is the primary force driving the political and economic fortunes of a country; to still others, state intervention, though necessary, can and does encroach on basic liberties. There is also need for discussion about how corporations handle their responsibilities to society. Business is not all bad and not just about profit and the interests of shareholders; governments and civil society are compelled neither to treat corporations as immoral nor to behave as though poverty and disadvantage are the consequence of hegemonic power (Blowfield 2005; Hoogvelt 2001).

The western arc of the Pacific Rim—East and Southeast Asia—brought grist to the mill. In the 1980s, Hong Kong, Taiwan, South Korea, Singapore, and Japan were often seized on as evidence of what the free market can achieve; China, Vietnam and North Korea showed what happened under the 'dead hand' of government. By the end of the decade those same countries, with the one exception of

North Korea, were being used either as examples of what thoughtful and pragmatic action and planning by the state was capable of; or as evidence for those who turned modernization on its head in the belief that Asian values (primarily Confucianism), not Western values, determined economic success.

Marxist criticism of neo-liberalism did not vanish; but it did weaken, especially as China and Vietnam opened up and turned to the market, and as confidence and delight in Asian values grew. Taking up the slack was a generalized feeling that America and Europe (and more especially political and business elites in the West) were manipulating and controlling world events, pushing their agendas, and imposing their model of 'what should be' on the rest of humanity. In reaction to this growing sameness, the vernacular, localness, tradition, and historical experience, were championed. The non-western is intrinsically and unremittingly different and its development should follow its own path at its own pace, measured against its own criteria. A diverse collection of 'new' approaches soon made their mark, centering attention on grassroots movements, NGOs, gender, democracy, justice, citizenship, the environment, and local relationships. There was a shift away from large-scale theory to midsize or small-scale analyses—to the local within the general development process. Again, the accent fell on 'basic needs', 'development from below', and 'empowerment of the poor'—on people and their participation (see, for instance, Chambers 1983, 1997, 2004). And somewhat in sympathy with these efforts was New Growth Theory, which homed in on endogenous rather than exogenous growth. It supplied a theoretical framework for analyzing growth determined by the system governing production rather than by the forces outside that system. It restored the role of government policy in promoting long-run growth and development (Todaro 1997: 93).

The very idea that development is desirable also came under fire: development studies and its theory were regarded as irrelevant. These new revolutionaries included environmentalists; those from the left who, as they witnessed the ineffectiveness of dependency theory, lost faith in socialism and communism; those who, drawing on Said and Foucault, believe that development is a notion based on all sorts of colonizing ambitions; and those who oppose what they take to be the ethnocentrism of white, Anglo-Saxon culture (Crush 1993, 1995. See also Blaikie 2000; Tucker 1997). If development means anything then it is change; and change can be for better or worse. 'Good' development might be understood subjectively as economic growth, national progress, and modernization, and involves the provision of basic needs and better governance. But equally this might be thought of as 'bad' in that it creates and widens inequalities, harms local cultures and values, engrains poverty and dreadful working and living conditions, ruin the environment, violates democracy and human rights, and embroils whole populations in a dependent and subordinate process. In this relativity Herath (2009) sees hope: after years of evolution, development theory can now supply 'the tools to understand development in a more context- and culture-sensitive way' and, in this sense, has matured.

1.2 Approach and Argument

There is no ready-made understanding of a monistic society in which 'organization' describes the protection of social relationships through their psychological transformation into 'something else'. And so, questions remain: what does big society look like, and how is that account realized?

The answer, I contend, begins with a willingness to accept that writers have no choice but to interpret. The course of action left open is, in principle, uncomplicated: to interpret in the light of their preliminary ideas, but to do so without assuming the presence of independent forces such as structure or culture, or economics or history. Once stripped of these assumptions, a writer is required: to find out as much as possible about how actors see the world and how they behave; to portray that world as faithfully as possible; and to interpret it as one in which phenomena such as structure or culture or self are ideas that exert an influence only in so far as they are drawn into practice.

The aim of the approach taken here, then, is to reach explanation through an economy of ontology. It is to work outwards from initial observations and explanation of behavior in small businesses; to explore the broader implications of those ideas for development; and to sketch an understanding of society in which those ideas make sense—an understanding that sets aside, but keeps in mind, social theories' emphasis on structure, culture, or agency.

The next eleven chapters follows this sequence only partially. For reasons that I will to come shortly, narratives of small businesses are left until the latter part of the book, while the ideas which arose from initial observations of those businesses are formulated into an account of the 'play', or basic logic, of relationships. This formulation is set out in Chap. 2 and in other places and drawn together in Chap. 12 . I argue that relationships occupy an inexact state. The actions, sounds, and symbols which are interpreted as expressions of relationships only have meaning when set within a mental context. That is to say, relationships do not exist in the 'outside' world. But that mental context—and so ideas of self, you, they, and us, and about how people think about and treat each other and the wider world—is derived from and sustained by constant interactions with that outside world. Indeed, that mental context exists and coheres only in so far as those interactions are being performed.

Emotion plays a vital role in these interactions. Emotion is what is experienced when the mind reaches a conclusion that is suggested by patterns of interactions but is not explicitly confirmed. Only in this way can the mind be sure that it is connected to the outside world and to a community of other minds. In seeking out these experiences, the mind is driven toward an affective state—a state in which relationships and the natural world are treated *as if* significant and important in themselves. This makes it both possible and necessary to transform relationships *psychologically* into what are taken by actors to be 'non-social' phenomena. This in turn enables the patterning of those relationships as the organization and as collections of organizations. It is this involvement in organizational life which eventually alters emotional dispositions again, further modulating the qualities of organizations and their arrangement.

An appreciation of this logic or play is broadened over the next five chapters through its use to strain debates central to the notion of development. In this way, an understanding of how big societies emerge and evolve is pieced together. Chapter 3 concentrates on the idea of informality—a quality that is widely thought to characterize less developed countries. In its everyday, colloquial usage, informality conveys well enough the sense of the particular, the unconventional, and the inimitable. When it is said that "John is very informal in his dress and behavior" it is recognized that John does not always follow the expectations and rules of the wider community; that he may be somewhat wayward, idiosyncratic, unpredictable, unsystematic, and perhaps even a little unreliable. But when informality is used to describe John and his friends and their generation, then its meaning is far less clear. Their behavior might, to some, appear informal and Bohemian and yet, within their set, it is collectively agreed upon, regular, fairly predictable, even conventional. This is one problem with 'informality': there is no functional distinction between the informal and formal; it is quite possible for the informal to regularize and bring predictability to practice. The chapter goes on to argue that this is so because there is no difference in substance between the informal and formal: the latter describes a psychological distancing of social relationships. Put another way, it is not what is done (practice) that matters so much, but the emotional coloring of what is done.

The question which must then be asked is why, in developed countries, does practice seem to be so predictable and systematic in comparison to life in the developing world? Chapter 4 argues that the West, most especially since the 1970s, has been going through a period of emotional change in which relationships (and ideas and practice more generally) are treated more as absolutes. Growing intolerance and inflexibility, masked by instrumentalism and corruption, have strengthened undercurrents of instability in both north and south. This social view of 'formal' society and its economy also reveals that the market, wherever and whenever it is found, is inherently destructive. Growth over the long term is nothing more than an inadvertent and frequently unacknowledged effect of attempts to avoid the fallout that the market would otherwise yield.

This line of argument raises still further questions. If today's modern, developed societies do not rest on formal structure and process and have only become more Puritanical, a quality that is destabilizing, then how do big societies come to be? How do they hold together? And how do they industrialize? These questions are considered in Chaps. 5 and 6.

Examined through the emerging understanding of big society, the debate on state origins throws up several matters of some interest. One is the Weberian quality frequently assigned to bureaucracy whose presence defines the early state. Another is the emphasis given to war and violence. A third is the relatively weak accent placed on mobility and trade as explanations for the appearance of settlements and states. In dealing with these matters, an understanding of state origins is returned that has relevance to commercialization and industrialization. It suggests that patronage, at first, works (if only gently and when populations densities are low) to encourage human populations to move. Over the long-term, however, patronage brings increasing pressure to bear on leaders both to dispense materials and services in return for compliance, and to attract still more followers whose number serve as an index of status and whose labor provides the wherewithal to secure yet more followers. This pressure to acquire ever-increasing numbers of followers: acts as a drag on the movement of groups; increases the density of population; stimulates both trade and the gradual domestication of crops, livestock, and people; requires the introduction of democratic elements to reduce tension and conflict; and prompts more complex organization. Emotional change is wrought by, and facilitates, evermore compact living and sophisticated organization. These events are reflected in more substantial architectures for shelter and living and settlement. At first, mobile populations establish way stations to victual so aid their movements along migratory circuits. These stations are occupied for short periods by transient populations who gradually attract peripatetic, nascent artisans (from cultivators to tool-makers). As the logic of patronage is worked through, the population swells and the frequencies of these visits increase. Only as human groups multiply, as each grows, and as their traffic intensifies, is the continuous occupation of these places by the *same* people and the arrangement of settlements into hierarchies more likely. 'Settlements' and state, then, are better understood, in their earliest forms, as relay stations in the movements of human populations. And in their evolution, emotional change is critical.

Additional grounds for a social interpretation for business organizations and the rise of the market are proposed in Chap. 6: neither Weberian qualities nor a market economy are features peculiar to Europe since the nineteenth or eighteenth centuries; and uncertainty over the distinction commonly made between 'social', 'economic' and 'organizational' spheres. The organization, I argue, describes changes in the emotional content of social relationships, such that social and openly affective relationships are protected even as commercial and technical objectives are pursued. (Consequently, the organization may appear to harden or soften—to the extent that seemingly it either turns into an impersonal entity or melts back into society and seems to disappear altogether—as the emotional states of actors change). These emotional changes also help shape the wider patterning and density of populations which in turn have a bearing on industrialization. Sharp geographical circumscription accentuates changes in emotion and the patterning of relationships as organization and market, and so makes industrialization possible. It becomes highly likely where there are sufficient densities and numbers of people, and where there is relative ease and speed of movements amongst population centers. Industrialization is not 'inevitable' in the presence of these circumstances; but since the general movement towards these circumstances *is* 'built in' to relationships, then given the appearance of these circumstances on enough occasions, industrialization *is* inexorable.

Chapter 7 considers the broad patterning of relationships in both China and the Philippines. These patterns—such as factionalism, commercialization, oligarchies, and financialization—which describe China and the Philippines (or any other big society) are an expression of the working through of everyday relationships. These patterns or contexts are not explanatory. Constraints and opportunities exist as *particular* instances of relationships, not as the indentations and convexities of structural or cultural templates able to imprint themselves on all and sundry.

How relationships are 'worked through' and shaped in the case of small businesses is described over the last four chapters. This material is drawn from a large number of interviews—around two hundred—conducted over many years in the Philippines and China. Often these were held more as conversations, sometimes with people I have known for a good many years. Verbatim transcripts, written in the original language with English translations, allow me to quote extensively. I use only selections of this material, not all of it (this would have meant a very different book), enough to illustrate the wider points being made. The interviews were necessarily very personal at times, but I do not think identities are compromised; and it will do no harm to say that the majority of the interviews used here were held in Project 7 (Manila) and Davao City in the Philippines and Nanshan (Shenzhen) in China.

The resulting narratives are placed in the latter part of the book simply because the details of what are otherwise common and garden relationships give up their true importance more easily once their implications for big society have been brought out. It is not big society that explains what goes on in small businesses, but what goes on in small businesses that explains big society.

Chapter 8 describes how relationships, often through a kind of happenstance, reveal new dimensions that lend themselves to business. Even a desire to salve emotional trauma may stimulate the creation of the business, as Chap. 9 illustrates. Chapter 10 examines how the business organization is put together through a more deliberate and sometimes explicit 'distancing' of relationships. Chapter 11 illustrates further how the relationships from which the business is shaped drift in and out people's lives, indistinguishable from any other aspect of the everyday. The logic of relationships must be uncovered, recognized, and worked at over and over again before there is any prospect of success.

The final *Conclusion* (Chap. 12) brings together a number of these arguments into an idealized account of the logic of relationships and the evolution of big societies. It also considers what this account means for both 'development' and the social sciences more generally.

Part I
Creating Society

Chapter 2
Emotion, Organization, and Society

2.1 Introduction

Observations of behavior in small businesses in the Philippines and China threw up the same two questions time after time. Why, even in very different contexts, do people unwittingly come together as organizations in remarkably similar ways? And why do they lean toward collective action? The reply to this last question might appear obvious: to concentrate and coordinate efforts to defend, to cultivate, to irrigate, to build, to govern, to administer, to barter, to eat and to drink, as well as to trade and to reduce costs, amongst many other reasons. But why lean towards *collective* action? Why *that* response? Why not circumvent or ignore problems that require such complex behavior? This chapter argues that a desire to protect relationships underlies a willingness to confront problems with collective action; and that the similarities in this response are also seated in the qualities of relationships.

2.2 Relationships

Relationships describe representations of how "you," "I," "we" and "they" feel about, think about, and behave towards each other. Although referred to separately, 'representations', 'practice', and 'emotion' as aspects of mind are to all intents and purposes fused together.

Representation is a term laden with meanings. Amongst these is "*intentionality*"—a conceptualization or construct of a thing or, more accurately, the direction of mental states at something which may exist or which may only be imagined but which, in either case, informs actions. In other words, a representation is a mental state encompassing ideas, objects, beliefs, imaginings, desires, and emotions. To understand the world is to understand it first as it is perceived and those perceptions acted upon. This "take" treats a "mental state" as more than a picture or map or

© Springer Nature Singapore Pte Ltd. 2018
R. Hodder, *Small Business, Big Society*,
https://doi.org/10.1007/978-981-10-8875-9_2

structure and, as such, it is closer the usage of the term "representation" in these pages. Here, representations are held to be states of mind about things—whether objects, practice, natural processes, or other representations. They may be reasonably accurate and provide a serviceable description of reality, or they may be inaccurate or entirely imagined. Either way they inform subsequent practice and the subsequent interpretation of practice. As a state of mind, a representation is necessarily *experienced* and, therefore, cannot exist independently of mind. Representations, then, are not artifacts to be picked over and examined scientifically. Written words (such as those now being read), conversations, sounds, movements and pictures do not constitute a recording or facsimile of a state of mind, let alone a representation. Rather, they prompt other people to form particular states of mind and, for the most part achieve this reasonably effectively. As states of mind, representations are also dimensional—that is, they have multiple meanings and implications.

Practice is informed by representations. Practice also encourages particular states of mind. This is achieved either by design or as a consequence of attempts to set up, avoid, take advantage of and close down constraints and opportunities through actions that are tangible and powerful especially if repeated, made routine and executed with physical force. It is also realized entirely unintentionally. Representations—including those of 'self', 'others', 'world' and 'self in world'—emerge, and are sustained, only through constant interaction with other people and with the natural world. Consequently, they color all subsequent interactions upon which the stimulus and development of all representations depend. Relationships, then, are not so much a category of representation and practice as they are an aspect of all representations and practice. In this view, the social world comprises strings of practice and representation—of dimensional events, meanings and understandings such that each practice or representation simultaneously forms points on many intersecting strings.

No distinction is made between actors' and scholars' representations (including those of structure, self, and others): they are necessarily treated equally. This shifts the focus of interest and analysis to what might be called the surface features of the social world—features which are to be understood in their own terms (that is, with reference to the strings from which they are shaped) rather than with reference to "deep" or overarching structures, though the possibility that strings of representation and practice may reflect such forces is left open.

Each mental context (or mind) emerges from interactions with other minds and the natural world. The revised self which is constantly emerging is constantly being re-integrated back into these understandings of others and world and informs subsequent practice. Each context, then, is in its details unique, for none of this can be repeated or replicated precisely. Thus it is only through trial and error that collections of different selves can arrive at a rough working agreement on the world and the place of others and each self in that world—an agreement aligned sufficiently enough that the group can coordinate practice. The consequence is that were it possible to see the patterns from afar, they would be extremely fuzzy and fragile, no matter how sharp and clear the world might otherwise appear.

This concoction is also extraordinarily sticky. Relationships, mental contexts, representations and practices and their multiple dimensions are so closely inter-dependent that altering one aspect is likely to change other aspects in ways unexpected and unpredictable. It is too sticky for, say, Mead's pre-existing society to imprint a given pattern onto one actor after the other, and too sticky to be shaped and planned to suit the will of any individual or collective. The constraints and opportunities which actors come up against, then, comprise particular instances—specific patterns of relationships that are neither clearly defined, nor entirely stable or predictable, nor large in scale. As for emotion, this is understood as a quality that representations take on, rather than as a collection of feelings.

2.3 Emotion

Attempts at the scientific and systematic analysis of emotion stretch back to the last quarter of the nineteenth century. Over a similar period the place of emotion in the organization has attracted occasional glances. In the last thirty years or so, literature on this matter has proliferated and more nuanced and more positive views of its role in the organization have emerged. Yet there remains little consensus either on what emotion is or on its significance, and few integrated theories of emotion in the organization have been offered, perhaps because there is also little accord on whether or not such theory is needed. If any general agreement is to be found in these discussions, it is that emotion can have a constructive role in the organization as well as damage or destroy it.

Amongst the great range of questions with which the study of emotion in organizations has been concerned, four matters stand out.

(a) The first—*the nature and mechanisms of emotion*—is derived largely from discussions in psychology (where it is a classic topic) and in neuroscience (where it is of growing interest). Do physiological responses amount to emo-tion, or does emotion trigger those responses? Are the meanings of physio-logical sensations pre-programmed or innate, or do actors search for external cues to interpret those sensations? Is emotion different from cognition? Does emotion follow specific pathways in the body (and brain) and, if so, do these differ from those for cognition?

Numerous accounts of emotion have been formulated to deal with these questions. Many overlap to some extent though, for the sake of convenience, they may be separated into three groups. The first understands emotions as social constructions or representations. These representations are arrived at by communities and used by actors to interpret their bodily sensations. Often a different meaning can be given to the same or to a very similar collection of sensations. Emotions, then, are publicly created.

The second group understands emotions—or at least some of them (see Jarymowicz and Imbir 2015)—to be innate and discrete and to describe functions critical to survival (Fridja 1986; Levenson 2011). These hard-wired (rather than, as Darwin believed, habitual) emotions are labeled 'basic' and together form a special class of mental phenomena. As such, they 'have a central organizing mechanism, and have the capacity to influence behavior, thought, and other fundamental processes' (Levenson op. cit., p. 1). There are, Levenson believes, six basic emotions—enjoyment, anger, disgust, fear, surprise, and sadness. Three other candidates for possible inclusion in this class are relief, contentment, interest, and love.

A third group of accounts places emotions somewhere between the innate (biologically structured) and representational, though precisely where is open to a deal of interpretation and debate. Schachter and Singer (1962)—drawing on James (1894), Lange (1922), Cannon (1929), and Maranon (1924)—argue that in order to explain their physiological state, actors will look to their social context. At the same time, the structural and chemical root of emotion is recognized: introduce a pharmacological block and actors will be less likely to respond emotionally regardless of the social context (Schachter and Wheeler 1962).

The view that emotion is partially determined biologically, and partially representational, suggests that it is not easily separated from cognition if at all. Certainly, more recent studies point very strongly towards emotion as an elaborate, coordinated, and extremely rapid integration of information from many areas of brain as well as the body. Any simple relationship (or correlation) between emotion, parts of the brain, body and its genetic material is becoming more elusive as more discoveries are made (see Lang 1994). One can reasonably argue, write Bevilacqua and Goldman (2011), that the task of disentangling genes, complex neural circuitries, endocrine systems, and environment may not be possible (p. 405). Others maintain that cognition and emotions *have* to be intimately entangled (Damansio 1994. See also Easterbrook 1959). The speed and complexity of decisions and consequent actions is such that they cannot take place unless precursors (emotions) are first laid out in advance (much like runway lights in the dark) to guide or lead thought.

In his study of emotions and its relationship to music, Budd (1985) treats all this implicitly as a distinct possibility. Emotions are a class, but a heterogeneous one whose membership is far from clear (p. 14). Emotions are experienced with greater or lesser intensity; they have no clear location in the body; an emotion does not have to be made manifest but when it is, the same emotion can show itself in many different ways; emotions may be unfounded; they can be judged as desirable or undesirable; they are often mixed; and they have no clear boundaries. Emotion is simply a thought or belief experienced with pleasure or pain and, adds Scruton (1971), involves desire.

(b) A second—*the stimuli believed to prompt emotion, and the effects of emotion on behavior*—has a direct bearing on the organization's performance, efficacy, and ability to learn and change and, consequently, has attracted much interest (See, for instance, Vince 2004; Isen and Baron 1991; Rafaeli and Vilnai-Yavetz

2004; Brief and Weiss 2002). Stimuli may be short-lived or enduring and stable, and include: prior emotional experiences (Stanley 2010); physical features (such as temperature, noise, colors, smell, symbols, layout, and architecture); and interactions with other people (especially with superiors) inside the organization and outside it (especially family). On the whole, there has been a shift: from the view that emotion should be kept out of the organization altogether; to the belief that more productive and creative workers are happier (Hersey 1932) and emotionally expressive (Lofy 1998); to an emphasis on context, for the demands of certain tasks—such as critical evaluation or negotiation (Overbeck et al. 2010)—do not always favor a positive mood.

(c) A third—*the communication of emotion*, how it is read, and the question of its authenticity—is also directly relevant to the matter of an organization's performance. Whether through words, facial expressions, smell, vocal tone, body language, mood, touch, or physical distance, communication is commonly understood today as an evolutionary response necessary for social living. Emotion conveys information about actors' reactions to their social and physical surroundings. It evokes responses, rewarding some and punishing others, and so works to keep groups together. For instance, anger can persuade others to modify their behavior, and gratitude encourages cooperation (Morris and Keltner 2000). One issue of particular interest is the link between a given emotion's social function and the channels (verbal and nonverbal) for its transmission (App et al. 2011). Another is whether or not emotions and their expression must be spontaneous or whether they can be communicated deliberately? Ekman (1972) argues that if expression (and emotion) is not immediate and automatic, then it is not emotion. The general run of the literature, however, appears to lean towards the view that the need to convey intentions and to appeal to an audience is fed into spontaneous feelings and their expression (Elfenbein op. cit.)

(d) A fourth—*the regulation and manipulation of emotion and its stimuli, meanings, experience, and communication*—is also of considerable interest, again because it has a direct bearing on the efficacy of the organization and its management (Maroney and Gross 2014; Krause 2012; Zapf and Holz 2006; Hulsheger and Schewe 2011; Callahan 2002; Gross 2001; Fineman 1996; Fridja 1988; Rafaeli and Sutton 1987). Regulation would appear to pre-empt any conclusion on authenticity. Indeed, there is a case to be made that any kind of regulation demands that emotion is staged and manipulated. Actors suppress, neutralize, or prescribe emotions. They re-arrange their own social and physical surroundings in order to avoid emotion or to control its stimuli more effectively. They buffer or compartmentalize it so that emotion takes on no visible expression. They normalize emotion by dissipating or re-framing it; by adapting to it (through repeated exposure); or by standardizing it through rituals (Ashforth and Kreiner 2002). And they devise organizational structures to order and re-route it.

Clearly, the study of emotion in organizations draws readily from many different fields. But there are other areas of interest that do not receive quite the attention they probably deserve. The relevance of some is not always immediately apparent. These include: theatre studies; interactions amongst place, emotion, and homeland; training in teaching and caring; and historical analyses of emotion, often as part of broader social history (see, for instance, Nicholson 2013; Pile 2010; Anderson and Harrison 2006; Gao 2002). Others could not be more directly relevant. This includes most notably emotion in family businesses —a matter which is given surprisingly little coverage in the study of organizations (Rafaeli 2013). A related matter is whether or not groups feel. 'While we tend to think of emotions as "belonging" to individuals … it is not just individuals who 'feel' … the family not only brings emotion to the family firm, but also "gets" emotion from the family firm' (Rafaeli op. cit., p. 297). Actors' emotions shape what they say and do, and shape the behavior, thought, and emotions of others. These emotions 'cycle' through organizations, amongst organizations, and between organizations and wider society (Hareli and Rafaeli 2008).

Profusion and Cohesion

There is, then, a profusion of ideas on emotion in organizations, but there have been few attempts to structure these themes and debates into distinctive approaches let alone theoretical models. One approach is to construe the debate on emotion in organizations as an expression of the arrangement of power. Domaglaski (1999), for instance, views the relative lack of interest in emotions as an indication of an 'emphasis on rationality and more deliberate modes of performance in organizations' (p. 833). In her view, emotion is, or should be, socially constituted and negotiated. The false division between emotion and rationality—and the association of these qualities with women and men respectively, and with those less able and more able to absorb stress and retain judgment—is symptomatic of a desire to control and maintain status.

Another approach (Elfenbein op. cit.) is to think of emotion as a process comprising a number of stages. The first is the registration or appraisal of stimuli. Sensory organs must be oriented to take in stimuli, and sense then has to be made of them. Actors do so partly through five hard-wired emotions (appraisal, achievement, deterrence, withdrawal and antagonism). But whilst automatically coded, there meaning is also 'deeply contextualized. Being hit by a ball could be an attempted injury, clumsiness or an invitation to play' (p. 323). Rules about how an actor in that context *might* feel have to be applied. The second stage in the process is the experience. That is, actors enter a 'feeling state'. This comprises physiological and psychological arousal. The two are not easily separated. Physiological sensations are interpreted, and these interpretations may in turn produce further physiological responses. Moreover, prior emotional experiences may also have a bearing on interpretation. The third stage is expression. Up to this point, the process has been entirely private. But now, physical cues to internal states find expression according to display rules. This is one of the most powerful forms of social influence (p. 330). During each of these three stages the emotion process is regulated. This regulation is frequently described as emotional labor, and has become increasingly important in organizations because of the rise of the service economy (p. 340).

One further approach, developed by Rosenwein (2002), is critical of emotion as an individual attribute and emphasizes complexity. She argues that historians have tended to treat emotion as 'great liquids within each person, heaving and frothing, eager to be let out' (p. 834), turning all experience in Europe before the eighteenth century into the 'directness and absoluteness of the pleasure and pain of child-life' (Huizinga 1924, p. 9, cited in Rosenwein op. cit. p. 823). True, there were some writers who did not adhere to this 'hydraulic' model; but they were concerned with the actions of those few people with legal and royal power. To all intents and purposes the emotional history of the West was one of gradual restraint and rationality preceded by a cold, calculating, loveless and violent existence stretching back over the millennia. All this was despite the appearance of non-hydraulic (that is to say, cognitive and constructionist) models of emotion of the 1960s and 1970s. Late though it is, Rosenwein argues, the emotional history of the West has to be revised. The unit of analysis should be emotional communities: these are similar to social communities (such as families, neighborhoods, guild and monastery), but the aim of research is to uncover systems of feelings: the feelings and behavior that communities judge to be helpful or harmful; their evaluations about each other; the nature of their affective bonds; and the accepted modes of expression (Rosenwein op. cit., p. 842). Cast in this light, emotion during Europe's long development is now exceedingly complex, without clear form, and opaque to any single grand narrative or explanation.

2.4 Emotion as Organization: A Model

It is plain that discussion on emotion in organizations has long-since moved on from stark, mechanistic visions of the Weberian kind. Emotion has an important, even central, role in effective organizations, though exactly what emotion is, and what role it plays, remains wide open to debate. Nevertheless, it is probably fair to say that a good deal of effort centers on the extent to which emotion is a biological mechanism or representation, a private or public phenomenon, and open to manipulation and useful to the organization; and on how it is coded and read.

This book points discussion along a slightly different path. This is so in a number of respects. It holds, first, that emotion is non-representational (as well as representational and physiological) in that it describes how representations and physical sensations are treated. Secondly, that emotion constitutes the organization. Emotion's defense requires a conceptual distinction around which the organization is built. Thirdly, that emotion is public and easily transmissible precisely because actors cannot achieve and experience it for themselves unless the cues and conditions which allow this to happen are arrived at communally. And, fourthly, that actors quickly become alienated when emotion is either manipulated or idealized.

More expressly, emotion describes the emergence of an irreducible conclusion for which there exists a choice to treat it *as if* significant in its own right. Emotion is necessarily public; and its communication is dependent upon a capacity to evoke rather than to declare. These qualities signal to the mind that it is intimately connected with other minds. Without emotion, mind becomes alienated and is gripped by anxiety. Emotion thus encourages actors to cooperate. And while the further intensification and expansion of cooperation fosters alienation as the nascent organizations begins to form, actors then defend their emotional states by creating a *conceptually* distinct affective sphere. This happens to enable more effective cooperation and the construction of a *conceptually* distinct 'organization'. I go on to raise the possibility that both organization and emotion co-evolved from primal biological mechanisms into a kind of cognitive niche.

Emotion Is Non-representational and Irreducible

Emotion, I suggest, refers in part to a general state of mind or mental context described here as affective—that is, a state of mind in which matters contemplated are treated *as if* significant in their own right. In part, also, emotion refers to that moment when mind becomes aware of a conclusion at which it has arrived at by itself; and at which it arrived because that conclusion is in itself entirely reasonable. In other words, it is a conclusion which—as far as mind is concerned, and irrespective of whatever other explanations might be formulated and proffered (through, say, the application of natural selection or neuroscience)—is irreducible. Thus the mind is, say, fearful because—and *only* because—it is reasonable in the circumstances that it should be. Take, for instance, a man who comes face to face with James' bear in a forest. Given the qualities of the man and the bear, and given the circumstances which brought them together, it is entirely reasonable that the man should be afraid and that he should be afraid on this and on no other account. He is afraid not because he believes the bear will attack him, cause him pain, and end his life (though he may have this belief); nor is his fear a side-effect of his body's instinctive response—its release of chemical and electrical impulses to quicken his breathing and heart beat and to re-direct the flow of blood (though all this may be happening). He is afraid because when all qualities (his and the bear's), circumstances (bringing man and bear together), and explanations (likely pain and extinction) have been razed, it is entirely reasonable that he should be afraid. It is the moment of his awareness of that conclusion which gives depth to his experience. Put another way, the realization that (for him, here and now) there can only be fear, is the point from which all else follows and gives intense depth to explanation (likely pain and extinction) and sensation (racing heart, quickening breath, and the coldness of his sweat).

This understanding of emotion—as the point at which an irreducible conclusion is arrived at and treated *as if* significant in itself—holds implications for a number of questions asked, and assertions made, about emotion. Two are of particular significance.

Emotion Is Freely Chosen

First, is emotion feigned still emotion? Perhaps the most helpful answer is that the premise of the question is misleading, for it assumes that emotion is either true or not true. Yet, as just indicated, it is how a particular mental event (*reaching* an irreducible conclusion for oneself) is treated that imbues it with the quality of being an 'emotion'. The event *becomes* an emotion when it is treated *as if* significant in its own right. If, for whatever ends, actors are being pushed, cajoled, and persuaded into a position in which they *ought* to have certain emotions; or if an actor is merely behaving in a way that mimics an emotion; then, in these instances, emotion is presented as a fact—as something that is worn as one might wear an item of clothing. The converse of this—that emotion should not be manipulated or feigned because it is sacrosanct and must remain genuine if it is to retain its quality and meaning—leads to the same conclusion: that emotion is an item that can be grasped and, in this case, revered. In each instance, whether revered or manipulated, the event is treated as an absolute and set apart from actors. Yet the one single quality that *makes* emotion, and makes it so inscrutable, is that it is *experienced*. If an event is emotional, then there exists the condition that it is treated *as if* absolute—*as if* it is important and significant in its own right. This cannot be an absolute condition, for if it were then emotion would be turned once again into an objective phenomenon. The condition is voluntary: there exists the *choice* to treat an event *as if*[1] it is important in its own right.

Emotion Is Public and Easily Transmissible

Secondly, does emotion remain a private experience until it is communicated through facial expressions and other means (Elfenbein op. cit.)? Clearly, one person's heart beating faster is not another person's heart beating faster; the desire of one person to get away from some terror is not the desire of another person. Yet is it possible for these to be anything other than *public* experiences? 'This' actor might be able to comprehend in a detached and intellectual way, or simulate, the meaning of angry, happy, sad, or fearful; but 'this' actor cannot appreciate what 'that' actor feels in a state of anger, happiness, sadness or fear unless 'this' actor has also shared that state. And for each to know whether or not they have shared it, both have to be able to communicate that state with one another. The effective communication of emotional states is necessarily indirect. Since emotion is experienced and not an object that can be handed about, it cannot merely be reported. Communication is realised by establishing cues—behavioral, linguistic, and symbolic (including art,

---

[1]'As if' is therefore far more than just a technique for normalizing (see Ashforth and Kreiner 2002), and therefore regulating, emotion.

music, dance, and literature)—with reference to which an audience can arrive at the state intended by an actor. Rather than simply report anger or love, a context must be established by an actor which allows the audience to reach for *itself* the conclusion intended and, in *reaching* that conclusion, experience the emotion intended. Emotion, then, cannot be communicated directly *because* it is an experience. I can know that I have the same experience as other people only if they can establish the conditions in which I can experience it for myself; and this, I now know, cannot but be confirmation of an experience that is public. If I am told by others that what I am experiencing is happiness, there can be only doubt. If they establish the conditions in which I can for myself reach the conclusion that I am happy and so experience happiness, I can have no doubt that I am sharing in a public experience. For this same reason (that it can be communicated only indirectly), emotion is easily transmissible: conditions are always being created quite unintentionally which spark emotion in others.

Alienation and Anxiety

Any irreducible conclusion or representation takes on the quality of emotion when actors reach it for themselves when in an affective state of mind. By the same token, any representation and sensation—even those usually associated with emotion-which are merely reported or realized in a non-affective state of mind will seem either distant, peripheral, indistinct, and numb; or overwhelmingly physical and absolute and thus little different from physiological reflexes such as thirst, hunger and pain.

This sense of ennui and physicality is a foretaste of what is to come if alienation is not relieved. My contention here is that self (a construction or representation) is dependent upon constant—and if it is indeed constant then, at some level, cooperative—interactions with the social and natural worlds. Starved of this, the self begins to unravel, and the result is a psychological state of anxiety, sometimes preceded by ennui, flatness, and sluggishness. If not eased the actor reaches a point at which anxiety becomes so intensely physiological that it reignites—in a way that cannot be ignored—memories of an affective state of mind in which experiences possessed color, dimension, vitality, and immediacy. This drives actors in one of two directions. One (ultimately doomed to failure) is attempt to establish their own entirely self-centered world in which thought and emotions are absolute, and to draw into it other people who must either accept that world or be excluded from it entirely. The other is to re-engage with the community once again.

Anxiety's role in pushing (in what can almost be a physical sense) the mind back towards an affective state derives in part from its place at the heart of constructions of self. López-Ibor and López-Ibor (2010) believe that the very word 'anxiety' derives from an ancient linguistic interjection which may originate in a universal human experience—the restriction of air flow through the throat and, ultimately, the struggle to take those first breaths at the start of life. The state of anxiety, and the word itself, is linked thus to sensations of choking, pressure on the chest, and breathlessness [Kierkegaard (1957), it should also be noted, argues that actors are prone to anxiety once they become aware of the *choice* to breathe or not to breathe]. And it is alleviated eventually by sharing the sensation and finding some kind of logical explanation for it. It might be inferred that as actors withdraw from the public creation of meaning, they regress to a point at which they can interpret physical sensations as well as thoughts *only* in the light of that earliest and most basic experience and, consequently, are inundated by their own everyday sensations.

Anxiety's significance also derives from the relative ease with which the constant interaction needed to maintain the construction of self is disrupted by either physical or social isolation. Without sharing, without taking part in, the public creation of meanings for thoughts and sensations, and without public confirmation, actors will be unsure of what is experienced by others and of what their own thoughts and sensations mean. Sharing and communicating emotion is by no means given. Not all actors will have experienced a particular emotion or a particular intensity of emotion. Not all are necessarily able at all times to establish or register those cues effectively. If, for whatever reason, actors cannot understand or cannot be understood, then alienation begins to deepen.

Emotion, Anxiety, and the Organization

It is for these same reasons—its place in constructions of self, and the ease with which it is induced—that anxiety is important to understanding the origins and changing qualities of organizations. Whatever practical solutions it offers, and even if these solutions are uppermost in their minds, actors turn to cooperative behavior (and to organization) for basic psycho-physiological reasons: to sustain interactions, maintain constructions of self, and stave off alienation. However, the subsequent development of the organization in both scale and complexity has quite the opposite effect. The instrumentalism and authoritarianism compelled by attempts to strengthen and focus a corporate body, interrupts the dependency of 'self' on community and its members' interactions and, in doing so, engenders alienation.

In mitigation of this effect, relationships with people outside the organization are treated by actors *as if* absolute or, in other words, *as if* important in their own right (This implies a choice to treat relationships in this way and, therefore, recognition that the choice is not always made). As a corollary, the organization and its rules, procedures, roles and practices are similarly treated *as if* absolute, masking the manipulation of relationships from which the organization is in fact engineered.

As the unintended practical benefits (increasing stability and flexibility) brought to organizations by this conceptual distancing accrue, explicitly social relationships and greater compassion may be admitted into the organization. Over the longer term, however, as actors become inured to the distancing of relationships, both the technical quality of the organization *and* the social quality of relationships outside the organization are increasingly reified (The organization and its processes as treated as absolute and social relationships are idealized; and in this there is understood to be no choice).

Under these conditions, the repression of alienation and anxiety builds. In response, actors begin to carve out pockets of illicit activity where room is given to instrumentalism, imperfection, selfishness, experimentation, and more affective relationships. If these outlets are blocked, then more generalized corruption and violence is likely to erupt, returning actors to a state in which instrumentalism and authoritarianism is prevalent, and so to conditions in which the affect is more likely to be re-asserted more generally.

These shifts from affective to puritanical, instrumental, and authoritarian states are neither inevitable nor mutually exclusive, but they are *mutually dependent.* Effective organizations (in that they are more stable, humanitarian, flexible and creative) most likely to be found during periods of liminality: that is, *amongst* conditions of settled affect (which risks drifting into Puritanism), Puritanism, disorder, instrumentalism, and authoritarianism. It is here—on the cusp of each of these conditions—that an affective state is at its most vibrant and its meaning most intense.

2.5   Conclusions: Emotion and Organizations

Three conditions under which thought takes on the quality of being emotion have been proposed. First, that the process of reaching or arriving remains a matter of choice; second, that the *experience* of reaching or arriving is treated *as if* significant and important in its own right; and, third, that it is a *public* experience. Without these conditions, actors retreat into a state of alienation, numbness, and anxiety. Understood in these terms, emotion is strongly and necessarily bound up with the development of corporate bodies from the family and the lineage to Weberian-style organizations. This is so in a number of respects.

(a) Emotion favors cooperation and the evolution of organizations partly because it signals that mind is integrated into a community of other minds; for only when emotion is experienced is there certainty that the mind is *of* community. Emotion also supplies the motivation to defend relationships when cooperation is scaled up, and when manipulation, compulsion and alienation set in. To protect their relationships with one another, actors distance the nascent organization conceptually from a social (and emotionally-laden) sphere. This is done by masking or re-presenting the highly instrumental and often authoritarian relationships from which 'the organization' is formed as its process, procedures, role and routines. This conceptual dichotomy—once it has become a well-established and generally accepted world-view—is soon transformed conceptually into a 'fact'.

(b) The organization is a means for the dissemination of emotion. This is so in a number of senses. First, its existence and operation demands changes in its participants' states of mind and practices. For instance, the emergence of a fairly coherent and effective organization presupposes an affective state of mind. Secondly, changes in states of minds amongst the organization's members will have a bearing on people outside the organization. Thus, members who have become increasingly Puritanical are likely to encourage changes of some kind in their families and friends. Thirdly, the mere presence of an organization is also likely to influence even those people who have no contact with the organization or its members. This is because they may build the organization into their representations of their world. For instance, a government organization characterized by highly instrumental behavior, instability and uncertainty might readily be incorporated into representations of a corrupt and untrustworthy government. And fourth is the need for actors to adjust their states of mind and representations such that they can coordinate their practices with each other more effectively. This might enable them to synchronize with one another cleanly enough to form a surge powerful enough to produce observable and large-scale effects. Thus, a Puritanical and conformist organization which has, say, a pivotal role in government may foster similar states of mind and practices in other parts of government.

(c) Emotion has an influence well beyond the horizon of any corporation or collection of corporations. I am invoking here not some kind of action-at-a-distance, but the necessarily complex manner and the direct and apparently unrelated ways in which emotion is communicated. The details of the technical representations of organizations, of self in the organization, and of organization in society, are always being rubbed together for practical effect and their details and original intentions easily lost. Emotional states help prepare the ground in which similar kinds of organizations are likely to emerge even if those blueprints are lost. For example, an affective atmosphere is more likely to encourage more stable and flexible organizations. Emotion, then, provides behavior with the grain to align itself.

Chapter 3
Informality

3.1 Introduction

One repercussion of the argument that the organization describes the protection of social relationships is to turn the informal-formal debate inside-out: it is not the social quality of the developing world but the apparently unsocial nature of the developed world that requires explanation and a solution. Another is to render patronage—the hall mark of informality—a central principle in the patterning of big societies.

3.2 Meanings

'Informality' came into common usage in development studies in the early 1970s, not quite twenty years after Europe and its industrialized offshoots began see economic development as a global problem for a global society (Worsley 1978). As a loose, everyday description, informality is uncomplicated. It refers to any facet of life from housing and politics to education and health. When attached to private economic activities, informality marks a discrete sector that is quite the opposite of 'organized' (one of 'formality's' equally various nomenclatures). 'Bazaar', 'lower sector', 'barter', 'emerging exchange economy', 'traditional', 'small-scale', 'trade', 'hidden', 'unofficial', 'non-market', 'black', and 'underground': all these, and other terms (such as 'community practice') carry its meaning. It describes work that is irregular, unregulated, illegal, and untaxed; employment in unstable and small (often family) groups, usually without pension or health or other benefits; behavior that is personal, familiar, spontaneous, off-the-books, and outside established routines and practice; and a wider context in which capital and advanced technology are scarce and labor is used intensively. Measures of the extent of informality in the developing world also vary but are striking. About 50% of employment and 30–40%

© Springer Nature Singapore Pte Ltd. 2018
R. Hodder, *Small Business, Big Society*,
https://doi.org/10.1007/978-981-10-8875-9_3

of all economic activities are thought to be informal. Figures are higher for some activities and in some regions. A good proportion (60–70%) of manufacturing across the developing world is said to be informal. In Latin America, about half of the salaried workforce is informal, while figures for the urban workforce alone range from 30–70%. Proportions of the labor force in informal employment rise to 72% in sub-Saharan Africa and to 65% in Asia (See Galiani and Weinschelbaum 2012; Maloney 2004; Moreno-Monroy 2012; Funder and Marani 2015).

With these attempts to define informality and to establish a reasonably distinct and tangible phenomenon for analysis, collections of features which are necessarily recurring and predictable are required. These features are numerous, but they allow discrete accounts of 'informality' to emerge. Of these, four are especially influential.

The **first** is informality as a barrier to progress. It delineates a detached sector producing different (and inferior) products with different (and inferior) labor and with little capital (see, for instance, La Porta and Shleifer 2014). Enterprises are inefficient and poorly managed, have low employment growth rates, seldom evolve into formal organizations, and see formality as a menace (ibid.). Thus, informality closes down opportunities, suppresses motivation, discourages freedom and creativity, inhibits and distorts communication; and—as markets expand, the division of labor deepens, and the number, scale and complexity of transactions increase—it becomes less cost effective (Balogh 1966; Bardhan 2002; Bauer and Yamey 1963; Olson 1982; Sobel 2002). The only remedy is economic development. The informal will only wither as more competitive, effective, and formal organizations replace it. In government and its bureaucracies, too, the presence of informality is thought widely to be symptomatic of features such as patrimonialism, clientelism, sultanism, and bossism. Personalistic and self-centered actors and special interest groups working for their own advantage (and at the expense of the wider citizenry) ignore the rules and processes of organizations and succeed only in producing a state which—even if democratic in name—is unstable, fragile, weak, captured, corruptible, inadequate, and unconvincing. The only solution is to engineer a clean, transparent, and formal government.

A **second** account portrays informality as a useful stopgap where capital is scarce and unskilled labor is abundant. Informal traders establish new outlets and new inlets; create new wants and new markets; store up capital; build up new infrastructure; and encourage subsistence producers to turn out new goods and buy in new wares (Bauer 1991). These channels and nascent organizations are often based on the extended family—'a social institution which has many advantages in one stage of economic development' (Bauer and Yamey 1963, p. 64). As informal traders and producers work to integrate and commercialize rural and urban economies, so they also 'train' for entry into the formal sector. The notion that it is a sink for disadvantaged workers who cannot make it in the formal sector is a caricature. Informal workers are no less rational and no less capable of deciding whether, to what extent, in what ways, and for how long it is in their interests to remain in that sector or to participate in the formal one. Indeed, the informal sector, writes Maloney (2004, p. 1159), can be understood as the 'unregulated, developing country analogue of the voluntary entrepreneurial small-firm sector found in advanced economies'.

Informality may also benefit political and bureaucratic organizations, and it may do so even if it is equated with corruption. This is because it opens up opportunities; invigorates and motivates; encourages freedom and creativity; and facilitates the communication of ideas, information and decisions. And it does so at little financial cost (Bayley 1966; Klitgaard 1991; Leff 1964; McMullan 1961; Nye 1967). There may be a thin line (Haggard 2000; Jomo 2000) between the collusive relations of the strong state and those of the captured state but, in East and Southeast Asia at least, strong bureaucracies, intimately embedded in wider society through informal relationships, are commonly thought to be crucial to any understanding of the general processes of economic development (Evans 1989, 1995; Weiss 2000; Wade 1990). De Soto (1989) goes a little further. Informality lies between the formal (which describes a largely hostile, oppressive and exploitative bureaucracy) and activities which are immoral as well as criminal. Informality may be illegal from the bureaucracy's perspective but it does not offend moral conventions; it comprises the initiative, creativity and entrepreneurial drive of ordinary people; and it is the key to survival (see also De Soto 2000).

A **third** places informality in even the most formalized societies. Defined as unwritten codes of behavior and conventions which underlie formal rules (see North 2004)—and easily stretched to cover 'social capital' and, therefore, 'social networks', 'values', 'norms' and 'trust' (see, for example, Bourdieu 1990, 1980; Fukuyama 1999; Granovetter 1985; Putnam 1995, 2000)—informality helps to explain in what ways and to what extent societies diverge. Institutions, believes North, are any form of constraint that humans devise to guide and shape their interactions, reduce uncertainties, and bring structure to everyday life. Like institutions, organizations (such as political, economic, social and educational bodies) structure and regularize practice; but they are consequences of the institutional framework. There are, North (2004) believes (p. 4), perfect analogies to be drawn between institutions and the rules that define the game, and between organizations and the teams which play the game. In short, institutions determine the opportunities in society; while organizations are created to take advantage of these opportunities. Change emerges from the interaction of institutions and organizations. As organizations evolve to deal with the game, they alter the underlying institutional framework. Institutions can be formal (as in the case of rules) or informal (as in the case of social conventions). Informal institutions give way to formal ones as systems of exchange become more complex and transaction costs rise. A key theme in development in the Global South, then, is to work out how rules and regulation governing, say, urban housing and land use are best formulated, understood, and implemented (Chiodelli and Moroni 2014).

The notion that informality and formality are best understood as a dualism rather than as a dichotomy is a common one. For instance, Marlow, Taylor and Thompson (2010) agree with much of the literature—formality strengthens with the size and complexity of organizations. In smaller organizations idiosyncrasy and prerogative have their place, encouraging commitment, quick decisions, and a willingness to solve problems collectively. Even within large, bureaucratic organizations degrees of informality are essential for labor processes to operate effectively. But there must be change. Authority must be re-distributed and associated interactions and procedures will have to evolve. The question is how such changes are handled. Informality and formality may be different but they are co-dependent.

Hart (2009), too, views informality as part of dialectic—one between the people (informality) and bureaucracy (formality). Certainly, informality creates problems (such as criminality, corruption, and patronage); but it is also important, even essential, within formal bureaucracy (which would otherwise grind to a halt) and outside it (where informality can often be equated with freedom, creativity, flexibility and horizontal relationships). The trick, believes Hart, is to enable a constructive partnership to emerge between formal bureaucracy (which is necessary for large-scale coordination and regulation) and informality. Such a partnership, however, has been stymied and its significance obscured time and again, by long and damaging swings between centralized state control and excessive liberalization. Fears of unemployment in Third World slums, and concerns about political instability, were projected onto informality. When those fears proved to be unfounded, informality became synonymous with 'bootstrap' development (an idea which Hart (1973: 89) treated with caution). When neo-liberalism swept across the world, capitalism itself was 'informalized' and given free rein. Informal economies in the Third World were ruined through competition, whole states collapsed to become entirely informal, and the scope of informal activities expanded hugely, such that the term became almost meaningless. And now—with economic crisis and a swing back towards state bureaucracy, standardization, and regulation—informality is suffering once again.

It is self-evident from these accounts - despite terms such as unregulated, unwritten, social, unconventional, corrupt, criminal and patronage - that informality refers to behavior that is patterned, regularized, predictable and structured. When understood as a barrier to progress, 'informal' enterprises might be inefficient and poorly managed; yet, clearly, they exist as distinct entities in numbers large enough and stable enough to make up sectors efficient, cohesive, and resistant enough to stay outside the sights of government and its revenue collectors. At the same time, complex relationships are patterned and structured into discrete phenomena—such as patronage—powerful enough to determine the modes of government and the directions of its policies. Understood as a stop-gap, 'informal' behavior is rational and arranged repeatedly into family enterprises, cost-effective practices, and training activities. In government and bureaucracy, too, informality describes sophisticated, predictable and effective arrangements to which many writers have attributed east and south-east Asia spectacular economic success over the last fifty years or so. Understood as social, collective, horizontal, civil, and bottom-up behavior, informality is again systematic, predictable, prearranged, and effective, as well as flexible, creative, and democratic.

The cohesion and regularities which characterize these three categories of informality are further highlighted by a **fourth**—an 'anthropological' or 'cultural'—account. Western social scientists, western governments, and western agencies, 'see' problems such as 'corruption', 'underdeveloped', 'poor', 'transitional', 'developing', and 'filling the gaps' left by weak states, only because they have an arbitrary 'cultural category' (formalism) locked into their heads. And it is when this category is imposed and practiced in developing countries that difficulties arise. 'As Gupta's (1995) analysis of state officials in northern India illustrates, Western assumptions about the rational activity of office-holders simply do not translate. An official's role as public servant and private citizen is collapsed not only at the site of their activity, but also in their styles of operation' (Haller and Shore 2005, p. 5). If observers are able rid themselves of this category, then they will begin to appreciate the complex and nuanced 'ritual', 'conversation', 'poem', 'narrative', 'form of exchange', or (as in practice of Chinese *guanxi*) 'art' which ties individuals and state together (Vivanathan and Sethi 1998; Yang 1994, 2000, 2002).

3.3 Problems

Categories and sub-categories of informality are contradictions in terms: the existence of each category demands recurring, predictable, rational and methodical patterns of behavior such that each category effectively describes its own realm of formality. As a consequence, these categories share an inability to accommodate many features of behavior encountered in the field and reported in the literature.

(a) The **first** is the ambiguity of formality and informality and their interactions. Informality can certainly corrupt, or support, the formal; and yet legal-rational behavior is to be found *alongside* predominantly informal behavior in administrative bodies widely characterized as weak and corrupt. In Africa, for example, 'it is a daily experience that *not all* political and administrative decisions are taken according to informal rules determined by private or personal interests. The distribution of jobs, administrative careers, as well as credits and licenses is also exercised according to fixed procedures, rules, and laws that follow the formal course of legal rationality' (Erdmann and Engel 2006, p. 17–18).

Moreover, formality can bolster modes of informal behavior that are generally thought to be undesirable. Turning again to Philippine bureaucracy, strict adherence to process and principles of merit has the effect of strengthening kinship and other personalistic networks. This is not hard to understand. Criteria for merit, when rigidly applied, limit the pool from which appointees can be drawn allowing explicitly social considerations—including kinship—to come into play without shame or guilt. This is evident in (but not restricted to) the Department of Foreign Affairs. The entry exam is notoriously hard but, once passed, candidates' social relationships with their superiors, and with politicians outside the Department, may strongly influence the distribution of prestigious (and often lucrative) posts (Hodder 2014).

Formality also has an indispensable role in supporting more positive modes of informality. For instance, Meagher (2006, 2007) argues that informal businesses and their networks in any part of the world are quite capable of operating across ethnic, gendered, religious, regional, and national divides, but cannot substitute for the state. It is essential that the state fosters linkages with production systems nationally and internationally, provides infrastructural and technical support, and serves as a catalyst for cooperation. This is especially true during times of economic stress. This kind of analysis sits well with any broad strategy in which the ultimate goal is to expand and deepen the formal sector. Lal (2008) argues that in those developing countries where the informal sector is already extensive, a two-pronged strategy is required. One is to expand the formal economy and draw into it as many people as possible from the informal sector. The other is to improve conditions within the informal sector by upgrading infrastructure, financial services, social security, technology, and production and marketing linkages. In East and Southeast Asia, too, it has been noted that informal market activities and entrepreneurs, and local-state society relations, can be important precursors to, but do not guarantee, successful official transitions (Kim 2012). The difference between 'subsistence-coping' and transformative informality is marked by increases in productivity; and this, in turn, reflects three important informal processes. The first, and most important, is the amount and kind of discretion exercised by local government in regulating informal behavior especially amongst developers, local government, consumers of real estate, and current occupants of under-developed land. The second is when and how quickly new ideas form and spread. The third is a level of trust sufficient to allow risk-taking (ibid.).

It is also the case that informality and formality may coexist indefinitely (and even during rapid industrialization). Take for instance what is held to be 'the engine of development' in many societies—the family (Au and Kwan 2009). This is widely believed to be a critical source of funding for new businesses in Chinese communities around the world and, partly for this reason, helps to explain their remarkable economic success. Yet it is also widely observed that the role of the family has been changing at least since the 1980s as Chinese entrepreneurs turn elsewhere to secure start-up capital. Although many Chinese entrepreneurs believe that the family increases transparency and lowers transactions costs, many others are sure that the opposite is true. This observation should be placed in the context of a long debate over the continuing role of *guanxi* and Confucianism despite the speed with which so many societies have industrialized and modernized in East and Southeast Asia (see, for instance, Yang 1994, 2000, 2002).

It is also acknowledged that in many parts of the world 'the management of the state comprises stable political systems based on forms of governance that incorporate elements of … patronage-based governance and rational-legal models. After 50 years or more of independence the governance … of a number of countries in sub-Saharan Africa and South Asia continue vigorously to display both sets of characteristics' (Blunt 2009: 94). It is hardly surprising that there has been 'a rethinking of "good" governance possibilities' (ibid).

(b) A **second** feature is informality's persistence in the developed world. The neat divisions, observe Portes and Sassen-Koob (1987, p. 41), 'between Third World countries, in which the informal sector is large, and advanced economies, from which it has nearly disappeared, is wrong.' An important reason is the 'juxtaposition of extensive labor legislation, frequently copied from advanced countries, and an abundant supply of labor' (Portes and Sassen-Koob, op. cit., p. 39). Firms have every incentive to dodge legal restrictions on the use of labor, and these incentives sharpen with competition. In advanced economies, too, flexible production and labor costs (and acquiescence on the part of state) describes a basic logic which cannot be ignored especially in the face of competition from Third World countries. Still another part of the explanation is welfare. Benefits are paid for by workers. In developing countries the reliability of welfare is uncertain and delivery is inefficient. Workers may well decide to stick to, or enter, the informal sector and evade taxes. Galiani and Weinschelbaum (2012) make a very similar point, arguing that the extension of formal sector jobs (and benefits) only to the worker and not to the worker's family is likely to constitute an incentive to work informally. In the developed world as well, write Williams and Nadin (2013), the majority of businesses in western economies start up trading wholly or partially off the books. This is especially pronounced in deprived areas. Owners keep their operations intimate and hidden, fearing they will otherwise lose small but relatively stable incomes derived either from the business itself or from benefits.

On the other hand, there is also an extensive literature (see for instance Goffman 1983; Whyte 1948; Sayles 1958) which treats informal behavior even in larger organizations in the developed world as a fact of life. Morand (1995) identifies formal and informal behavioral minutiae—linguistic, conversational (turn-taking and topic selection), spatial, gestural, emotional, physical (such as dress) and contextual (such as office desk and chair). Whether these are viewed, following Goffman, as interaction orders or as illustrations of the re-introduction of explicitly social relationships into the professional sphere, they appear to be critical to effectiveness in even the most modern and successful organizations.

(c) The significance of informality's persistence in both developing and developed countries is reinforced by an extensive historical literature on Europe. This raises a **third** feature: the emergence of informal practices which subsequently came to define Europe. The case of Europe is critical because the drive to impose formal and, it is assumed, stronger organizations on developing countries originates in, and is modeled on, Europe and America and their offshoots. Yet both continents experienced long and very creative, periods of what is commonly described as informality prior to, during, and after industrialization.

One of most obvious instances is the appearance of revolutionary Christianity (see Turner 1969) under the domination of Rome and proscribed until a few years after the conversion of Constantine the Great. By the end of the fourth century, the

Church had been brought into union with the Empire. It remained strong enough to pick up the pieces following the slow collapse of the western half of the empire, and capable enough to service Charlemagne's ambitions.

A second is the informal relations of dependency and subordination strung amongst leaders and followers after the fall of Charlemagne's empire. Smaller neighbors willing to 'commend' themselves were often attracted to the strongmen who were busy accumulating territory. This appears to have been part of a blend of practices (including elements of slavery in both Roman and Germanic societies) which constituted a system universalized by Charlemagne through his edict *Capitulare*, and through which he turned the estates he himself had lent to his followers into fully inheritable property (Postan 1976; Bryce 1901).

A third is described by the commercial networks, businesses, and supporting collectives that appeared from the eleventh century onwards. The new feudal kingdoms which had been slowly pieced together in the wake of Louis the Pious' disastrous rule needed revenues to maintain the support of their subjects and to pay for their adventures overseas (most especially the crusades). Only merchants could supply these in sufficient quantity. Towns were designated as pockets of freedom. They became 'non-feudal islands in the feudal sea', places 'where merchants could live in each other's vicinity and defend themselves collectively and which enjoyed or were capable of developing systems of local government and principles of law and status exempting from the sway of the feudal regime.' (Postan 1976: 239) By the fourteenth century the networks woven by merchants among competing towns had helped to shape a sense of national identity. By the fifteenth century, the expansion of foreign trade, the Company of Staples, and various associations of merchants (the forerunners of the Company of Merchant Adventurers) had transcended the urban gilds. By the late sixteenth century, the regulated companies—that is, organizations designed to regulate the trade of its constituent individual merchants—were being replaced by joint-stock companies. Only in the nineteenth century did businesses encouraged by limited liability start to incorporate. These changes (the rise of the regulated, joint-stock, and incorporated businesses) focused efforts, lessened risk, supplied more capital, and produced more stable entities no longer so dependent for their existence of an individual merchant and his family (Ekelund and Tollison 1980). Even so, these organizations rested on a sea of informal practices. The gilds and regulated companies were shells within which individual and families operated; and the joint-stock could survive only as an organic part of a matrix of informal behavior. Merchants in the seventeenth century in, say, Chester did not make a distinction between personal and business networks: business *was* personal, and these networks of relationships were vital to maintaining local and long-distance trade (Stobart 2004). As for the modern corporation today, the more informal are among the most successful (Morand, op. cit.).

Two further instances of informal practice which came to define Europe deserve comment. One is the provision of welfare. Turbulence and then plague on the Apennine Peninsula in the mid sixth century left Christians with little choice but to seek refuge in the countryside. Amongst the most notable of these exiles was Benedict (c480–c543). In the rural communities he established, mixtures of ex-slaves, peasants, petty nobility, and aristocracy labored in the fields, shared the chores of everyday life, and studied. They were places of orderliness, routine, humility, and compassion where service to God was an end in itself (Davis 1988; Kennedy 1999; Tredget 2002). Benedict's Rule (his instructions for the organization of his communities) was later absorbed by the Church as Gregory the Great (c540–604) reformed its administration and government such that it could take on practical responsibilities as parts of the Roman Empire fell away. By the eleventh century, welfare provision had become extensive in many parts of Europe. With a population of some 2–3 million, and more than 1000 monasteries (each with infirmaries), England could boast one monastery to every 2000–3000 people (Furniss 1968). There were, in addition, some five hundred hospitals. Infirmary and hospital were places where the old and the sick prepared for the end rather than sought a cure. But, within the limitations of medical knowledge at that time, extensive health provision was offered until the Reformation. Another four hundred years would have to pass before similar levels of provision were restored (ibid.).

The other is the arrival of universities between the eleventh and thirteenth centuries. They began informally—even spontaneously, argues Kunstler (2006)—amongst the medieval guilds. Networks of students clustered around itinerant teachers; the clusters became faculties; and faculties became the university whose relationships with former students could be both a curse and a Godsend. It was no coincidence they appeared when towns and cities were multiplying. Professionals of all kinds were needed in these dense and complex societies. While for its part the Church desired to reconcile Christianity with Plato, Aristotle, Euclid, Archimedes, Porphyrus and others whose original texts were being discovered or re-discovered; the uncertainty of individuality, the perishability of the soul, the eternal nature of the world, the bare and impersonal perfection of God, and Man's existence for the polity, were views not easy to square with Christian beliefs.

The universities, like the Church, quickly became conformist and staid. Renaissance humanism grew up in Italy from the thirteenth century outside the universities, and did not enter their curriculums until the fifteenth century (Bebbington 2011). The dramatic change in thought which described the Enlightenment more than two hundred years later was also generated in far less ordered contexts mostly outside the universities (Martin 2012; Brockliss 1996). Not until the late eighteenth and nineteenth centuries did universities become more secular; and even then so many of the discoveries which helped drive the industrial revolution were not theirs or were made only in loose association with them.

Similar comments can be made of the role of learned societies (see Fay 1932; Hartmann 1996; Eknoyan and De Santo 2012). These started out during the Enlightenment as informal groups of talkative intellectuals who, as learned societies, went on to do little else but talk. Nearly all the great scientific discoveries were made outside them. And they remained highly dependent upon informal arrangements—the patronage of a sovereign or local aristocracy or a local university—for their survival. Yet their part in spreading new ideas and attitudes—and in establishing for the scientific method and its breakthroughs a comfortable atmosphere of acceptance and normality—was decisive (Fay, op. cit.).

3.3.1   Refocusing Informality

'Informality', 'formality' and the distinction between them raise a number of problems, but not the means to deal with them. If informality is inimical to development, or is left behind as an inefficient anachronism in an increasingly sophisticated economy, or is a useful conduit between a developing and developed condition, then why does it continue to flourish in economies that are mature as well as in those that are industrializing successfully? If informality is culturally 'different', then why is it found across developed and developing worlds past and present? If informality dissipates with the size and complexity of organizations such that it retains an important but residual function oiling the cogs of the formal machine and its connexions with wider society, then why is it so often damaging to large organizations, entire governments, and whole states, and why is it also to be found in some of the largest and most successful and modern organizations as well as at the very top of governments including those of the most powerful and apparently durable states?

These problems, however, do begin fade once filtered through the argument set out in Chap. 2. Informality is not just to be expected, a norm; it *is* society. 'Informality' (social relationships) is the material from which 'formalized' behavior and the organization (with its processes and rules) is shaped, and by which it is sustained. To the extent that social relationships alone are the substance of the organization, then it accommodates Morand's rather technical description of organizations as 'social constructions whose facticity is generated and maintained by virtue of ongoing patterns of face-to-face social interaction' [Morand, op. cit., p. 860; see also Burrell and Morgan (1985), Silverman (1971)]. But it goes further: the apparent distinction between informal and formal is a purely conceptual one driven by emotional change. Scholars are not immune from these shifts. At the start of the twentieth century, point out Aldrich and Cliff (2003), the word 'business' meant family business—the adjective 'family' was redundant. Today, those studying family businesses feel compel to use the term 'family' despite the fact that most businesses owned by households are family ones. This vision of family and business as disconnected systems reflects 'the influence of socio-cultural changes on the way scholars think' (p. 575). It is, then, not so much the social quality of the non-western or developing worlds but rather the seeming lack of that quality in the West that has be explained. This is a question to which Chap. 4 returns.

3.4   Patronage: Dimensions and Doubts

The argument that emotional change is bound up with the propensity of humans to organize, and that organizations (even at their most formal and impersonal) *are* social relationships, also holds implications for an idea closely associated with informality—patronage. The matter is of some importance to development.

Relationships classed as patronage are often thought to be unequal, vertically-aligned, manipulative, and personalistic; to convey a sense of dependency and control; and, therefore, to be different from purely social relationships and from interactions of the kind that pervade formal organizations and democratic politics. As such, patronage carries many negative connotations. It is a traditional pattern of behavior (Sultana 2009; Jeffrey 2002; McCourt 2003) which describes the skillful manipulation of ambiguous and pragmatic relationships (Rocheleau and Roth 2007). It is often accompanied by fear. Miquel, for instance, argues that in states riven with ethnic divisions patronage is used by leaders to compensate their own ethnic groups after having taxed them and the rest of the population heavily (Miquel 2007). Supporters are kept in line only through the fear they may fall under equally venal and ineffective rulers who favor other ethnic groups. Patronage also explains organized corruption in strong states. It vests arbitrary power in the hands of unaccountable appointees who emerge from and disappear back into 'a secret world in which corruption can be practiced with impunity' (Flinders 2009, p. 550). By encouraging particularism in organizations, it provokes distrust, shirking, and poor organizational commitment (Pearce, Branyiczki and Bigley 2000; Gambetta 1988; Putnam 1993). In these and other ways, patronage undermines attempts to reform organizations and governments and to improve the lives of the poor and disadvantaged (Aufrecht and Bun 1995; Laguna 2011; McCourt op. cit.; Nunberg and Taliercio 2012). It disrupts formal politics at both national and local scales (Benit-Gbaffou and Piper 2012). It breaks up horizontal connections, disorganizes people, and perpetuates inequality and dependency (Das 2004). It interferes with the fair and impartial management of the economy. And, as in the Ukraine, it increases the risk of financial crises and the collapse of the state (Faccion, Masulis and McConnell 2006; Rajan and Zingales 1998). In Africa, too, post-colonial rulers more often than not bought loyalty by redistributing resources and assets as patronage. This was effective in building power bases initially; but it soon meant that less was available for the wider population; and it eroded the organizations through which those goods and services were supplied. As these channels withered, rulers begin to rely more and more on parceling out economic opportunities and markets to their loyal supporters. They, in turn, bought up people who might otherwise have participated in reformist movements, or marginalized others with more overt ideological agendas. In this way local networks of patronage were strengthened at the expense of the ruler's, and formal organizations were undermined (Reno 2002).

Not all writers, though, equate patronage with ineffective government and corruption. It is a means to secure votes; to bind one group to another; and to establish, fund, or control political parties and bureaucracies. It is even compatible with democracy. And it these accounts which take on prominence when strained through the arguments set out in Chap. 2. The nature and significance of patronage alters markedly once its unequal, vertical, particularistic and instrumental qualities (along with the impersonal and technical interactions that characterize organizations) are recognized as *aspects*—rather than as *different categories*—of social relationships.

Understood in these terms, a number of observations which indicate that patronage is the very stuff of democracy and organizations may be gleaned from the existing literature.

One is the persistence of patronage. Although its eradication in the developing world is widely regarded as preferable, this is a slow business; and in fragile states, such as Timor Lestee, patronage-based government is necessary if political instability and violence are to be prevented (Blunt op. cit.). Chabal and Dalozmake (1999) a similar point, arguing that in Africa—where informality, patronage and clientelism are everything and determine access to resources and influence—western institutional models are of little relevance and the notion of a 'rhizome state' is more apt. In China, too, 'phenomena such as corruption, gift giving, and patron-client relationships, which are part of the sphere of personal transactions, play a pivotal role in mediating the transactions between market and bureaucracy and in integrating society at the level of social action' (Pieke 1995). The result is a new type of social formation—'capital socialism'. Patronage was also a persistent feature in the evolution of government in Europe (See, for instance, Join-Lambert and Lochard 2011) and America, and is still found in modern states. In the UK in the 1970s British ministers were responsible for some 10,000 politically selected appointees (matching the number thought to be at the disposal of the Philippine president today); and during the 1980s and 1990s both Labour and Conservative parties continued with 'clientelistic practices whereby public sector appointees were distributed as a means of maintaining and rewarding political or electoral support' (Flinders, op. cit., p. 555). Even after the Office of the Commission on Public Appointments was established (with the intention of constraining the power of ministers) allegations that appointments to the House of Lords were being made in return for donations did not end. Over this same period family ties within the British parliament and government, and attempts (often successful) at handing on seats to kin, also strengthened. The families involved were known nationally as well as locally and included names such as Benn, Blair, Cooper and Balls; Dunwoody, Eagle, Gould, Grieve, Gummer, Hames and Swinson; Hoyle, Hurd, Jenkin, Johnson, Martin, Maude, Miliband, Mitchel, Morris, Prescott, Sandys, Sarvar, Sawford, Soames, Straw, Vaz, and Harman and Dromey.

A *second* observation is that patronage is not just a one-way street: it is fundamentally reciprocal, interest-based and frequently voluntary (Landé 2002); and it is layered with sentiment, obligation and loyalty. It is both possible, and quite common, for the same actor to possess laudable qualities *and* be motivated by selfish ends. As Kerkvliet puts it, politicians may not be 'totally altruistic or selfless, free of playing factional politics, or inexperienced in playing personal favorites. But at the same time other ideas and values are important to them' (Kerkvliet 1995). Patronage is far more than just a form of political behavior (Bearfield 2009); and, even when used politically, it is often entangled with horizontal ties as patrons try to organize and support collective action. It can serve as a means of resistance against centralized and despotic power. Notes Belge (2011): 'the disproportionate stress scholars place on Weberian notions of order … obscures the ways in which subjects of disciplinary power navigate multiple moral orders and create pockets of order that often operate according to radically different logics.' As such, patronage is entirely congruent with democratic principles. Clients will work to cultivate in their patrons a sense of trust and a desire to extend support; and patrons who do not meet clients' expectations may lose respect and face opposition (Auyero 1999; Scott 1976). Buck makes a similar point, arguing that by openly praising specific politicians and bureaucrats for the help received, and by publicly denouncing them when they fail to do so, clients help to sustain patronage as a way of organizing the polity and the moral climate in which patrons feel compelled to extend support (Buck 2006, p. 21). Omobowale and Olutayo's (2010) study of clientelism in Nigeria, too, describes complex relationships between patrons and clients. Here, clients operate less as individuals and more as members of groups (such as trade associations, friendship associations and cooperative societies) so that together they can wield more clout. They are then in a position to exert pressure—by changing or threatening to change patrons—sufficient to ensure that even though patrons may use coercive power 'the most important tool for retaining the loyalty of clients is acceding to their demands' (Omobowale and Olutayo op. cit., p. 467).

A *third* observation is the arrangement of patronage into patterns with democratic or democratic-like features, such as forums for debate or processes to share power or rotate the leadership. These are pragmatic responses to tensions generated amongst competing groups, each vying for influence. One small, though significant, illustration of an organization shaped from patronage is the search committee which aids the president of the Philippines in the selection of political appointees at the highest level. The body is not a constitutional requirement. It is thrown up to deal with the many interest groups fielding their own favored candidates for high-level posts. It appears and dissolves with each administration and has done since the mid 1980s. Much the same can be said of the Commission on Appointments. Although constitutional discipline gives it permanence, it has an energy that pulses with the rise and fall of administrations. In both organizations it is as favors given and taken as part of relationships that information and assessments of appointees are transmitted and approaches to candidates and deals on appointments are made. It is also worth noting that groups of patrons and their respective clients are also found within private businesses. Kondo, for instance, describes the heads of Philippine corporations as closed elite groups who encourage competition and monitoring amongst their clients at subordinate levels (Kondo 2008). Patron-client relationships also function as an organizing principle in small and large factories in Turkey (Dubetsky 1979), and in overseas Chinese businesses all over Southeast Asia.

The circumstances which bring about larger scale democratic-like *patterns* seem to be a growing density of patrons and sharper competition amongst them. A similar effect is produced as patron-client relations are stretched through trade and aid (such that donor governments, overseas businesses and international NGOs add to the number of local patrons), or as local or central politicians target development grants, public goods, or fiscal policies directly at their followers and reduce their dependency on local middlemen (Pepinsky 2007; Calvo and Murillo 2004). The Malay states shortly before the British assumed control of the peninsular in the last quarter of the nineteenth century furnish one illustration of the effect of competition.

Under the sultan (who embodied and symbolized unity) chiefs exercised leadership over administration, justice, defense and revenue collection within areas often defined by river valleys (Gullick 1958). A chief usually emerged from the aristocratic lineage that customarily provided the holder of that office. But to attain and hold power he needed both followers and the means to support his following. This required an increase in the productive population. This meant an increase in the number of mouths to feed, loans to be made, favors to dispense, and bodies to clothe and protect. Wealth was channeled to the chief but then had to be recycled. And a balance would have to be struck with other chiefs in the club under their acknowledged leader—the sultan. In essence, political authority was dependent ultimately on the willingness of those were ruled to be ruled (ibid.). Similar arrangements were noted in many parts of Africa (Evans-Pritchard 1940; Kuper 1961; Butt 1952) and in what would come to be called the developed world. Moore (1966), for instance, argues that the strong parliament which arose at the expense of the crown after the English civil war was monopolized by a landed gentry who also filled the cabinet. Parliament settled disputes peacefully amongst the gentry's competing factions, and made for an arena into which new social groups (primarily traders and manufacturers) could be drawn. Both old (landed gentry) and new (business) proved willing to alleviate mass distress; and both, during the nineteenth century, took part in a popularity contest for mass support by making concessions. The pressures brought through the rise of new entrepreneurial wealth (most especially of the Chinese overseas) in Southeast Asia could well have a similar role today (Sidel 2008). European sovereignty in practice (the pre-eminence of political power at home, and its independence from outside actors) might also describe the emergence of democratic-like patterns on a grand scale. Europe's history, argues Sheehan (2006, p. 4), is one of shifting boundaries along which claims and counterclaims are made, and one of an 'unstable blend of law and violence with which they are settled.' Today the European Union (neither state nor collection of autonomous states) is a new expression of the practice of sovereignty: a nested arrangement of competing interests and groups focused in national parliaments who together now exercise their claims and counterclaims within a new transnational forum.

A *fourth* observation is that patronage goes hand-in-hand with the emergence of programmatic policies. A further consequence of the reciprocal nature of patronage —combined with the increasing density of patrons and clients, and tougher competition (such that each patron finds the resources available to them to redistribute shrinks)—is that more leverage is handed to clients. If agreements among competing groups to share power are to hold together, then a willingness to distribute goods more evenly to each patron's client base is essential; and exchanges necessarily become less personal and more programmatic. By the same token—when faced with circumstances in which territory is fixed and there is no possibility of further expansion and the resources available are in decline—it may prove difficult for a collective leadership to avoid targeting resources and assistance at particular groups, most especially the poorer ones.

In practice, then, the distinction between public and private goods, and between programmatic and personalistic behavior, is often far from clear. Calvo and Murillo's (op. cit, p. 743) understanding of patronage as 'a redistributive tool which transfers resources from net payers of the tax system to the poor' makes plain the difficulty in disentangling patronage from the programmatic. The considerations underlying policies and programs targeted at particular groups are, in the end, very similar to those underlying the targeting of patronage. People with lower incomes and with less training and education are more sensitive to clientelist transfers than those with higher income, better training, and better education. Returns from impersonal transfers to wealthy and educated people are also likely to be much weaker and less extensive. Both patronage and welfare are directed more at the poor than at the rich (Calvo and Murillo, op. cit.).

Moreover, leaders do not always behave in this way. Even in a more programmatic polity, some parties are driven by prior linkages to funnel patronage towards high-income, high-skilled constituencies and so do not benefit as much from patronage as other parties (Calvo and Murillo, op. cit., p. 755). It is also the case, argues Gordin (2002), that personalistic leaders spend *less* on patronage. All parties tend to deliver benefits to their loyal followers, but party leaders who are personalistic in style 'seem less compelled to divide up state revenues and jobs as spoils to be disbursed to partisan followers than those of more institutionalized and ideological parties. Rather, personalistic leaders tend to marginalize the role of their party and establish unmediated links with followers. Generalized benefits to a more diffuse following, mainly through social assistance programs, are preferred over the provision of a more limited number of targeted goods in the public apparatus' (Gordin, op. cit., pp. 541–542). After all, why limit the electoral base?

In short, patronage is wielded in a manner very similar to impersonal welfare payments, and both have the potential to be as effective or ineffective as the other. Moreover, personalistic leaders can be just as efficient, if not more so, than formal and ideological parties in the delivery of benefits to the widest possible base.

A *fifth* observation is that negative features of patronage (such as corruption, favoritism, and particularism) reveal something of the energy that propels democracy. That is, these features describe fault lines amongst competing groups who are attempting to reconcile their interests and who, as a consequence, happen to excite the emergence of organizations and democratic patterns. The view that corruption in the Third World is the product of formalism imposed by the West on non-western societies, and signals fundamental cultural differences, might also be indicative of those lines: formalism and 'mature' democratic patterns merely describe a re-casting of patronage and its many blades.

In Somalia, for instance, patronage and kinship which rested on publicly negotiated rules constituted an effective mode of organization and the framework for corporate political groups (Mohamed 2007). That foundation, however, was ignored and left it to rot by colonial and post-colonial rulers, freeing actors to use kinship for their own selfish ends and behave as they saw fit.

Patron-client relationships may also provide the lift for economic take off—a condition often regarded as a prerequisite for a stable democracy—just as efficiently as Weberian bureaucracies (Ha and Kang 2010). China, for instance, has its own informal arrangements which are intertwined with more formal ones and stimulate market exchange (Yao and Yueh 2009, p. 760).

Or look at America where patronage was used to plant within the bureaucracy civil servants both capable and committed to the regularization of recruitment and promotion based on merit (Johnson and Libecap 1994). Conversely, the formalization of merit can provide a useful means of establishing protected cliques within which patronage can be freely practiced, as the case of the Department of Foreign Affairs the Philippines alluded to earlier illustrates. A further example is the professionalization of accounting by Filipinos which, under American rule, was a means of capturing the work, identity and status of the CPA (Dyball, Poullas and Chua 2007).

3.4.1 Refocusing Patronage

Patronage is generally treated as a discrete phenomenon through which political, bureaucratic, and wider social behavior may be analyzed and explained. As such, it is often seen as an obstacle to (or as a stopgap for) effective administration; as a feature that is in some respects compatible with (and may aid) democracy; and as behavior that is quite simply different from practice within Weberian bureaucracies. But once the arguments set out in Chap. 2 are taken on board, patronage soon takes on quite another look.

Explanations for the organization revolve around the extent to which it is seen as a collection of individuals or nexus of contracts, or as a phenomenon in itself. Thus, the organization is brought into existence by, the interaction of individuals (Wieck 1995; Alchian and Demsetz 1972; Fama 1980). Or it is an open system which reflects the wider environment (such as new technology or changes in population and economy) in which it is embedded (Lawrence and Lorsch 1967). Or it possesses the properties of social actors and, as such, has a life of its own (King, Felin and Whetten 2010, p. 298). Indeed, it is so much like social actors that organizations as a kind of species may be understood to have evolved though natural selection (from nodes of kinship, to social orders, to specialized formal entities) as the wider environment changed (Kieser 1989). Cast as a means to protect relationships, the organization (and its hierarchies, mutual dependencies, and modes for defusing tensions) is easily understood as an expression of relationships one aspect of which—patronage—is of some moment.

Discussion on the emergence of democracy is complicated by uncertainty over its meaning. It is believed widely that associations or correlations exist between democratic characteristics and their economic and social prerequisites, such as levels of urbanization, education, industrialization, and wealth. It is assumed, for instance, that a wealthy and more educated population is more likely to make rational choices. Another explanation concentrates on competition amongst interest groups and classes (Dahl 1989; Lipset 1983; Rustow 1970). The place of elites may be crucial in this: struggles amongst them, resolved through compromise and a willingness to share in the polity, are enshrined by ideals and beliefs and, later, by habit (Moore, op. cit.). Changes in constraints and opportunities and in the structures of power are also identified as causes. Treated as a dimension of social relationships, patronage takes on a seminal role. Its fundamentally reciprocal nature; its emotional layering; the dependency of patrons on their clients; the willingness and ability of clients to control, weaken and dismiss their patrons; the need for programmatic-style policies, especially as the density of patrons increases and competition among them for clients intensifies; and the need for forums to moderate competition and rotate leadership: all these features are very close to what is often classed as democracy.

Something of how big societies come together now begins to show itself. The desire to protect relationships betrays a need to cooperate, experience emotion (a state that signals to the mind that it is integrated into a community of other minds), and avoid alienation. Cooperation shades into organization; and as both the organizational and social spheres becomes routine, there is the risk that the conceptual distinction is, from the perspective of actors, reified. This is most likely, though not restricted to, dense and settled populations with more specialized and complex organizations. In bringing this about, one aspect of relationships—patronage—is vital. In the right geographical circumstances, patronage aggravates mutually reinforcing increases in population density and competition amongst groups, one consequence of which is a growing reliance on commerce. With these changes (in population density, competition, and organizational complexity), alterations in the quality and patterning of organizations become more distinct. There are two reasons for this. First, patrons must find ways of cooperating and serving broader sets of clients. This requires a means of sharing and distributing authority, and finding distribution methods that are as much programmatic as they are personal. Secondly, as the social and emotional spheres strengthen and an interest in relationships in themselves deepens, so does a sense that ideas and practices more generally— including the artistic, musical, and literary, and those concerning the natural world —are also matters of importance in their own right.

3.5   Conclusions

To treat patronage as a discrete phenomenon conceptually while attempting to accommodate its complex dimensions in the field, artificially separates it from social relationships and produces unwieldy analytical categories. A more nuanced approach (and one closer to everyday experience) is yielded when patronage is regarded as a dimension of social relationships; and when organizations, rules, and procedures are understood as a re-casting of social relationships underlaid by changes in the emotional disposition of actors. In these terms, democracy is patronage regularized, and a timeless feature of human society; the efficacy of formal organizations and innovation is dependent upon informal behavior; and even

—or especially—those patterns of behavior and organizations that seem the most entrenched, permanent, structured, and routine are always on the verge of rapid and radical change. An obvious question, then, is why should developed countries appear to be so formal and stable?

Chapter 4
Puritanism

4.1 Introduction

The answer to that last question is Puritanism—an affective state of mind that indurates such that relationships and behavior (and the emotion, beliefs, values, conventions, rules, procedures, regulations, and laws which pattern them) are reified. Neither Puritan nor affective states are entirely absent from collections of organizations, the actors who populate them, and their dependents and neighbors who together make up what might be termed 'emotional communities' (Rosenwein 2002). Through the alienation it generates, Puritanism readies the ground for more affective states of mind (wherein relationships and emotion are treated very much *as if* important in their own right) just as affective states through habit prepare for the drift into Puritanism. As each community swings from one state to the next, an atmosphere that is more strongly affective or Puritanical establishes itself; and, occasionally, one community synchronizes itself with others, creating a tidal surge. It is not going too far to suggest that organizations and patterns (democratic or otherwise) treated as manifestations of puritanical absolutes (which it is asserted with great passion *must* be adopted) are likely to be short-lived creations.

Today's Puritanism is nothing new. In the middle of the nineteenth century harsh new creeds had attached themselves to the industrial revolution. Free enterprise, the individual, the survival of the fittest, self-reliance, utilitarianism, the economic laws of Ricardo and Smith, and the population thesis of Malthus—stopped politicians from taking even the most basic and remedial humanitarian action. Government should have no sympathy for the poor; nor should it have any role in planning, sanitation, housing, or controlling slum landlords and jerry builders (Trevelynan 1980).

By the end of the century, three sets of particularly malicious dogma had become ingrained. One was the industrialization and bureaucratization of the military: huge machines running to their own implacable logic. They were, the Schlieffen Plan counted on, slow to start; but they drew entire populations into their operation and

© Springer Nature Singapore Pte Ltd. 2018
R. Hodder, *Small Business, Big Society*,
https://doi.org/10.1007/978-981-10-8875-9_4

once activated, Moltke argued, could not be stopped. A second was a hardening of the concept of war. For Napoleon it had been an art. Clauswitz wondered if it might yet become a science. For Ludendorff, war in the twentieth century was a natural state of affairs, and peace its continuation by other means. The approach to geopolitics also changed. The strategic positions and ambitions of states and their desire to control and counterbalance each other through changing alliances had long played into the calculations of political and military leaders; but now these matters congealed into something akin to a natural law. Mackinder's (1904) pivot region and the 'number, virility, equipment and organization of competing peoples' (p. 437) formed part of a world organism that shaped world history. Were Germany to ally itself with Russia, vast continental resources could be marshaled for fleet building and the empire of the world would be in sight (p. 436). Mackinder's idea fed into the mind of Haushofer—one of many who believed in the geopolitical principle of the heartland (Wolkersdorfer 1999; Herwig1999; Diner 1999). A third string of rigid certainties—'from the exaltation of the heroic leader, the racial myth, anti-Semitism, the community of the Volk, and the attack on the intellect, to the idea of the ruling elite, the subordination of the individual and the doctrine that might is right'—was to be 'found in anti-rational and racist writers (not only in Germany but France and other European countries) during the hundred years which separate the Romantic movement from the Foundation of the Third Reich' (Bullock 1990: 408). The working out of military machines, principles of war, the laws of geopolitics, and other 'certainties', was left unfinished at the end of the First World War. It would resume a mere twenty years later.

   The industrial age was not the first time Puritanism had shown itself. In the late sixteenth century, Puritanism began to take hold of large parts of Europe. Urban communes inspired by Luther (1482–1546) in Germany and Switzerland refused to tolerate Rome; while the Netherlands, the Rhineland, northwest Switzerland and south and southwest France turned to Calvin. In southern Europe, in response to northern puritanism, the Church harmonized the education, the practices, and even the dress of its priests; and through the confessional box found a way into the most intimate thoughts of its congregation (Davis 1988; Bryce 1901). Meanwhile, in England, during the first half of the seventeenth century, the Puritans' resentments slipped into open rebellion and, at end of the civil war, into nearly twenty years of rule. Ordinary lay courts were charged with the suppression of sin; adultery was punishable by death; soldiers entered private houses to ensure the Sabbath was being observed (and being observed correctly); Sunday sports in villages were prohibited; Maypoles were cut down; and, as in many other parts of Europe, 'witches' were persecuted. Counter-revolution followed: anti-clerical feelings were in large part responsible for the Restoration of 1660 and for the anti-Romanist or Glorious Revolution of 1688 after James II had tried to foist Catholicism on a people already tired of religion (Trevelyan, op.cit.).

   In the decades that followed, and well into the latter part of the eighteenth century, memories of Puritanism continued to worry and bother. For Hume, it was enthusiasm which marked out the Puritans. They first struck the spark of liberty and then smothered it. Fanatical in their celibacy, fasting, penance, mortification, the

Puritans harangued and launched invective with noise and vehemence, proscribing human learning, wit, and gaiety while encouraging cant, hypocrisy and intolerance (see Seed 2005, pp. 451–452 *passim*). Might Puritanism raise its ugly head once again? Others still wondered about its origins. Did these lie in disputes with the established Church over clothing ceremony, worship, godliness, and true belief? Was it the consequence of an escalating sequence of non-conformity or doctrines? Or did it reflect a particular world-view within the Church of England? (Knappen 1939; Trinterud 1951; Hill 1988; Dickens 1982). Nearly a thousand years earlier, Louis the Pious attempted to model his world on a monastic community in which everyone knew their place and performed their duties properly. He appointed subordinates whom he judged to possess sound Christian qualities. And he demanded public atonement from rebellious aristocrats. His own penance at Attigny in 822, if not forced humility, exuded astonishing confidence and indicated something of the intensity of those same principles upon which rulership had come to be based. (Noble 1980, p. 313; de Jong 2009). He had wanted to build God's Kingdom on earth, or at least conjure up a reflection of it; but succeeded only in hastening the collapse of his father's empire.

Four centuries earlier still, Puritanism had worked against the later Roman empire in the West. A regimented caste-system it was not; but there was throughout all levels of society a concern for status and wealth. Taken up by Constantine, and then by the aristocracy, Christianity became earthly and very established—a far cry from its revolutionary days—while the Church became as effective as the imperial bureaucracy at squeezing the peasants. By the sixth century, the Senatorial aristocracy and others possessing inherited wealth had blocked off any opportunities for bureaucrat, Roman soldier, or barbarian to rise through society. Thus was 'the fate of the Empire sealed by Christian prejudice' (Brown 1967, p. 333). Even the transformation of economic matters into 'isolated and specialized objects of concentrated and systematic effort' or 'independent and authoritative standards of social expediency,' though this took place on a grand scale only recently, was 'familiar enough in classical antiquity' (Tawney, op.cit.: 228).

The periodic billowing of Puritanism is often followed by instability and violence or an affective revolution and surge in creativity or both. During the Great Crisis, pockets of affect which, in northern Europe, found expression through Milton (1608–74), Locke (1632–1704), Wren (1632–1723), Vermeer (1632–75), Hooch (1629–78), Voltaire (1694–1778) and Bach (1685–1750) and, in southern Europe, through the remarkable works of Caravaggio (1569–1609) and Titian (1570–1650), had, by the late seventeenth century, coalesced into 'the Enlightenment'. The affect—now prized apart from reason and especially from politics (Nicholson 2013)—permeated European societies. In the mid fifteenth century, love had had little to do with marriage. Discipline within the family was harsh and children were still 'counters in a game of family aggrandizement, useful to buy money and estates or to secure the support of powerful patrons' (Trevelyan, op.cit., p. 80). A century later, matrimonial freedom and the 'love marriage' was viewed more sympathetically at least in literature and on the stage, though in practice child marriage was still very common. Not until the Enlightenment had family relationships moved decisively toward greater intimacy during what Stone (1977) calls an 'affective revolution'. Love was more likely than not to be accepted as the basis of marriage, and children were treated no longer as pawns in a game of power.

The surge of affect during the latter part of the seventeenth century and at the opening of the eighteenth century helped to establish larger and more effective industrial organizations; and more effective organizations worked to intensify the affect. In the latter part of that century manufacturing began to move into factories, aided by new technology (such as the spinning jenny, Compton's mule, Arkwright's water frame, the Darby family's innovations in iron smelting, and Watt's steam engine). Factories were concentrated at certain places; and if there was no coal or water or people to feed the machines, then machines would be taken to the raw materials and towns thrown up around them. Buildings were shaped by the demands of accountants. Hundreds and thousands of machine-patterned houses arranged in machine-patterned streets occupied the cities—houses for the working poor who became separated geographically from the rest of society. These organizations—and the extent to which the mechanization of production, commerce, transport, and time began to dehumanize life—saw the affect deepen still further. Yet it was the smaller family business which, up until at least the 1820s, lay at the heart of the industrial revolution and engaged a large part of the growing urban population (see Barker 2017). Each of these was a group of people bound to each other by duty and emotion (most especially love) far more than it was ever a knot of interests, politicking, and negotiation (Barker, op.cit., p. 226). Throughout society, emotions were explored, experimented with (see, especially Hunt and Jacob 2001), concentrated and poured into the arts, literature and music. Alongside the Romantic Movement, humanitarian concerns tightened their grip; and society began to heave. In France, the republicans had come to value 'the unmediated expression of the heart above all other personal qualities' (Hunt 1992: 96–97). In England, one year before the poor law of 1834, slavery was abolished and limits on the working hours of English children were introduced. By 1875 English trade unions had received their charter of rights, while in Germany social reforms had already been enacted to an extent and depth that would not been seen in the rest of Europe for many more years.

But it was the intense alienation and anxiety generated by the industrial wars of the twentieth century which fostered an affective revolution perhaps greater than those of the industrial revolution, the Enlightenment, the Renaissance, and even revolutionary Christianity itself. (A similar point is made by McGrath (2006) who looks to post-traumatic growth to help explain the emergence and resilience of Christianity after the death of its leader and its continued persecution.) Only in the nineteenth century—in the wake of industrial slums, and with the smell of revolution in continental Europe still in the air—did national governments begin to legislate for relief in any meaningful way. Not until the start of the Great War was the notion of a welfare state floated as concerns for children and mothers gathered momentum (Gente 2001). And not for another thirty years or more did the welfare state became a reality, while 'in British social work what might be called the "rediscovery of the family" in all its aspects … was very much a phenomenon of the 1950s and 1960s' (Sutherland 1973, p. 421). Governments, which had learnt through total war to involve themselves in the lives of citizens intimately, now placed center stage the family, children, education, health, relief from cruelty and from economic hardship, the importance of emotions (especially love and compassion), and freedom of expression: all this was now paramount and guaranteed, it was thought, by democracy and stable organizations. Welfare states emerged; new generations were sent to schools and universities in numbers never seen before; employment kept growing; more of those people entering universities and the workforce were women; and merit, now more than ever, was replacing kinship and other social ties. The weakening of the family, the rise in divorce, falls in Church attendances, the increase number of people living alone, the emphasis on self-indulgence, and the burdens all this placed on welfare and health were lamented and still are. Yet all this *also* signaled that family and marriage were no longer only, or primarily, a social instrument and a duty to be endured. They were now treated *as if* matters of importance in their own right. So, too, was political freedom; democracy; fairness; human rights; freedom of expression; emotional well-being; physical security; gender equality; sexual freedom; and freedom from hunger, thirst, and violence. At the same time, the world economy jumped: the production of manufactures increased four-fold while their trade increased ten-fold; grain yields more than doubled; lakes of milk and wine collected; technology helped to alter everyday life and economies; and growing affluence in developed countries became the norm and remained so well into the 1960s. Internationally, and despite the apparent ideological certainties of the cold war, security was provided by a voluntary alliance—NATO—in which the greater power allowed smaller ones much authority, while the number of democracies worldwide more than doubled even before the collapse of the Soviet Union (Gaddis 1998). These decades were, Hobsbawn (1997) wrote, 'a golden age'.

4.2 Expressions

The generations born after 1945 were quickly inured to this new world. Peace, democracy, freedom, relationships, emotion, society, individual, market, and equality were transformed into Puritanical icons and suffered the consequences. Security, re-presented as an absolute, is now eating away at liberty. The absolute sanctity of family and relationships now requires the supervision of behavior to an extent, and a level of distrust, that is rarely seen except in the most distressed societies. Democratic process has become a facade behind which the polity has been captured by the very few. Extraordinary efforts to realize the ideal of economic freedom has brought extraordinary concentrations of wealth; and peonage for the have-nots. The absolute importance of education has turned schools and universities into places where the 'game' is played. Merit and credentials, hardened into absolutes, have become commodities for which the highest prices are paid, such that social mobility has begun to seize up. A formal and highly structured world has begun to undermine its own foundations.

Puritanism is today quite plain in many aspects of everyday life. In politics the crystallization of absolutes removes space for possibility, argument, demurral, and compromise. Sentiment could have gravitated in quite the opposite direction but, with reform in China and the fall of the Soviet Union, magnanimity in victory was forgotten and a timid and conservative left was dragged toward an extreme form of libertarianism. Democracy no longer lives and breathes through bustling, make-do, rough-and-ready performances on the street. It has been turned into a stone effigy, distant and esoteric, to which the elected appeal. In America the Obama administration focused on domestic policy (where executive action is constrained by the legislature and webs of rules and regulations) while anchoring foreign policy (which is subject to fewer such limitations) to his own legalistic world view (Horowitz 2010). This led him, carefully and rationally, to construct a 'disposition matrix' in whose light he acted as judge, jury and executioner of US citizens. David Cameron, the former British Prime Minister, claimed very similar powers for himself, and did so with barely a whisper of criticism from parliament. In Europe, governments are struggling to gain traction with their electorates while unelected technocrats who staff huge transnational bureaucracies cite rules as they cleanse entire countries (mainly Europe's southern Latin members) of their profligacy and rob whole generations of hope. On both continents, most people find themselves without effective representation (Berman 2014). Political action is being replaced by rule of law such that recourse by state to legislation and by citizen to litigation is now *de rigueur*. In the UK around two-thirds of all legislation generated by English parliaments since the thirteenth century has been manufactured over the last forty years or so. And the lion's share of this takes the form of statutory instruments, allowing scrutiny by the House to be circumvented. Determining rates of litigation is notoriously difficult but these, too, appear to have risen throughout large swathes of the developed world since the 1970s (Hoover and den Dulk 2004; Yates et al. 2001; Yates et al. 2010). This is so even in Japan where rates increased by 30% in the last fifteen years of the twentieth century (Ginsburg and Hoetkeer 2006).

Puritanism also lends itself to the functional and mathematical nature of commercial transactions and accounting, transforming commerce from servant into master of the collective. To survive, the business must bring cash through the shop front to keep the organization working and meet its obligations. To grow, it must develop what accountants call 'goodwill and intangible assets' and trade through the shop's backdoor. Maintaining a flow of cash sufficient to keep it working, and a sound reputation for doing so, will allow the shop to make and receive investments, to trade in real estate, shares, financial instruments, and so contribute to the development of these markets. To improve the flow of cash, the business must introduce efficiencies which lead to reductions in the number of workers and in their relative costs per head. Other businesses will do likewise. Some businesses will survive, but many will go under, further reducing labor costs. This makes sense from the perspective of a single business, even though it will eventually reduce the overall amount of cash coming in through the shop front. Consequently, transfers will have to be made by the collective to those without income. Transfers will have to take place for other reasons, too. Backdoor markets—trading in 'products' which are notionally secured by cash but in practice may be redeemed only after days, weeks, months or years—can help the shop front draw in more cash to sustain its growing operation, and allow it to intensify further its activities in backdoor markets. But these backdoor transactions also create severe instabilities. One is a gradual squeeze on the amount of cash available. Another is the growth and concentration of wealth in backdoor markets in quantities far greater than can be met with cash. This is risky because the reputation of businesses can always be questioned. If faith collapses, obligations will be called in which, as the cash runs out, cannot be met. The collective will then have to find ways to erase or set aside these obligations. A third is pronounced disparities in wealth between those who work in the backdoor markets and those work at the shop front and in the rest of the collective. The former will, at best, take the latter for granted—as vehicles for currency but immaterial in every other respect. These instabilities build if transfers from the backstreet to the front street are not made; and it is by dressing up a reluctance to do so as 'efficiency', 'profitability', 'competition', and the 'invisible hand', that Puritanism disrupts economic life. Transfers cannot be made, it is asserted, because these would interfere with market signals and undermine confidence in the government and its understanding of the market. It would also be seen to reward laziness, and chip away at the mystique of wealth and its creation. The hard-working and self-reliant, the creative and entrepreneurial, the 'talents' and 'leaders', the Dagney Taggarts and John Gaults, are pitted against mean-spirited, envious, and chattering critics and scroungers - people who want something for nothing, people who are mere products of a dependency culture. Working or not, those who depend on wealth creators are not be trusted with transfers or higher incomes because it would be bad for them and for society, much as it was once thought that women are more content if left out of the dirty game of politics and that slaves imbued with an indefinite desire for something they cannot properly comprehend (liberty) no longer know how to be happy.

Economic puritanism is nothing new in Britain. Time and again governments have been averse to transfers, fearing inflation and the loss of any confidence that backstreet players might have in them. The first of these fears is a product of governments' own action or inaction. The inflation suffered during the first war could be managed through price controls and rationing (Fig. 4.1), as the second war showed. The inflation of the 1960s and 70s was in part a consequence of oil prices; and, in part, arose from wage controls which led to resentment, lower production, and lower productivity, generating the very problem the government was trying to avoid. The second fear was also self-defeating. The refusal of government to make transfers when faith in the backstreet markets evaporated in 1929 ended in a depression. The determination of governments throughout the eighties, nineties, and the early twenty-first century to 'squeeze out' inflation and limit transfers (such that narrow money fell to about 3%) while stoking up the backstreet economy, turned faith in financial products into the corner stone of the whole economy. When that faith evaporated in 2007, liquidity had to be injected into the backstreet on a vast

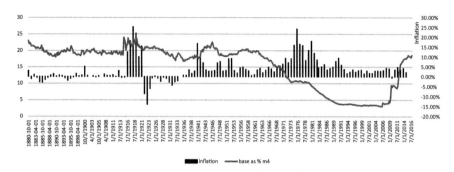

Fig. 4.1 Narrow money and inflation (UK). *Source* Bank of England

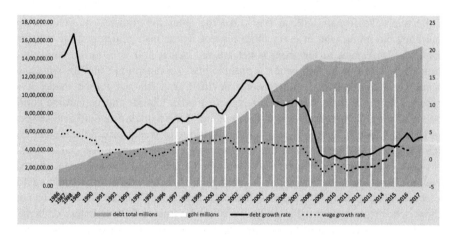

Fig. 4.2 Personal debt and income (UK). *Source* Bank of England

scale in return for bad assets that were parked outside the economy on the central bank's balance sheets. Even then government still worried primarily about its own standing in the eyes of backstreet players. 'Austerity' was needed to counter the liquidity that would leak into the front street: welfare was cut and wages in the public sector were frozen, only for personal debt to continue its rise (Fig. 4.2), all to the advantage of the backstreet.

Crisis, then, is simply an extension of rationality and efficiency, of squeezing the amount of cash that come in through the front door, of fueling the backstreet market, of refusing to make transfers from the backstreet to the front street, and of dressing up those refusals as rules and laws through which it is asserted the economy works as a phenomenon quite separate from relationships. Lathering those rules in moral certainties is nothing more than intolerance. When real growth stalls and stagnates, when profitability comes to an end, when competition gets too tough, when wages fall, when business leaders and shareholders get impatient and lazy, when regulators no longer care, and when the real economy reaches out to the financial one, chaos ensues.

Large public organizations are unusually sensitive to Puritanism, for their very existence goes hand-in-glove with a hardening of ideas and practice. The hospital *is* a regularization of processes essential in the complex business of diagnosis and treatment. Ideas about the wider natural and social worlds *are* the university's internal divisions (the department of this and the school of that), its academic hierarchies and external walls; and they take on those bureaucratic functions only when they leave their personal, subjective, and uncertain qualities behind and become publicly agreed upon certainties and givens. These organizations readily draw on surges of Puritanism within the wider community and contribute to those swells.

One striking feature of the debacle at the Mid Staffordshire National Health Service (NHS) Foundation Trust was the emphasis placed on targets and cost reduction to the exclusion of all other considerations. Procedures which enabled targets to be hit at the lowest cost—and on which staff felt their jobs and prospects depended—were all that mattered; other procedures (governing, say, complaints, staff appraisal, and communications between management and staff) were at best secondary concerns; and the sick were more often than not ignored. Even when enough staffs were on duty, patients were time and again roughly handled, deserted in stages of undress in full view of passers-by, abandoned without food or water, and left in their own feces and urine (Francis 2010).

One equally striking response to this, and to other reports in a very similar vein, was to set out additional sets of absolute criteria which must be met and, above all, must be shown on paper to have been met. The Dudley and Walsall Trust (Dudley and Walsall Mental Health Partnership Trust NHS 2013) supplies one instance. At the start of the Board's '*Winterbourne, Francis, Cavendish, Keogh and Berwick Report Overview Report*' a chart (with the equally ungainly title *Patients First and Foremost-System Response Timeline*) is presented. It notes the publication date of each report and the consequential measures taken by the Trust. 'Overarching themes' are then named and 'mapped' to those reports. A table of initiatives follows, linking each theme backwards to a report and forward to action taken by the Trust. For example, 'increased staff engagement' (a theme mapped to the Francis report) is met in part by 'service line quality groups,' 'team meetings,' and a 'trust escalation framework'. Thus another set of absolutes ('care' as defined by documentable criteria) is added to the first set (an organization capable of high turnover at least cost).

Universities responsible for training nurses reacted in a very similar way—by establishing new sets of absolute criteria and by documenting processes to meet those criteria. In the case of the University of Plymouth—renowned for its teaching and learning excellence—compassion is turned into an itemized and measurable 'skill'. This is achieved in two ways. First, students are required to write 150–200 words on an aspect of the 6Cs (care, compassion, courage, communication, competency and commitment) identified by Britain's Chief Nurse in the wake of the Francis report. An example of a possible question is 'why do you think compassion is important in nursing?' (Plymouth University 2015a). A pass—without which a candidate will not be accepted onto the University's program—is set at 40%. The second is through establishing clear sets of program aims (of which there are nine) and Intended Learning Outcomes (ILOs) which are 'mapped' to criteria defined by the NMC. ILOs number close to forty and are divided into five groups: knowledge and understanding; cognition and intellectual skills; key and transferable skills; practical skills; and eleven employment-related skills, one of which is to 'engage and interact with patients and clients of all ages in a sensitive, kind, and compassionate manner' (ibid.).

This emphasis on process, and the easy use of anodyne language, runs throughout university education in the UK. A further illustration comes from Geography at Plymouth. Here, as in nursing, the emphasis on process is such that data on students appear to be more important than the students themselves (see also Wood 2014); and the *process* of instruction is more important than content. ILOs (with itemized skills arranged into the same categories) are paramount. 'Substantive knowledge and understanding of geography' is provided only in a limited number of option modules (which also reinforce the ILOs) in second and third years, and amounts to no more than thirty percent of the degree (Plymouth University 2015b).

No longer about ideas treated *as if* matters of significance in themselves, a degree now describes a repertoire of distinct skills and, still more importantly, the 'evidenced' processes through which those skills are delivered. Any remaining attention which might be paid by students to the development of ideas is diluted by bureaucratizing what few opportunities are left to forge extended debates. The student is faced with an array of distinct pieces and asked to combine these into an acceptable narrative. These parts include, for instance, 'content and structure', 'critical evaluation and development of arguments', 'literature', and 'presentation and written style'. Each of these categories is sub-divided into a collection of others. 'Critical evaluation and development of argument' comprises 'developed and sustained argument', 'logical and realistic argument', 'critically evaluated material', and 'original thought and initiative'. 'Content and structure' includes 'logically organized material' and 'clearly defined aims and scope'. 'Good English' (a sub-category of presentation and style), 'logical and realistic argument', 'logical organization of material', 'critical evaluation', 'original thought and initiative', and 'literature' are all separate and distinct from each other. A good 'essay' is one which sets out all these items and, quite literally, allows all those boxes to be ticked. Each of these items can also be mapped, conveniently, to ILOs: a student can demonstrate an ability to, say, work independently and organize their own learning (key transferable skills 2) or to 'develop a reasoned and sustained argument' (cognitive and intellectual skills 3).

Who or what is to be studied, as well as how and under what conditions, is also defined ever more sharply and not just through a hardening of disciplinary boundaries and bureaucratic identities. Ethics committees, for instance, are becoming increasingly assertive and enforcing their views through elaborate rules and processes. Funding bodies demand to know in advance what will be discovered, how long this will take, and its value to 'stakeholders'. Once it was thought necessary to spend months or years trying to get to grips with social phenomena outside the university; now it is entirely proper to spend a few days or a week or two to glean what is needed to illustrate the operation of local, national, or international political structures which, it has already been decided, will explain an issue and benefit society in ways that were identified even before the study began.

This marginalization of student and content is now almost obligatory in many state and private schools: time in the classroom is dominated by lesson plans, assessments, mapping, and 'evidencing' which on occasions includes taking photographs to prove that practical lessons took place. This herding towards process begins at very early age. In nurseries in the UK, children's actions and mental states are treated as interconnected but discrete blocks of phenomena to be broken apart, categorized, analyzed, and recorded. 'Learning' is underpinned by 'play and exploring', 'active learning', and 'creating and thinking critically' (British Association for Early Childhood Education 2012; see also Department of Education 2014). A child's development is divided into two blocks. One is 'prime areas', comprising three separate sub-categories—'personal, social and emotional', 'communication and language,' and 'physical' development. The other, described as 'specific skills and knowledge', includes literacy, mathematics, understanding the world, and expressive arts and design. Each of these sub-categories is again split into two or three further categories. Thus 'playing and exploring' is divided into 'finding out and exploring', 'playing with what they know' and 'being willing to have a go.' Each of these third-level categories is then fragmented into several fourth-level categories. Attached to these collections of fourth-level categories are numerous sets of behavior to be performed by adults. These are organized into two kinds: 'positive relationships' and 'enabling environments'. Thus 'having their own ideas' is associated with 'respect for a child's ideas and efforts' (positive relationships) and 'planning of linked experiences' (enabling environments). These fourth-level categories, and attached sets of adult behavior, are split yet again into age groups. There are, for instance, categories of practice held to be indicative of third-level mental states that a child of a certain age ought to experience. Under the 'prime areas' and its second-level category (personal, social and emotional development) and third-level category (making relationships), a child at 16–26 months should play alongside other children and should play cooperatively with a familiar adult (ibid.). If they are to survive this barrage of tautological categories, then child and teacher must perform their assigned roles in a defined process and do no more than that.

Puritanism also shapes advanced countries' development efforts in the third world. The conditions fastened by the West to its aid and loans and the expectations often attached to its policy advice—that developing countries should build strictly formal organizations and implement strictly formal processes—appear to be almost satirical at times. Take, for instance, a project to decentralize primary and secondary education, health, and rural development at Khyber Pakhtunkhwa in Pakistan. A 'functional assignment methodology' was applied. This involved: establishing principles and criteria (such as subsidiarity, externalities, economies of scale, and the capacity of receiving levels) to aid decisions; unbundling sectors and functions into 'substantive' areas (such "water" into irrigation, clean water supply, and hydro-generation); disentangling management functions (such as planning, policy formulation, financing, implementation, and regulation); the assignment of managerial responsibilities; defining the precise mode of decentralisation (devolution, delegation, or deconcentration); making a clear distinction between the obligatory and discretionary nature of functions; and delineating stages of the functional assignment process, including 'functions mapping' and 'functions review' (see Ferrazzi and Rohdewohld 2010a and b; Ferrazzi 2008).[1] The Pakistan government felt it did not have the capacity to spend the money, let alone complete the project successfully, and refused it and the accompanying loan from the ADB. The government then came under pressure from the bank to accept even larger subventions. According to the bank, the project subsequently failed (and the Pakistan government was left with an additional loan to repay) because political leadership and coordination amongst government departments were absent while powerful development partners ignored the project's devolution agenda and funded their own vertical programmes (ibid.).

The issue here is not just one of 'pushing' loans by an institution whose new headquarters in Manila is a wonderful example of conspicuous consumption. The problem is much broader: development is seen as a rational and mechanical bureaucratic process which, if correctly operated, produces clear 'outcomes'. To all intents and purposes governments in the west—which experienced very lengthy and highly creative periods of informality over many centuries—are asking developing states to dismiss the ambiguities which informality brings and to treat those ambiguities as unwanted, corrupt, criminal and dangerous. These expectations, and the beliefs that go with them (for example, that a rule matters more than a person) throw up problems in developing countries which go beyond the suppression of creativity. It is an attitude likely to spawn resentment and counter-movements against what can only seem like western intolerance—movements whose significance and strength developed countries are unable to gauge accurately precisely because they are 'informal' in nature. Striking similarities can be drawn, as Phillips (2010) does, between today's jihadists and the confessional militants (especially the Calvinists) of Reformation Europe; though he believes the solution is the spread of the 'dense' institutionalism which already characterizes the global North (and the international order) across developing countries where more 'robust state structures' need to be constructed.

Once idealized absolutes are established, then any departure from that perfection will be thought to resemble its nemesis; where there is deviance from the perfect state envisioned, there must be correction, supervision, and surveillance. What applied to the economy, applies to society as a whole.

The case of the Mid Staffordshire Trust has already been alluded to: once the absence of compassion was identified and traced to a failure of rules and process, a bureaucratic response and more careful monitoring was inescapable. Or take what might happen in a British nursery if a child does not manifest the categories of

---

[1]For a broader overview of international donor activities in the area, see Elahi et al. (2015).

mental states that it should when it should. A departure from these absolutes (from what *is* or should *be*) *inevitably* signals a problem, and another bureaucratic process which extends way beyond the nursery may be set in motion. A child whose interests seem too focused in one area and insufficient in another, or who is unable to form 'balanced' relationships with peers and adults, or who constantly misbehaves, or who in other respects departs from the established 'absolute' mental states and practices, becomes a matter of concern for staff, parents, and authorities and is likely to require special 'intervention'.

Indeed, relationships and behavior more generally throughout society are watched carefully. Once transformed into absolutes, emotions are first categorized and then judged: love, sadness, and loss are moral imperatives which *ought* to be felt and which, for this reason, *ought* to be displayed (and this is so even when they are about public figures who are otherwise complete strangers), while others (such as prejudice, frustration, anger, and insecurity) are deemed to be offensive and their expression in public subject to legal sanction (provided by say, the Public Order Act 1986, the Communications Act 2003, and the Malicious Communications Act 1988).

There is a growing body of opinion that smacking children under any circumstances is harmful and immoral and should be made illegal. There is another which blames many of society's imperfections on parents and their sins of omission. With loosening bonds in family and civil life, opined Blair, a radical new approach was needed to make life as it should be for the model law-abiding citizen in a model community. Anti-social behavior was to be eradicated. This meant 'reversing the burden of proof' (Blair 2006): the accused would now have to show that they were innocent. It meant swift penalties and punishment. It meant re-education classes for children and their parents. It meant problem families had to be identified.

Interventions are even applied by the state to behavior towards oneself. Conceptions of the perfect bodily form and life-style are various. Take, for instance, the Barbie and Ken people, the models of the catwalks and glossies, the Hollywood actors, the contestants paraded by 'extreme makeover' TV shows, and those who populate the waiting rooms of cosmetic plastic surgeons. But whatever the details, those who do not at the very least keep to an ideal weight are either pitied or chastised. As I write the British government is exploring the possibility of removing benefits from people who are either obese or dependent on drugs or alcohol, and who refuse treatment for their condition. The government's argument is that such people are a drain on the exchequer and must be made fit enough to work. The same holds true for the disabled: those who can work should work. In this big push to construct a perfect economic state, 'imperfect' minds and bodies must prove through a minimal-cost process that they are too imperfect to contribute. In the service of absolute ends and absolute process, distress and fear, inequities and harm, and deaths hastened, are as nothing. Monitoring and restrictions are also imposed on organizations whose behavior departs from idealized economic practice. Under the proposed Trade Union bill (2015–16), a picket will have to inform the police of its plans two weeks in advance of any proposed action, and for any picket a supervisor must be identified by the union. Supervisors will be required to wear a badge or armband or other item that allows them to be easily identified as a supervisor; carry a letter of authorization from the union and produce it when asked to do so by a constable; supply the police with their name and contact details; and attend the picket at short notice. Failure to meet these requirements would render the picket illegal.

The layering of surveillance and control in society, which had been thickening even before 9/11, became especially noticeable after the attacks. Methods were formulated to accumulate information; and supporting legislation, from the Regulation of Investigatory Powers Act to the Digital Economy Act and the Prum Treaty (Bunyan 2010), was enacted. During the first fifteen years of the new century, 111 statutory instruments related to terror were produced, compared to 30 over the previous three decades when anti-terror legislation was first introduced. CCTVs are now found everywhere on urban streets and public transport. Personal data are stored, traded, and distributed by companies (such as airlines and banks) and government; fingerprints and DNA are routinely harvested and stored; and watch-lists are drawn up. There was some watering down of these measures after 2010 and, more especially, the Protection of Freedoms Act of 2012. *ContactPoint* (the data base accumulating information on all children) was switched off; and DNA records for hundreds of thousands of people without convictions were destroyed. But the trend has not been reversed. *ContactPoint* was replaced by a sign-post system (Bellamy 2011); and, under the Counter-Terrorism and Securities Act of 2015, organizations from schools to local authorities and universities to NHS and trade unions had imposed upon them statutory duty to prevent terrorism (HM Government 2015; Houses of Parliament 2015a and b). For universities this means vetting and monitoring external speakers, promoting British values, binding these values into their curricula, and ensuring that all staffs are trained to recognize those individuals susceptible to radicalization (ibid.).

That terrorism and its process (radicalization) is now perceived to be one of the greatest threats to the UK is not surprising given the reification of democracy and democratic process. Nor is it remarkable, given the reification of family along with emotion and wider social relationships, that child abuse and its process (grooming) is seen as another. It is no longer 'just' a crime like murder, but a corruption harbored by a significant proportion of the male population. The National Crime Agency puts the number of men who are potentially capable of sexual abuse of children at 750,000. The number of pedophiles is estimated to be more than 250,000 (men), to which another 65,000 women can be added. This works out at nearly four times the current prison population (for all offenses, men and women) or around 3% of the adult male population. These figures, it is said, may be under-estimates. (Indeed, Wurtele et al. (2014) suggest that in the United States nearly 10% of males and 4% of females have a sexual interest in children.) It might be expected, therefore, that in any large organization of say 30,000 people (such as a university or police force or government department), somewhere between 500 and 2100 people are pedophiles. In the UK it would appear to be a threat that is frequently realized. Around a quarter of young adults are reported to have experienced sexual abuse as a child (Radford et al. 2011) while some 5–15% of boys and 5–30% of girls across the developed world have suffered sexual abuse

(Townsend and Rheingold 2013; Gilbert et al. 2009). The incidence of abuse may be on the rise. Although a small drop was noted in 2009 (over 1998/9), the overall trend seems to be in the other direction. Increases of 80% was reported in 2002 (over 1994), and most recent figures indicate sharp increases in 2015 of 31% over 2012, and 165% for reports of non-recent cases over 2012.[2]

It would seem that the sexual abuse of children is waiting to be found, quite literally, everywhere. Not to find it is unacceptable—a corruption and, in fact, a crime in itself. In some countries in the developed world, designated groups of workers and, in many national or federal jurisdictions, *all* citizens are under a legal obligation to report their suspicions. There remains as yet no such obligation in the UK (where citizens have no legal duty to report *any* crime or suspected crime), though legislation designed to protect children has multiplied. Between 1989 (when the Children Act was passed) and 2013, more than 40 legislative items were introduced compared to 17 over the previous century (1889 and 1988). Similarly, the number legislative items related to sexual offences between 1985 and 2013 number 12, compared to six over the previous century (Gray and Watt 2013).

One consequence of these fears and their associated legislation is that organizational life for children and adults has become one of suspicion and surveillance. Staff (all of whom must undergo police checks) are contractually obliged to inform a designated child protection officer about any relationships between child and any other member of staff that seems to be, or could be interpreted as, a little too close or abnormal in some way; and schools have a statutory duty to ensure that such measures are in place. Within mixed sex communities it is not uncommon for public demonstrations of affection (such as holding hands) or relationships between students whose ages differ by more than two years to be banned. Classrooms must always have a glass door or opening through which the room may be observed from within the building. Teachers (and this is especially true in boarding schools where children see them as stand-in parents) must be very careful to behave in ways that cannot be misrepresented. A child should not sit on an adult's lap. Consoling a crying child by patting him on the back when witnesses are present is possible; but hugging a child with or without witnesses is not; and doors should always be left open. In nurseries a staff member cannot change a child's diapers, nor train them to use the toilet, unless another member of staff is present, and charts of which staff changed which child and when are kept. There are log books, too. Any visible blemish (such as bruise or red mark) on a child is noted along with its size and position on the body. The child's general physical and mental condition is also examined and recorded. Is the child dirty? Do her clothes need washing? Is the child wearing the same clothes as they day before? Is he wearing enough clothes and proper clothes? Does the child smell? Is the child withdrawn and quiet? A list of parents, with a photograph next to each name, is drawn up just in case one or the other should lose 'access'.

---

[2]National Police Chiefs' Council, May, 2015, and widely reported in national media.

The alienation generated by Puritanism is not hard to understand. Whole groups in society are being told that much of what they eat, drink, and smoke, what they look like, how they express themselves, what they might or might not feel, and the language they use, are not just unacceptable but outlawed or ought to be. Moreover, every citizen is both suspect and informant in battles against crimes which are said to threaten the very foundation of state and society. Alienated, thought capable of both terrorism and abuse, and with the minutiae of their behavior closely watched and tightly proscribed, actors try to reclaim some autonomy by becoming more instrumental and manipulative or finding surrogates who are and who will act on their behalf. The most dramatic expression is the rise of political mavericks from the left and right—such as Trump and Farage, Corbyn and Sanders, Le Pen and Petry, Wilders and Michaloliakos, Vona and Akesson, Hofer and Kotleba, Tsipras and Grillo. But it is also manifested directly in all kinds of other behavior which is often deliberately aberrant. Systems of law, welfare, and education are played for advantage. The extent of cheating in schools and universities is very hard to determine and there are few studies longitudinal studies (cf. Diekhoff et al. 1996). There is also the danger of accepting too easily unnecessarily restrictive definitions preferred by university administrators (Barnhardt 2015). Nevertheless, there is strong support for the view that cheating as understood by students is indeed on the rise and has been for some time (Jones 2011; McCabe et al. 2001; Klein et al. 2007; McCabe 2009; Trost 2009), especially in business studies (McCabe et al. 2006). Very similar comments can be made about corruption more generally in society, from the sharp practices exposed by the banking crisis, to the pedantry and brass used by MPs to claim expenses; from the apparent fabrication of evidence for WMDs in Iraq to the daily shenanigans of Metropolitan Police; and from the stratagems and contrivances devised by universities during research assessments exercises, to the magazines who sell copy by selling university ranking tables.

4.3   Conclusions

Puritanism describes a tendency to reify concepts and practices and to behave accordingly: it is to treat them as absolute rather than *as if* absolute (and to admit doubt and choice) for practical effect. It is at the same time a desire for perfection: since concepts and practices are absolute, they must have a specific shape and content to which they conform meticulously; and mechanisms for surveillance and oversight must be faultless if that state is to be maintained. Puritanism is also alienating: concepts and practices—independent, set apart, perfect, and unattainable—are transformed psychologically into icons under which actors must labor. Alienation evokes anxiety; behavior grows increasingly manipulative and self-centered.

Puritanism takes many different forms at many different times and places. In England, the great rush of legislation since the 1980s and 1990s (and through which we are still living) was preceded by others. One swept across Victorian England; another through the latter part of the eighteenth century as the industrial revolution gathered momentum; and still another through Cromwell's Protectorate. There were two other such waves of legislation which, though comparatively less marked, were nevertheless significant. One rose gently during fourteenth century; and the other during the first half of the sixteenth century. The first was followed by the Renaissance; the second by a remarkable burst in literary creativity known as the English Renaissance.

True, a complex of influences probably accounts for the rise in litigation since the nineteenth century. Changes in agriculture, changes in technology (such as the railways), the growth of complex cities, and colonialism, among a hundred matters other than Puritanism are more direct considerations. In America, the availability of lawyers and funds; growing social complexity and a breakdown of informal practices for resolving disputes; perceptions of the justice of managerial decisions; the appointment or election of judges; and whether or not courts have the power to decide constitutional rights, invalidate legislation, and serve as alternative focus for political action: all probably constitute part of the explanation.

Alternative explanations can also be suggested for other manifestations of Puritanism. Tumult in American society at the end of the nineteenth century and start of the twentieth century is often explained by Trachtenberg's 'incorporation'. Private enterprise mechanized the means of production and the circulation of goods; it co-opted a state which now organized violence on its behalf; and, together, enterprise and distributed power hierarchically, suborned the citizen, and polarized rich and poor. Expansion was wrought through systematization; unification through division, and standardization through dismemberment. Globalization today is just incorporation writ large: inequalities amongst nations are sharpened and the public is ferociously dumbed-down by a spectacle of celebrity and entertainment (Trachtenberg 2003, p. 762). Enmeshed in vast structures, citizens now have little choice but to play the rules of the game (Kroes, op.cit.; see also North 1990).

Bureaucracy, though its psychological effects also helps explain a slide into instrumentalism. By extending the childhood experience of dependency way into adulthood, argues Lasch (1980, 1984, 1985), bureaucracy and its professionals (such as doctors, lawyers, and social workers) encourage delusions of self-sufficiency, omnipotence, and self-importance: the world is, or should be, as *I* want it to be. This narcissistic condition is sharpened by advertisements peddling unrealistic and childish dreams of success, authority, and importance. A desire for leisure supplants a desire to work; and even if a hedonistic life-style should materialize it ends in feelings of numbness and emptiness.

Kilminster (2008) looks for an explanation in a re-balancing of id, ego and super-ego during waves of informality. Social conduct loosens and new symbols (such as less formal language, dress, haircuts, music and dance) emerge as power gradations weaken and social distance lessens in a society that is becoming increasingly differentiated. Negotiation displaces prohibition, and freer rein is given to primal instincts (id) and experimental relationships. These new groups begin to merge with the old and there return to more formal (but now hybrid) ways. Such waves coincide with the 1890s, when the term 'narcissism' was first coined, and in the 1920s and 1960s when narcissism was extensively discussed (Kilminster, op.cit., p. 141)

If self-centeredness describes excessive individualism, then it is to be explained, or so Tawney (1963) believes, by the separation of economic matters from religious and ethical affairs. This, he argues, became evident, at least in England, during the eighteenth century. More than two decades after Tawney's original 1926 publication, Mumford (1952) raised his own concerns about the West's obsession with technological mastery of the objective world and its relative disinterest in the subjective (and artistic) one. Flanked by Tawney and Mumford is Sorokin's (1937) *Social and Cultural Dynamics*. Focused very largely, though not exclusively, on the West, he argued that cultural change rests on movements back and forth between ideational and sensate mentalities, driven by a kind of immanent self-regulation. These mentalities find expression in myriad ways, from architecture to patterns of social behavior, from philosophical treaties to art. Ideational mentalities are concerned with faith and the immaterial; the sensate only with what can be perceived directly, with the physical, and with self-gratification. A third state, which Sorokin terms idealistic is a combination of the two guided by reason. It is their superior because it takes faith and intuition to be as important as observation and empiricism. None of these states exists in a pure form, but one or the other can dominate, often for centuries. The early middle ages was ideational, the thirteenth century idealistic, and the twentieth century sensate.

Power is the dominant theme in Deleuze's (1992) work. The disciplinary societies which took the place of societies of sovereignty are now, in their turn, being superseded by societies of control. Prison, family, hospital, factory, school and other enclosures—are under constant reform because they are on their last legs, kept going only until new forms are ready. The corporation is being replaced by the factory, the school by perpetual training; the examination by continuous control, acquittal by limitless postponement, and the individual by code. Debt, too, is becoming a mode of social control.

Culture is preferred by Hofstader (1964). The early Puritans' world view of good and evil, and revolution against George III, were seminal experiences. Always wary of government, and determined to separate powers amongst their own politicians and bureaucrats, Americans continue to pit themselves against evil of one kind or another. Driven by a belief that some group or other—cosmopolitan, intellectual, suburbanite, businessmen, freemason, intelligence agency, White House, military, industrialist, communist, liberal, Christian, mafia, or political dynasty—is accumulating excessive power at everyone else's expense, Americans constantly fear dispossession. Just as for Hume enthusiasm (rather than their ideas) marked out the Puritans, so for Hofstader conspiratorial fantasy, suspiciousness, and heated exaggeration characterize American politics. Larkin (2014), too, sees Puritan values being reasserted more generally in the West through welfare legislation and policy in common law welfare states, though his 'take' is less cultural and more historical.

For Hobsbawm, the 1970s and 1980s mark the beginning of what he calls the Crisis Decades. The automatic rise in real incomes ended; inequalities increased; ultra-liberal economists came to dominate policy making; technology priced human beings out of large slices of the labor market; and transnational business undermined the nation state. Society fragmented, communities dissolved. Politicians seem increasingly helpless and necessarily evasive. The electorate in general withdrew from politics, magnifying the interests of the more committed, and often more extreme, minority pressure groups. As politicians' frustration at their own impotence grew, their desire to weaken the constraints on their behavior strengthened. Technology came to their aid. With it came ready-made justifications apparently quite separate from their desire to recover some kind of initiative: the flow and collection of data makes life more convenient; goods and services can be traded more efficiently; children and other vulnerable groups can be protected more easily; health care and welfare can be targeted more effectively; and fraud, anti-social behavior, and other crimes can be deleted more quickly (see, for instance, Bunyan 2010; Meyer and Van Audenhove 2010). Chief among these other crimes is terror which, as it evolved into both a generalized threat (a war) and a non-specific process (radicalization) defined by an opposing and equally vague set of absolute standards (British values), has become the most powerful justification. But technology also constitutes the means for control. The storage and retrieval of data and word processing can simplify and speed up, and also create far more complex, bureaucratic procedure. It can both centralize and devolve bureaucratic process such that entire populations are made functionaries of government bureaucracies, increasing dramatically government's ability to monitor and control its citizens' day-to-day affairs. Thus micromanagement of the populace was substituted for effective national policies and clear political direction.

Yet whilst these ideas might help to account for some aspects of what I take to be manifestations of Puritanism, they do so for the most part only on a grand scale and for specific periods. They do not account for the many dimensions or instances of behavior that do not fit, such as the resistance to Puritanism or the continuation or resurgence of affective states of mind during times of extreme intolerance. Nor are present or past features of Puritanism easily aligned with, say, the economic, objective, technological, or sensate—a problem which is not helped by cycles that, for Sorokin at least, endure for centuries. As for those explanations which are specifically cultural, it is difficult to make the case that a unified cultural entity describes either the "the West" *in toto* or any of its constituent states; and what can these accounts say about Puritanism in non-western societies, especially those in which a social emphasis is otherwise strong and pervasive? It is also quite possible to have bureaucracies that work effectively and flexibly, that do not treat rules and processes as both the means and the end, and that do not dehumanize actors. Weber's rational bureaucracy is but one of a very wide range of approaches which include, say, public choice and bureau-shaping models (see, for example, Mosca 1939; Blau 1973; von Mises 1944; Michels 1962; Katz and Kahn 1967; Downs 1967; Niskasen 1971; Dunleavy 1991) and other still more generic theories of organizations and society. Of particular interest are: the concept of organizations as social—rather than as purely, economic, political, or technical—processes (a quality emphasized by role of informal social relationships in undermining the official); and the view that organizations are social systems which interact with other social systems. Some writers go further, taking the view that organizations comprise human beings who, as they interact and attempt to give meanings to the wider world and self [which is shaped by interactions with other people (Cooley 1962, 1964)] produce streams of activities in constant change.

Puritanism emerges from, and melts back into, the affective. It is a regular and unwelcome feature of society. The commercial revolution of the sixteenth century, and the industrial age that would later follow, were not the offspring of Puritanism nor was Puritanism a tonic for those developments. Emotional change, wrought by organizational life, and intensified by the concrete demands for revenue, led to the compartmentalization and focusing of practice and thought. The affect deepened, concentrating energy and creativity within multiple spheres of interest and activity, before the drift towards the uncompromising certainty and intolerance began once again.

The developed world is once more gripped by a resurgence of Puritanism. A predominantly affective mood will return sooner or later in its wake; but, in the meantime, without spaces where dissent, the bizarre, the experimental and the affective can flourish, the twenty-first century may, with hindsight, come to resemble something of the Great Crisis of the seventeenth century.

Chapter 5
Emotional States

5.1 Introduction

If 'formality'—especially the rigid, Puritanical, or absolute kind that characterizes large swathes of the West today—is not what allows big societies to come into existence and hold together, then what does? How and why states emerge are questions which have drawn attention from disciplines as varied as archaeology, international relations, sociology, classical studies, and environmental science (Engles 1910; Oppenheimer 1926; Childe 1936; Adams 1966; Carneiro 1970; Rosenberg 1992). The answers are widely thought to lie in inchoate forms described variously as proto-state, semi-state, segmented societies, and chiefdoms. If there is a difference among them it is that a proto-state has the potential to mature into a state proper. 'Chiefdom', however, is in more common usage and this is so whether or not it is regarded in any particular instance as a proto-state.

The distinction between chiefdom and the state proper is often described in the following terms. Chiefdoms exhibit hierarchies in status and class whose membership is ascriptive. The selection of the leader—whose role is to serve the collective by redistributing goods and materials—is determined usually by kinship. There is also little or no specialization of authority, no formalized coercive organs at the center (Southall 1957), and no distinct bureaucracy. By contrast, the state proper features a central bureaucracy which survives on the tribute it extracts from the rest of society. The bureaucracy is internally specialized, closely integrated, and capable of monitoring and regulating its various components. There is, in other words, a hierarchy of control (Wright and Johnson 1975) effected through a hierarchy of settlements (Isbell and Schreiber 1978) which are, at its apex, urban in quality (Childe 1950; Li 2009). Here, prestige and ritual objects are produced; and metallurgy and writing are practiced. In these and other ways (such as the construction of large public architectures) rulers establish the culture by which they define themselves. They govern in its own interests and have the means and

© Springer Nature Singapore Pte Ltd. 2018
R. Hodder, *Small Business, Big Society*,
https://doi.org/10.1007/978-981-10-8875-9_5

legitimacy to coerce the general populace and to defend the state's territory (Isbell and Schreiber 1978).

The state proper, then, describes an elite class and complex and comparatively impersonal organizations (political roles are often free of kinship), both of which are capable of operating even though the people who comprise them change. As Runciman (1982) puts it, the state *is* the accretion of three forms of power—control over the sources and distribution of wealth, attribution by subjects, and command over the technical and organizational means of coercion—in the hands of incumbents in specialized, permanent and non-kin government roles. Nevertheless, the exact point at which chiefdoms become states is unclear. If it is an essential quality of the state that men are more likely to come to power, rather than construct it around themselves personally, then it is a quality which, for Sahlins (1974), also characterizes more advanced chiefdoms.

5.2 Explanations

Few, if any, writers look to a single cause for the emergence of the state or treat any one of these as indispensable. For example, writing may be a definitional and causal attribute in Chinese civilization (Li op. cit.), but was never developed by the Inca (Dillehay et al. 1997). Answers, it would seem, are to be found in interactions among a number stimuli to which explanations return again and again.

One is conflict and the use of force by some to compel others to relinquish their autonomy. Indeed, for Weber, state formation describes the consolidation of a ruling warrior class (Weber 2003; Spencer 1898; Oppenheimer op. cit.; Carneiro op. cit.). A *second* is the production of an agricultural surplus. This allows the division of labor, specialization and, therefore, political integration (Childe 1936). A *third* is large-scale irrigation (Wittfogel 1957), or the construction of other large-scale works (such as city walls) or monuments (recording, say, victories in battles), and the centralization of authority this demands. A *fourth* is technological change, such as the introduction of new crops or metals or technologies. Along the coast of Peru the cultivation of maize and other crops allowed fishing communities to survive during lean years while making a gradual transition to arable farming that became the foundation of state societies on the Central Andean littoral (Wilson 1981). The discovery of lime—probably for use with cacao—may also have influenced the rise of Andean civilization at a very early stage (c7000). Extractive technology, suggest Dillehay, Rossen and Netherly (op. cit.), focused communal relations and ritually sponsored action, promoting group cohesion and identity. Festivities more generally may have had a similar effect and constitute a *fifth* stimulus. Such activities, argues Gernet, hold together communities of peasants from whose *conscious collective* evolves the legal and political institutes of the polis. A *sixth* is environmental circumscription (Carneiro 1970). Population increases on agricultural land enclosed by, say, mountains or deserts, intensifies competition. Larger or stronger groups absorb others until one is left—the state.

A variation on this—social circumscription—works in a similar way: sub-groups are forced to submit to a stronger one, their movements limited by the presence of another and entirely different social group. A *seventh* is the emergence of ideological or religious ideas and practices which facilitate the integration of groups and classes, legitimate these arrangements, and consolidate the leadership's authority. An *eighth* stimulus is interregional trade. Ur, for instance, was founded on abundant pastoral and agricultural resources and sheer manpower; but here, at the head of the Gulf, trade also mattered very much. The city, believes Reade (2001), evolved in part in reaction to demand for products from India (especially Monhenjo-daro, Harappa and Lothal) after 4500 BP, just as India would later (after 4000 BP) benefit from demand for luxury goods from Iraq. Very closely related to trade is a *ninth* stimulus—intercourse and competition among many inchoate entities. A *tenth* is a rise in population, though this is usually seen as a response to changes rooted in one or more of the other nine stimuli.

Precisely why any combination of these stimuli come together to produce a state is difficult to say; but 'the internal interactions necessary to transform a non-state society into one recognizable as a state do not vary significantly from one kind of state to another', or so argues Runciman (1982, p. 352), following Cohen (1978, pp. 12–13). Several necessary, though not causal, events and conditions are at work: relative stability; population growth; a geography (littoral and insular) that discourages the dispersal of population; a shift from stock farming to arable farming; changes in ideology; and improvements in armor and tactics. It is the *spark* that differs from one case to the next. In Greece the immediate trigger was defense or aggression, either by a single man or by a group sharing power (Runciman op. cit.). In pre-colonial Africa, too, what Monroe (2013) terms political entrepreneurs were instrumental in the formation of the state, though only after there had come about a productive agricultural environment, large population densities, local and long-distance trade, social hierarchies, territorial expansion and integration, economic specialization, control over labor and coercive power, and the promulgation of ideologies.

Unexpected change in one or more variables, such as a rise in population, which existing semi-autonomous units are unable to deal with, may also ignite state formation. On the southern Arabian lowlands the addition of new—and higher levels of—administrative hierarchies may have been a response to greater aridity after 7000 BP. This stimulated 'action' (more work and the application of more manpower) on the landscape, especially irrigation (Lezine et al. 2010, p. 427). This, along with other social changes, marked the beginning of the early Bronze age in the fifth millennium BP.

But these comparatively sudden and specific catalysts (such the ambition of 'political entrepreneurs' or a swift change in population or climate) might be rare. Wright and Johnson (1975) suggest that state formation more commonly describes piecemeal, 'additive' effects brought about through changes in interactions among variables, such as a lengthening or shortening of intervals before each variable is thrown into the mix. State formation, then, takes place over very long periods of time and is extremely uncertain. For example, Mesoamerica between 6000 and

5000 BP was still characterized by hunter-gatherers and a few, scattered horticultural camps and semi-permanent villages. Fully sedentary and complex societies did not appear until 5000–4500 BP, and chiefdoms not until 4000–2500 BP. The collapse of societies on the coastal plain and the rise of highland societies began around 2900 BP. And not until a few centuries later did the first states proper appear (Stanish 2001). Part of the reason for its long, slow gestation is that the state emerged not at a single point but from the eventual incorporation of a number of competing polities. The final sequence of events leading to the state proper can be measured in one or two centuries; but this is preceded by a long period of experimentalism or cycling during which networks of polities are built up and broken apart time and again (ibid.). In Madagascar, for instance, there were many failures and partial successes before a lasting union finally emerged (Wright 2006, p. 314).

5.3   Emotional State?

Strained through the arguments set out in Chap. 2, three sets of observations and questions of some interest emerge together with three sets of explanation.

(i) The **first** observation is that the qualities which define the state and separate it from chiefdoms are very similar to those which characterize a Weberian bureaucracy, most especially in its permanency, dispassionateness, hierarchy, and specialization of administrative activities (Weber 1997). And yet accounts of state formation provide little or no explanation for these qualities beyond a general recognition that they are a necessary and practical response: the emergence of complex organizations, it seems, describes the emergence of the state. 'The seeds of bureaucratic organization', writes Schott (2000, p. 75), following Waldo (1956), 'were planted early in the agricultural revolution when increased population and social complexity triggered the growth of specialization, social inequality and the beginnings of a rudimentary administrative hierarchy.' Urbanism—most especially the institutionalization of religion, private property, economic specialization, and organized warfare—then provided the nuclei for more complex organizational and administrative forms. Thus it is only very recently in the last 8000 years or so that organizations began to emerge, and only in the last 4000–5000 years that bureaucracy proper materialized (see also Hole 1966). The debate is made still more complex by a view widespread outside the literature on early states that bureaucratic organizations did not appear until much later. For instance, Stoelhorst and Richerson (2012, p. 552) argue, that a bias toward kinship and tribe acquired through natural selection explains why transitions to impersonal firms are so difficult. So difficult that if Coleman's (1975) definition is applied, then 'the organization' did not appear in Middle Europe until the fifteenth century (Kieser 1989).

A more coherent and consistent account of the organization is provided by emotion through which, it is argued in Chap. 2, mind is integrated into a community of other minds, and *indirect (*and highly intricate) communication is achieved. This implicates speech and other forms symbolism and iconography including art and music. It is in order to protect their sense of integration that actors: engage in cooperative behavior; and, as the group (the nascent organization) increases in size and complexity, begin to distinguish it conceptually from social (and emotionally charged) relationships. They do so in order to mask psychologically the fact that the organization depends upon the manipulation of relationships and emotions—a fact that, if not veiled, would lead to intense alienation and a state of generalized anxiety. This understanding raises the possibility that the shading of cooperation into organization was gradual and took place in concert with speech, abstract thought, art, and music whose development indicated the integration of emotion as a primal, physiological phenomenon into much higher levels of abstract thought. These attributes—and the new mental realm or cognitive niche they defined—were probably already well developed by 40,000 BP when material evidence indicative of such changes begins to appear (see, for example: Knight et al. 2000; Horan et al. 2008; De Leo et al. 2001; Conard et al. 2009; Einworgerer et al. 2006; Tooby and Devore 1987; Pinker 2010). Emotion, then, has always been central to cooperation and organization, and this remains so today.

(ii) A **second** observation of discussions on state origins is the emphasis given to war, violence, and compulsion; and to the necessity for a leadership that extracts from, rather than serves, the collective: just how compatible is conflict and oppression with the preservation of stable, large-scale social entities over long periods? A far more effective pattern of behavior in both simple and more complex societies is patronage. Rather than extract and oppress, patronage can work to redistribute, equalize, empower, and serve and, indeed, is fundamentally reciprocal nature and layered with emotion. Programmatic-style policies appear to be a logical response as the density of patrons increases and competition among them for clients intensifies; and so, too, is the arrangement of relationships (in which patronage is an important aspect) into forums to moderate competition and rotate leadership. These features are both ubiquitous and seem to foreshadow what is often classed as democratic practice. So what role might patronage have in state formation? There are three points to make here.

First, patrons are faced with a conundrum. On the one hand, their authority depends on building up a large following: more followers provide the labor to produce more goods and to protect; and, often, a large following is in itself a mark of status. On the other hand, a large following also means more mouths to feed, and more bodies to clothe, shelter, and protect, and this becomes more difficult as the size of population increases. Authority, then, is limited by the capacity to collect and distribute goods. Patronage both drives an increase in population and sets limits on how far the group can expand. Secondly, competition among patrons and their followers will intensify within any given area as the population grows. If there is enough physical space, groups will move apart; and, as the limits of authority are reached, expanding groups may at first segment and later split. Fissions may retain a common identity but are otherwise only loosely connected; and these connections are likely to become weaker over time. If, however, there is no room to move, then people are forced into a sedentary life. Competing groups must now face the uncertainty of conflict and possible annihilation; or accept a degree of tension, competition, and ritualized or actual (but limited) violence as ways to check and balance power. Or they must be prepared to cooperate and form what is, in effect, a single corporation. This requires them to share leadership in some way, distribute goods relatively evenly, and so disperse authority. Only through agreement and compromise—and by delivering to each constituency of those leaders who have come together to form the coalition—does the corporation remain viable. Coercion and conquest may succeed temporarily in bringing groups together under a single authority; but without the dispersal of authority, the corporation will be unstable over the longer term. In state formation, the avoidance of violence is more important than war.

Thirdly, this 'coming together' to share power describes elite formation. Behind the apparent cohesion of their ideology and culture, the groups which comprise 'the elite' are divided and fractured. They work as a functional unit only in so far as methods to separate and disperse power, and to rotate the leadership, are agreed upon; and they permit entry into their ranks from below only in so far as it is judged necessary either to reinvigorate, or to defuse tension, or insofar as there is a belief in merit.

Patronage, then, assumes two important roles. One is to encourage population increase and, at a certain point, fission and mobility. The other—once the choice to move is no longer open—is *to moderate* what Tocqueville (1968) believed to be an inevitable tendency for states to be drawn towards either complete fragmentation or complete integration (absolutism). For example, coherent and centralized polities, built around frameworks of agnatic lineages or shallow (and often fictive) lines of decent, or from an amalgam of different groups, whose leaders are duty-bound to provide for followers, have been recorded across many parts of Africa (see, for example, Middleton and Tait 1958; Evans-Pritchard 1940a, b; Bacon 1922). In more centralised societies, too, authority is conditional and dispersed. For example, the Swazi King shared authority with his mother and was ruled by his councillors, while village chiefs were 'owned' by theirs. Moreover, 'the expectation was that wealth should be expended to obtain and retain descendants such that the number of subjects was an index of political power and generosity' (Kuper 1961, p. 155).

It is very likely that this mutual dependency was also a feature of prehistoric chiefdoms as, for instance, the remarkably even levels of nutrition amongst populations in North America seems to bear out. In more stratified, centralized societies, the gap in nutritional status is readily apparent, though rates of morbidity between elites and commoners are unclear (Danforth 1999).

In mature, centralised polities, too, ways were found to disperse authority and power. In Japan this became especially clear from around the twelfth century from which point on it was neither feudal state nor ruled directly (Hall 1962, 1961). Power was divided between Emperor and Shogun each with their own courts and authority. Local military governors and, later, the *daimyo* exercised considerable local autonomy and control (MacFarlane 1997, p. 793). By the Tokugawa, local lords had further increased their control but maintained their allegiance to the centre such that Japan was kept unified. Even by the end of the Tokugawa, Japan was still neither feudal nor centralized. In many part of society, authority was exerted impersonally through legal or institutional channels (Hall 1962, p. 47). Yet the *daimyo* retained considerable independence; and kinship links (both genuine and fictive) amongst shoguns, *daimyo* and emperor—together with ranks and titles bestowed by the royal house—were thought the best way to control subordinates (Wakabayashi 1991). These arrangements gave the impression of a club whose members rotated, shared and delegated leadership and power among themselves. Ravine (1995), following Mizubayashi (1987) and Tilley and Ardant (1975), prefers to describe it as a 'composite state'—large domains (small states) arranged within a broader state system: 'although in isolation neither the shogunate nor any of the domains was a state, in combination they exercised most state powers: the organization of armed forces, taxation, policing, control over food supply, and the formation of technical personnel' (Ravine op. cit., p. 1017).

The lessons drawn from the unhealthy centralization of power were only too evident in China. Bouts of absolute rule—most especially between the third century BCE and the second century AD, the sixth and eighth centuries, and fourteenth and seventeenth centuries—ended in unrest, fragmentation and anarchy (Gernet 1997). A large part of the reason why these periods lasted as long as they did is that for much of the time, before they finally ossified, these 'centralised' regimes were strongly paternalistic and humanitarian. Moreover, outside these periods of absolutism and unrest, China was either fragmented among powerful clans, landed aristocracies and their clients, or governed centrally by rulers who understood the value of a clear separation of powers and competencies and effective service to the general population. Thus, under the Sung (and most especially in the eleventh century) 'plans and proposals of every kind, emanating from people of very different classes flowed into the office of the civil service right up to government' (Gernet 1997, p. 303).

Even at their height during the late seventeenth and early eighteenth centuries, 'absolutist' states in Europe were not all that they seemed to be. Monarchs faced resistance from government, obstacles of all kinds from uncertain bureaucracies, and doubts throughout many sectors of society about how much power the monarchy should have (Black 2001, p. 220). As the population of Europe grew and commerce expanded, monarchs and government discovered that more sophisticated bureaucracies than had existed hitherto would be needed if the populace was to be kept satisfied and revolution avoided. Absolutist states were rarely absolute or, if they were, did not remain so for long: overtaxing merchants and agriculturalists and alienating those with ambition was a recipe for instability. The state could not just take: it had to redistribute and cultivate. Patronage had to be regularised, institutionalised, and modernised.

(iii) A *third* observation is the comparatively limited role assigned to mobility. A mobile life spent hunting and gathering is generally thought to be the antithesis of a sedentary one based on agriculture. After all, the shift from one to the other entailed 'long-term changes in the structure and organization of the societies that adopted this new way of life as well as a totally new relationship with the environment … .While hunter-gatherers live off the land in an extensive fashion, generally exploiting a diversity of resources over a broad area, farmers utilize the landscape intensively and create a milieu that suits their needs' (Price and Bar-Yosef 2011, p. s171). Moreover, the transition, which began about 12,000 years ago, is widely believed to have driven rapid increases in population and laid the foundation for early settlements and states. Evidence that population expanded quickly after the 'invention' of agriculture seems clear. Genetic data, for instance, suggests a strong correlation between population growth and widely accepted dates for the rise of agriculture. As Gignoux et al. (2011, p. 6048) argue: 'genetic lineages associated with hunter-gatherers do not show the same dramatic expansion as those associated with agriculture' (see, also, Downey et al. 2014). The question, therefore, appears to be straightforward: why did hunters become farmers? So, too, is the frame in which this question and its answer are set: given that the new mode of life was so different from the old one, then the factors which brought it about must also be different. These may be *sui generis* or truly global, or endogenous or exogenous—anything from climate change to resource abundance, individual accumulation, or status differentiation (Price and Bar-Yosef op. cit.).

But is a settled (and agricultural) existence the antithesis of a mobile one? Is it not possible, even likely, for the former to have evolved from the latter? I want to reset the problem by asking what role mobility had in preparing human groups for settlement, and by proposing a solution which begins—as any must do—with a landscape comprising itinerant groups of hunter-gatherers. As occasional movements over long distances become regularized, and migratory routes established, way stations appear at intervals—common places, such as wells, or patches of vegetation easily harvested—to victual groups. These way stations are often coincident: with meeting places between different groups especially those whose circuits lie across or touch on different environmental zones (such as forest and savannah, highland and lowland, and coast and interior); or with mineral deposits; or with the raw materials for making tools; or with useful navigation points or points to measure time and changes in the seasons; or with places that offer animals water or pasture along their migratory routes.

It is here—in and around these places to victual, exchange, navigate, measure, shelter, mine, or hunt—that wild crops are cultivated, livestock reared, minerals extracted, and tools made, in a desultory fashion but, for the first time, in a fixed location and in order to service other transient populations. The new technicians who 'settle' here do so only temporarily: that is, they include this place in their own circuits and return to it only occasionally to tend animals, harvest crops, or extract or process minerals, or fashion tools and crafts, and exchange these materials and manufactures with other itinerant groups. As knowledge of the place and what it offers spreads, and as the population and number of groups rise, so does the frequency of their visits. These places become settlements with permanent structures periodically renovated by groups who, though bound by kinship or some other significant kernel of association, move separately. Thus a population larger than that which the physical structures can accommodate at any one time is rotated through the settlement.

These places, and the activities there, take on greater significance as peripatetic technicians are compelled to settle permanently or at least for extended and lengthening periods. Either this is because other lands are occupied or because a group is too large to move *en masse*. Or it is because the place attracts so many other dedicated itinerants that the rewards from servicing them out-weigh the drawbacks of permanent settlement and cultivation.

There is a number of comments to be made of current data which seem to point in this direction. First, both trade and the centralization of food and its subsequent redistribution precede the appearance of agriculture and the first states by a very long way. Both appear to have been common practices among early modern humans by around 150,000 BP and possibly among archaic human groups by 1.5 million BP (Ofek 2001; Gamble 1999; Isaac 1983; Horan et al. 2008). Trade also favors groups all kinds of ways. For instance, it supplies exotic goods that serve as symbols of authority and unity (Indeed, a physical place for exchange may itself become a symbol of status and—whether or not physical structures exist and a sedentary population collects there—a place of some importance amongst other settlements.) Trade also mitigates tension and conflict amongst competing groups by providing goods in addition to those which each group alone can produce.

Secondly, the relative lack of genetic diversity amongst humans—and the high probability that modern humans around the Mediterranean basin some 120,000 years ago lived in small and highly dispersed groups (Stiner et al. 1999)—

suggest that diverse, effective, and long-distance mating networks were necessary. Such networks would need to be in place even as humans first settled if those sedentary groups were to remain strong and viable.

Thirdly, there appears to have been a major expansion of population in the millennia immediately after the Last Glacial Maximum and before the emergence of agriculture, and this was so not only in Europe, but in Africa and North America too (Zheng et al. 2012. See also Aimé et al. 2013). This indicates the effectiveness of mating networks; and may have favored a shift to agriculture by encouraging peripatetic cultivators and hunter-gatherers to settle permanently.

Fourthly, the presence of sedentary villages is not synonymous with full-scale settled agriculture. In China at least, village settlements appear 'before cultivated plants make a significant contribution to diet and several millennia before agricultural systems with domesticated plants and prepared fields are in place' (Cohen 2011, p. s288).

Fifthly, hunter-gatherers, forager-farmers and, later, permanently settled agriculturalists probably co-existed. This appears to have been the case in the Levant where not until around 8000–7000 BP was subsistence based mostly on domesticated plants and animals (Belfer-Cohen and Goring-Morris 2011). That a mix of farmers, foragers, farmer-foragers and pastoralists occupied this section of an important route from Africa to Asia and Europe is undoubtedly significant. That this region is one of the earliest places for appearance of permanently settled agriculture and states also speaks volumes. It seems quite possible that nomadic technicians servicing populations dedicated to mobility emerged first in the Levant precisely because of the relatively heavily traffic in a world that was otherwise very sparsely populated. The manufacture of composite tools, decorated items and figurines, and the presence of silos, among Natufian groups who were not yet entirely sedentary between 15,000 and 12,000 BP is also suggestive. In Japan which, comparatively speaking, lay off the beaten track, hunter-gatherers persisted much longer than in the Levant. Not until about 2000 BP did the Jomon (hunter-gatherers) finally merge with Yayoi (agriculturalists) (Hammer et al. 2006).

Sixth is the presence of scattered 'assemblages'—or places where tools were made by anatomically modern humans—along possible routes from East Africa to northeast Africa, the Levant, and Arabian peninsula. One such place, known as Station One, is set on an inselberg overlooking 'the pre-Neolithic peneplain' suggesting that its inhabitants 'employed a subsistence strategy tied to larger game moving through the savannah' (Rose 2004, p. 212). Another, which clearly served as a way station more recently, is found on Iran's Shir Plateau at Maqta where the permanent availability of spring water probably always made it an important resting place for nomads and their herds; and, therefore, important place in millennia-old networks of routes from the Omani coast inland (Siebert et al. 2005). The place and the route is marked by tombs which date back to around 5000 BP found immediately above Maqta. This was a common practice throughout the rest of the Arabian peninsula (ibid.). It is in this light that Natufian cemeteries dating back to around 12,000 BP might also be cast.

Finally, there is no shortage of far more recent historical examples of way stations, 'empty' settlements, and empty (or periodic) markets in the literature which might be indicative of human behavior at much earlier times. In Morocco, argues Fogg (1940, 1939, 1938), periodic markets rendered market towns similar to those found in western Europe unnecessary. It was only following Spanish occupation that buildings of importance signaled market places which formerly were either left unmarked or found near a well or spring, or comprised a few stone booths unoccupied except for a few hours once a week. Yet in these empty places 'a large variety of goods ranging from live animals to grain, and from Oriental spices to North African medicines and charms, changed hands …' (Fogg 1940, p. 2). Similar places have been identified in China and Japan (Shiba 1970; Hayashi 1980; Spencer 1940). Of Kisimani, in East Africa, Gissing (1884) wrote: 'I call it a market village because no one lives in it, but the Wa-nika bring their produce here to sell'. A much larger settlement, deserted except when a market was held (when somewhere between 20,000 and 60,000 people attended) was Berbera. Here 'there is no fixed town, no resident population; and consequently no merchants to make purchases … at all seasons of the year. It is simply a place for commercial assignations: a place to which buyers and sellers come, and meet to transact business, by mutual consent, at certain seasons of the year' (Christie 1876, p. 124). Even when these empty places (way stations and markets) became permanently occupied (and closer in size to towns than villages), they may well remain distinctly agricultural in nature in that a good proportion of their population are farmers, while the remainder comprise streams of itinerants on the way to somewhere else, as in the case of the Yoruba town of Fiditi. Or empty places may evolve into large towns and cities. Bovil (1922) furnishes the examples of Bamako, Ouagadougou, Fada-n-Gourma, Gaya, Jega, Kano and Dikwa—seven of the most noted markets in the West Sudan. All were located in the intermediate zone separating savannah and forest, and all were essentially entrepots linking the two ecological zones. Timbuktu was also one of a number of trade centers (including Taouadny) running along the rivers and trans-Saharan trade routes from West Africa to North Africa, including Morocco (see Hallett 1965; Bovil 1970; Caillie 1968).

There are, then, good reasons to suggest that early technicians were peripatetic; and that they emerged long before permanent settlements and 'the invention' of settled agriculture. A sedentary lifestyle did not replace itinerancy, nor was it the consequence of entirely new causal factors. Rather, itinerancy fostered techniques that enabled settled life and, thorough complex networks for exchange and mating, provided flexibility, allowing small and scattered populations to survive and eventually grow to sizes that induced permanent settlement. These peripatetic technicians may also have formed the basis for the division of labor and classes which evolved as settlements grew in size and complexity.

5.4   Conclusions: Mobility, Patronage, and Emotion

This chapter focuses on three modes of behavior: emotional change; patronage; and the mobility of early humans and their engagement in trade. None—with the possible exception of trade—has a prominent role in current explanations of states or organizations. Nevertheless, the study of their interaction enables an appreciation of the origins of organizations by way of an understanding of the origins of the state.

Mobility encourages the need for places where different groups can meet, victual, navigate, measure and shelter; where techniques (such as crop cultivation, animal husbandry, tool-making, and the extraction of minerals) that eventually permit a sedentary existence are practiced and spread; and where trade can be conducted. As population densities increase, these places hold the potential to evolve from way stations temporarily occupied by transient populations into permanent settlements. Marketplaces in particular take on special significance because trade alleviates the pressures on patrons to service their followers as populations rise and their movements are restricted. There is no necessary causal connection between marketplaces and permanent structures and settlements, but they are likely sites for their growth.

Patronage drives competition between groups, sparks their migration, and encourages population growth and trade. Once movement is limited by the sheer weight of population or by other circumstances, patronage then works to stimulate increases in population density and the emergence of more complex arrangements to collect and redistribute goods. Patronage also compels competing groups to share power and authority behind a facade of unity (rather than to fight and wage war), and to devise what are essentially democratic elements.

All the while, *emotional change* permits growing complexity in organization. The eventual emergence of states is simply a continuation of this course as population densities increase and opportunities to move and to secure land diminish. It is only when organizational life becomes extensive and powerful enough that it begins to leave its mark on the landscape. This is most apparent in the remains of those 'pristine' civilizations which arose independently in Mesoamerica, the Central Andes Mesopotamia, the Indus Valley, and China.

This account of state origins in no way denies or marginalizes the weight often given to other explanations such as bureaucracy or war. To the contrary, it provides a framework within which those explanations might even work a little better. Environmental circumscription is certainly important, but it hastens rather than drives state formation. War and violence may have pivotal roles but cannot hold social units together. Bureaucracy is vital but needs some explanation itself. This account also highlights three further points often noted in the literature. One is that the landscape during and after state formation does not evolve in a linear fashion. It is a complex mosaic (see Monroe 2013, p. 24) comprising hunter-gathers, mobile pastoralists, semi-permanent settlements, settled farmers, and small food-producing villages on the best agricultural land. The other is the emergence of a succession of 'experimental' urban, or urban-like, settlements. The third is the diffusion of ideas: it is entirely conceivable (see Lawler 2006) that, as each spurs the other on, interactions amongst non-state units contribute to the formation of a state in an entirely different location.

These aspects of human behavior continue to play an important role after state formation. Competition amongst large, complex, and tightly-packed groups of patrons and clients demands trade; democratic-like practices are required to mitigate tensions; and emotional change goes hand-in-glove with the evolution of more sophisticated organizations needed to service a growing and increasingly dense population. Nor then does this account marginalize existing understandings of the organization's origins: it places them in context. No longer do organizations just 'appear' with transaction costs or a competitive advantage in one resource or another: rather, they are deeply rooted in the human psyche and simple practical logic—qualities which continue to underlie the genesis of organizations today whatever their immediate *raison d'être*. This seemingly plain statement—that organizations evolve with human relationships—also holds all kinds of implications their impacts and efficiency.

Chapter 6
Firm, Market, and Organization

6.1 Introduction

The case was made in the previous chapter that market*places* and organizations pre-empt settlements as well as encourage their subsequent growth and expansion; and that the emergence of the *market*[1] is a necessary response where population densities are high and competition amongst patron-client groups is intense.

These statements requires some elaboration given that today's business organization is generally thought to have emerged under European capitalism during the nineteenth century (most likely its latter half). This conclusion derives from three academic specialties—a theory of firms, a theory of capitalism, and a theory of organization. Each is well established and defined, each with its own set of approaches and perspectives; and each strengthens the other. The first is concerned only with firms under industrial capitalism; the second is tied to a very specific time in a very specific part of the world; and the third is frequently treated as a still more recent phenomenon.

Viewed more critically, however, each specialism reinforces the others' limitations. Each neglects a literature which suggests neither a market economy nor the mechanization of production is peculiar to Europe in the eighteenth or nineteenth centuries. Each fails to address the uncertainty surrounding distinctions commonly made between social, economic, and political organizational spheres in Europe today, while the presence of Weberian-style organizations found in many other parts of the world long before Europe's industrial revolution is barely acknowledged. In the light of these different (and often opposing) viewpoints, just how is the business organization to be explained?

---

[1]Exactly what is meant by market is not clear cut, though it is usefully described as monetized exchange between privately-owned entities or between these and the state, and where such exchange is prevalent or at least significant.

© Springer Nature Singapore Pte Ltd. 2018
R. Hodder, *Small Business, Big Society*,
https://doi.org/10.1007/978-981-10-8875-9_6

6.2   Firms, Organization and Market

Over the last eighty years one idea more than any other has come to dominate explanations of the *firm*. It is the belief that finding out what prices are involves a cost; and that firms are established to mitigate that cost (Coase 1937). This idea has been expanded: there are series of other transaction costs that also require the creation of firms (Williamson 1975, 1985; Barzel 1982). These costs are related to, say, collecting information and bearing the responsibility of decisions (Milgrom and Roberts 1988). The firm is essentially a governance body (Madhok 2002) which attempts to avoid or reduce transaction costs of one sort or another.

A second influential view is that firms are created to provide a competitive advantage (Teece et al. 1997; Barney 1991; Peteraf 1993). The essence of this advantage is, for many writers, knowledge (Conner and Prahalad 1996). People with somewhat different experiences and capabilities come together for mutual benefit. Arguably, the distinction between a firm that mitigates costs more efficiently than another, and a firm that has a competitive advantage, is a fine one. Nevertheless, transaction costs and resource-based explanations are held to be different because the former compensates for market failures, while the latter explains why one firm is more successful than another (Madhok op. cit.).

This emphasis on the market and its imperfections, and on competition, takes *capitalism* in Europe as the broad context within which firms emerge. It is explained by a mixture of events, including warfare, conflicts among classes, and the emergence of proletarian labor; production for the market; rationality; individualism; and the nation state and its ability to secure revenue. It is thought to be quite distinct from what came before (feudalism), and different in size, scale and technology from what comes later—industrial capitalism (Lachmann 1989; Dobb 1947; Brenner 1976, 1977, 1982; Moore 1966; Hobsbawm 1965; Merrington 1978; Sweezy 1976; Collins 1986; Chirot 1985; Hill 1972; Needham 1969; Wallerstein 1974, 1980; Lane 1979; Schoenberger 2008; Hall 1985; Mann 1980; Levi 1988).

Since the firm emerged under industrial capitalism, and since industrial capitalism is distinct from the shade of capitalism that replaced feudalism, it follows that *organizations* are very recent phenomena. For those who specialize in their study, organizations before the mid nineteenth century are a rarity. Humans have been creating organizations of sorts for thousands of years, writes Starbuck (2007); and organizationally relevant themes—the division of labor, specialization, and mass production—have appeared many times throughout this period. But entities such as governments, cities, and armies were too specific and idiosyncratic to inspire generalizations. They did not exist as discrete social systems. Not until sometime after European industrialization had begun did theoretical treatment of the idea become *de rigueur*. Only in the second half of the nineteenth century did greater interest in 'the organization' become generally perceptible. And only after 1850 did a growing population and enthusiasm for rationality, education, and new technologies (especially the application of steam power) create the basis for theorizing about (and explaining) organizations. Large construction projects demanded large-scale organizations; and returns from standardized production encouraged large factories to be built. By the early twentieth century the organization—a formal and defined social system—had taken on an identity distinct from its owners and the people in it. People came and went, but the organization—a distinct product of 19th century - endured.

Much of the debate on the organization focuses on what are taken to be its new forms in today's market economy. Setting aside transaction costs and resource-based accounts, explanatory models frequently overlap but, Romanelli (1991) argues, gravitate toward: random variations; environmental conditioning (and notions such as creative destruction, imprinting, and speciation); and emergent social systems or, in other words, embedded interactions between society and organization. It is in that space, where society and nascent organizations interact, that the organization first appears. Organizations help create the environment or context; they are constrained by it; they must adapt to it; and they emerge from it. The essence of this context is, for many writers, rationality.

It is fair to say, as Perrow (2000) does, that across the piece there is more interest in how organizations work and how their functioning might be improved than there is in the impacts of organizations on society; while, by comparison, discussion on how the organization as a general phenomenon (and not just a business one) came to be is neglected. Two further matters have also escaped the attention they deserve.

(a) The first is that dispassionateness, hierarchy, specialization, and other Weberian qualities which define the modern organization also define early (ancient) states, and separate those states from chiefdoms (Southall 1957; Wright and Johnson 1975; Isbell and Schreiber 1978; Childe 1950; Runciman 1982; Sahlins 1974). It is difficult to see how this can be reconciled with the belief that organizations are creations of the nineteenth century. An additional and related point—and one which goes some way to help account for that contradiction—is the uncertainty surrounding the distinction commonly made between what are held to be different categories of activities. Such doubts are nothing new. For instance, Polanyi's view that economic activities are enmeshed in social rela-tionships, argues Lie (1991), should be taken further: markets *are* social net-works or organizations made up of traders (see also Filani and Richards 1976). There exists no single dis-embedded 'market' but rather multiple communities of traders and customers. More social perspectives of organizations and their origins must also be acknowledged. Schiele (1990), for instance, argues that, from an African point of view, human beings are fundamentally good and non-material; social relationships matter more than anything else; and emotion is a valid path to knowledge. By refusing to accept that rationality is a category of western thought, organizational theories have 'fostered human service organizations that concern themselves not with the human needs … of their members and clients, but with becoming more efficient (rational) in achieving their announced, and often unattainable, goals' (Schiele op. cit., p. 159). Other writers point to the non-rational quality of modern organizations, even in the West. Abrahamson (1993) includes in his understandings of rationality a desire to satisfy ethical and moral beliefs. For Homans (1950) the mitigation of isolation is one important element driving the creation of newly formed groups. The firm, like any other organization, is a human community and as such has intrinsic social responsibilities (Melé 2012). Since 1945 rationality has found expression not only through scientism, individual rights and capabilities, education, professionalization, law-like arrangements, and accounting, but also through the world-wide expansion of organizations with non-rational features (Myer and Bromley 2013). For instance, the need for universities to meet ranking and accreditation doctrines compels them to evolve systems that are not clearly linked to their main functions. Their original objectives are subsumed by quite different ones. This might, as Perrow (op. cit.) suggests, help to explain why debate on the origins of organizations has been so limited: the demands of the organizations in which academics work have, especially through regimes for funding and promotion, skewed efforts towards more immediate and utilitarian questions.

(b) The second matter is the questionable distinction made between, on the one hand, Europe's capitalist development and, on the other, economic, political and social arrangements in other parts of the world (see Goldstone 1991; Goody 1996; Elvin 1973). Periods of Smithian and Schumpterian growth (and marked prosperity)—or efflorescences (as Goldstone 2002, describes them)—were normal and common occurrences in many civilizations long before Europe's industrial revolution. This new revolution (or efflorescence) differed from earlier periods in that engines fed by coal and oil released machines from their dependency on muscle and agriculture, concentrated energy on a huge scale, and drove self-sustaining and accelerated growth.

But was the increase in scale, vast as it was, a qualitative difference or one of degree? Collins (1997) argues that labor-intensive techniques are also innovative and used to exploit market opportunities. The point, an important general observation, is illustrated by markets in Tokugawa Japan. It is also worth adding that, if viewed in purely utilitarian terms, human labor—wage or slave—was just one form of energy converted into another form through machines. Human muscle was not the only reservoir of energy available in pre-modern societies. Wind and water power was applied widely. Gravity was used by the Greeks to drive automatons. Coal for combustion was also known to them as was the distillation of crude mineral oil and its transformation into different grades. Electricity, generated by batteries, was in use in Parthian settlements (near Baghdad) around the first century AD (possibly earlier) for electroplating or medical purposes (Keyser 1993). The installation of 27 furnaces (comprising 3000 smelting units) with a combined length of more than one kilometer, all to exploit copper at Seh Nasbt in Egypt during the Old Kingdom, is surely industrial in character rather than nearly so (Fluzin et al. 2011) and is just one of numerous metallurgical sites on the Sinai Peninsula, some of which date back as far as 2500 BC (ibid.).

Pre-modern societies could be industrial in other senses, too. Tools with jeweled tips for boring into rock, and copper saws with corundum teeth for slicing it, litter the vast flood-control and irrigation works capable of regulating the Nile and the sites of huge stone monuments, testament to the industrial quality of construction in Egypt (Hull 1939). In Greece, by the end of the pre-Christian era, the laws of levers, buoyancy, and center of gravity, and something of relative density and hydrostatic pressure, were known. Wedges, jack-screws, pulleys, windlasses, toothed gearing, compressed air and water pressure pumps were in practical use, and shipbuilding facilities and dry docks were equipped with moveable gates, valves, pumps and keel blocks (ibid.). The description 'industrial' must also surely apply to highly regimented teams of laborers, each charged with a very specific task, and placed in galleys designed to convert human energy into motion and capable of 12–15 knots for short periods. In Rome, *officina* (establishments for large-scale production, or factories) were a common sight. There were armories, mints, shoe factories, paper mills, glass factories; there were chemical factories manufacturing red and white led, indigo, dyes, and drugs; there were food manufacturers and perfumeries; there were factories producing lamp-black, incense, and surgical instruments; and there were stone cutters and weavers. Populated by slaves and trade unions of freedmen operating machines such as olive presses and wine presses, tasks were often specialized either within the factory or geographically by town segment or town (Wright 1917). In the countryside, too, mechanized harvesters (such as those found in Gaul) and other agricultural devices were in use. (White 1967).

These kinds of developments in technology and in the use of labor, set against high levels of commercialization which extended to factor markets, brought an unmistakable industrial feel to human activities. China's economy, for instance, was characterized by diversification and handicraft production and, in some parts of the Empire after the tenth century, by extensive and dense trade networks and by a lasting inclination towards privatization (Wong 2002). It was, to all intents and purposes, a huge market economy. Money penetrated backcountry villages, and many different types of credit were used. There were marked improvements in agriculture, water transport, and metallurgy. Cities grew in numbers and size, many predominantly industrial in nature (Elvin 1972, p. 141). By the fourteenth century Chinese society was probably the most numerate, literate, and advanced technically and scientifically in the world. Textile manufacturing had been transformed into an efficient industry of mass production: its machine technology was already equivalent to that used for re-spinning flax and spinning silk in Europe in 1700. China's iron and steel industry had long since expanded along an arc from south Hebei to northern Jiangsu. Indeed, none of the advances made by Europeans up to the mid-eighteenth century, nor their productivity levels, had been out of reach of China four hundred years earlier (Elvin op. cit.; Hartwell 1962, 1982).

If industrialization is viewed as a continuum—the further end of which is marked by the application of fossil fuels to manufacturing, transport and communications—then it is clear that varying degrees of movement along this continuum have occurred at many times and in many places. This being so, then it is highly likely that the conditions which make this possible are both common and straightforward: it is only their intensification which provides the final push into a state of modern industrialization.

Take, for instance, the application of steam which lay at the heart of Britain's industrial revolution. This was preceded by an extended lead time—some two thousand years—during which the organizational and commercial experience and sheer density and scale of population sufficient to encourage its use and absorb its impacts fell into place (The same might also be said of the batteries and application of electricity in Mesopotamia.). The steam engine appears, probably for the first time, in ancient Greece as a toy to illustrate the principles of converting steam into power. The piston and cylinder also emerges at this time (Petroski 1996; Scally 2011). Steam power was discovered again in the early sixteenth century to pump water through fountains or from the bottom of mineshafts or to the upper floors of buildings. Not until the late eighteenth century was it adjusted to power a mill, sometime after Hyugen had experimented with a gunpower-fired engine (the forerunner of the internal combustion engine [Petroski op. cit.]).

The conditions driving the steam engines' evolution and subsequent adoption were two-fold, and both roughly correspond with those detailed by Boserup (1987). One was high densities of population. By 1725, Leeds already had around 275 people to every acre (68,000/km^2), increasing to 365 in 1771, and up to 390 (96,000/km^2) by 1781 (Chalklin 2001)—densities greater than, or approaching those, found in the slums of Nairobi today. London, Manchester, Salford were at about half these levels by the end of the eighteenth century, but these were still very high. The other was the pattern of population: large and dense clumps at the nodes of commercial networks which had been laid down over the preceding six centuries. All lay within about 300 km of each other (or about three or four days on horseback or by coach when the weather was good, and about a week by wagon). Such distances were practical for keeping an eye on commercial interests and for supplying businesses with materials and transporting their manufactures.

These high-density clumps, set within striking distance of each other, presented a huge reservoir of labor and demand. They also made possible the comparatively fast exchange of information and ideas. The evolution of science and technology in Europe over many centuries owed a tremendous debt to commercial and other contacts with the near and middle east, and with India and China. But as important as this was, the generation and transmission of knowledge built up through trial and error by those who had more practical experience than formal or theoretical education was no less decisive. Even without a systematic understanding of the principles of nature, great things could be achieved as Europe's cathedrals demonstrated.

The importance of proximity and density in mixing up ideas, knowledge, experience, and information is also illustrated by the close link between patents and the production of raw materials in Fig. 6.1. Patents give only a very imperfect indication of inventiveness, but the connection between the filing of patents and output seems close enough[2] to indicate that, at the very least, information was

---

[2]Simple correlations between patents and each of the items produced (cotton, wool, pig iron and coal) are high (around 0.9). The original material is readily available in the sources cited in Fig. 6.1.

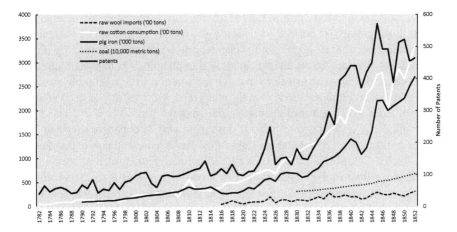

Fig. 6.1 Patents and production (UK). *Sources* Mitchell (1998), Woodcroft (1854)

circulating effectively; and that many hopeful inventors were keeping a careful eye on the production of base materials as an indicator of demand which they might be able to satisfy through some or other technique or device they had been working on.

The increasing density and scale of population, and prior commercial and organizational experience, also constituted favorable conditions in another respect. Only when the expansion of population and the specialization of the market reach a certain point, argue Goodfriend and McDermott (1995), are households encouraged to innovate such that production then shifts from households to firms. The state can have a role in all this by, say, integrating markets (Epstein 2000) or by providing stability and guarantees of protection for private property and patents (North and Thomas 1973).

6.3 Emotion, Pattern, and Illustration

Confining the origin of the business organization (and the organization more generally) to Europe since the industrial revolution is questionable on a number of grounds: the existence of Weberian-style organizations in different parts of the world long before their appearance in Europe during the eighteenth and nineteenth centuries; uncertainty over the distinction between social and other spheres of activity; and the ubiquity of industry and commerce prior to the nineteenth century. How, then, is the business organization to be explained?

The answer is simply that the business organization or firm is a means to protect relationships during the pursuit of commercial ends; and that it is most likely to appear when the movements of groups of patrons and clients are circumscribed and competition amongst them is intense. This answer emerges naturally from a synthesis of the arguments presented so far.

The motivation to form groups (any kind of group) is rooted in the material from which those groups are formed—relationships. Relationships describe streams of representations (of self, others, and wider world) which are informed by and, in turn, inform practice. Actors congregate as sets of relationships to solve a multitude of problems. But they are driven to that general solution by a psycho-physiological need to maintain representations of self, others, and wider world—a need which, if not met, leads into a spiral of alienation and anxiety.

Emotion has a pivotal role here. It describes what is experienced when mind arrives by itself at a representation, rather than has a representation communicated to it directly. Emotion implies choice and, therefore, the treatment of relationships *as if* absolute (that is, *as if* significant in their own right). This is called an affective state. To treat relationships *as* absolute or as a means to an end removes choice; emotion is dulled; representations of self, other and world are weakened, and actors begin their fall into a state of alienation and anxiety.

It is precisely this problem—descent into alienation—which intensifies with the size and complexity of those congregations of relationships; and it is precisely in order to protect their affective state of mind that actors mask and re-present their relationships as the technical routines, roles, rules, hierarchies and processes of 'the organization.'

These changes in the treatment of relationships, and the organizations that emerge, have an important effect on those aspects of relationships described as patronage and on the patterns of relationships. The patrons' dependency on the growth of population as the means to service their clients and as a symbol of status, encourages further growth and (where physical movement and land is restricted) increasing density.

When movement is restricted and new land is no longer available, and where patrons and their followers find themselves in competition with other such groups, trade and commerce will necessarily take on particular saliency if patrons are to continue to deliver goods and services and maintain support. Industrialization, including its modern form, is simply an extension of the increasing density of population, commerce, and competition. Indeed, where those circumstance prevail for long enough industrialization is very likely though not guaranteed. The emergence of democratic-like arrangements is also very probable. To avoid internal dissent and conflict with other competing groups, patrons come under irresistable pressure to cooperate with each other. This leads them eventually to find ways of rotating power amongst themselves and of distributing goods on a more programmatic basis.

England and Japan

This series of events is most likely to play out in full where the movement of groups is circumscribed. The sharply defined geographical boundaries of two islands— England and Japan—at opposite end of the vast Eurasian landmass worked to just that effect. On both islands the growing size and density of population, the competition to secure and provide materials, and the rise in commercial activity, called up an increasingly complex patterning of activities and organizations. The emotional pulses intimately connected with these changes were also vented through all kinds of apparently unrelated endeavors, not the least of which were artistic.

Pattern

In the centuries following the slow invasion and occupation by Anglo-Saxons, England appears to have 'filled up'. Greater population density meant greater competition among patrons to attract more followers to occupy or reclaim whatever land remained, to cultivate land more intensively, to defend territory, and to feed, clothe, and house more bodies. This in turn meant the accretion of still more clients which each patron would then have to service. Land reclamation continued up to the fourteenth century when the 'age-old movement of colonization came to a halt' (Postan 1976, p. 27); but the take up of secondary and marginal land was nearly complete by the eleventh century so that as the number and size of villages grew, the average size of holdings fell.

Growing competition amongst patrons at home and overseas also meant increasing dependency on commerce, less interest from landowners in direct farming, an expanding base of taxpayers, and, in response, a ruling club that widened its membership beyond the crown and its immediate supporters. All this found expression in changing patterns of activities. Three such changes are especially noteworthy.

One was the spread of the manorial system which, by the middle of the eleventh century, covered most of England. The manor comprised the Lord's hall; his demesne (home farm); and holdings let out to tenants (both un-free and semi-free) on whose labor he depended. It reflected more intense competition in that its boundaries were well defined and fixed, while its internal arrangements varied. During periods of tension and open conflict amongst patrons, lords handed their demesne over to important followers while developing alternative sources of income from mining to commerce. These periods were frequent and by the mid-fifteenth century very few home farms were left under the direct management of lords (Postan 1976).

A second was the rise of towns. Fixed borders and territories, and increasing densities of population, compelled a more settled life throughout the Anglo-Saxon era, though not an urban one. Between the eleventh century and the beginning of the thirteenth, however, towns proliferated. Kingdoms throughout Europe demanded revenues to fund their adventures against each other and in the crusades—revenues which only merchants could supply in sufficient quantity. Pockets of comparative freedom were needed, places where they could trade unhindered. It was on these 'non-feudal islands'—sometimes no more than small villages or even empty spaces—in the feudal seas' (Postan 1976, p. 239) that medieval towns grew. The larger ones would later receive their privileges as charters of liberties. Through the gilds, the towns' merchants exercised monopoly control over trade in their region; and through reciprocal rights which towns extended amongst each other, a national commercial network was woven together, centered on London. Similar principles and arrangements emerged internationally—in the Company of the Staple and the Company of Merchant Adventurers. By the fifteenth century merchants were circulating in the countryside, stimulating periodic markets, permanent markets and the annual or bi-annual or quarterly fairs, bringing English rural goods into the international market and bringing imported urban goods into England's countryside.

A third was the simplification of the patron-client hierarchy. Estates failed to keep pace with demands from followers and crown. At the turn of the thirteenth century additional and burdensome taxes were imposed, culminating in the Barons' refusal to pay any more. Over the next forty years, taxation began to move to all men in the country in possession of goods and income, marking the start of a direct relationship between crown and its lowlier and more numerous subjects. In broadening the tax base, the crown would have to make some concessions: the provision of Westminster of 1259 protected freeholders from abuse by the barons; and knights were summoned to parliaments between 1254 and 1294 after which time the practice was regularized.

Similar events took place in Japan. Here, fifty years or so into the seventh century—some little time after the Anglo-Saxons' slow invasion of England had come to an end—much of the good land had already been divided up amongst the chiefs of the great clans. One of these was elevated to Emperor and absolute monarch in imitation of the Tang model of government in China. But it was only an imitation. The attempt to centralize power was frustrated by disagreements amongst the clans. The arrangement which emerged by the early twelfth century resembled a club formed around a nominal chief patron—the Emperor—but led in practice by the shogun who, as *prima inter pares*, worked to hold the group together through the exchange of titles and favors. Ravina (1995, p. 1017) prefers to describe this pattern as a 'composite state'—large domains (small states) arranged within a broader state system. Power was dispersed; Emperor and Shogun had their own courts and authority; and local military governors (or the *daimyos* as they came to be called) exercised considerable autonomy and control (MacFarlane 1997, p. 793; Hall 1961, 1962).

The club was remarkably stable. It came apart only once. Competition amongst clans finally came to a head in the mid fourteenth century, aggravated first by Buddhist monasteries which had accumulated large tracts of land and built up their own armies, and then by Mongol invasions which, though repelled, drained government and put further strain on the manorial system. There followed a period of civil war, independent fiefdoms, and decentralization lasting some two hundred years before the club was fully reconstituted and the shogun exercised control over the entire country. On either side of this long hiatus, commerce and towns thrived, generating the wealth that agriculture could not.

The earlier, and more limited, burst of urbanism took place mainly along the coast where flatter land and most of the population were to be found. These commercial centers provided goods, exotic symbols of status, and wealth over and above whatever agriculture could offer, and so often enjoyed both self-government and protection. But the urge to create multiple and linked pockets of freedom for commerce was not yet felt. Most towns were places for administration or defense or belonged to temples: they might allow or possess a market though only as a useful appendage.

The later burst followed in the wake of a new, emerging, and centralized leadership and its policies. Surveys were ordered providing more accurate and detailed information on what each plot of agricultural land could produce and, therefore, on how much tax it could realistically bear. And those who in fact cultivated the land were designated as tax payers and given security over it. Thus, a body of independent family cultivators appeared who, slowly, also began to have more say over village affairs. At the same time, warrior farmers (the samurai) were given a choice: either stay on the land as farmers, or remain warriors and move to the castle towns of their lord. But they could do not do both. Some chose farming; many went to the castle towns under the patronage of their daimyo and—accustomed to a fine lifestyle and now with no other means of support—at great cost to him. Each daimyo had to bear other expenses, too, not the least of which was housing his own family and retainers in estates in Edo as a guarantee of his loyalty to the Shogun.

These fiscal demands, together with the freedom that cultivators now had to keep more of their own produce, were met by another round of forest clearance, irrigation and water conservancy projects; by land reclaimed from bays and tidal marshes (Toshio 1991); and by a drive to extract more from existing agricultural land. This, however, meant more investment, more labor, and more mouths to feed. Commerce provided another way of generating wealth comparatively quickly. The samurai (around a million of them who, together with their families and retainers, now swelled the towns) were not only a burden for the daimyo: they also constituted a new market for artisans and merchants. The marketplaces, once mere attachments to the castle towns, now *became* the towns. Initially the daimyos, like the patrons of ancient Greece, minted their own coins (Nobukio and McClain 1991). In response, and anxious to ensure free-flowing commercial networks, the Shogunate produced its own national currency and restricted monopolies such that towns became interconnected islands. Here, merchants could ply their trade. They could not work in the rural areas nor change profession, but then neither farmer nor samurai could become merchants. But as demands for an increasing share of their wealth grew and taxation increased, the merchants roamed well beyond the confines of the towns, commercializing the countryside too. By the latter part of the seventeenth century, commerce was the most vigorously growing part of the economy.

As competition—domestic and international—grew more febrile, Japan's ruling club became increasingly dependent upon commerce and towns. Continuity and stability was maintained not by widening its membership but (after the long civil war) by ensuring that the 'first' among all these 'equals' held the greater share of land and commerce. To this end an enormous bureaucracy evolved through which the Tokugawa family managed its extensive holdings of land, mines, and forests scattered throughout Japan; levied taxes on industry and commerce in those cities under its direct authority; and so controlled the wherewithal to forestall any challenge from the daimyo (Toshio 1991; Saxonhouse 1995; Fulcher 1988).

Organization

Were these changing patterns in England and Japan described by the activities of organizations? The answer to that must surely be yes. Even if organization is equated with an incorporated body and its narrower set of criteria, then many of its defining features were common in England long before the mid nineteenth century and legal incorporation. The craft guilds were originally fraternal and religious organizations which sometimes overlapped, and sometimes coincided, with the borough and with districts occupied by specific trades in London (and which later became known as livery companies). The guilds sought royal charters granting them monopolies, internal autonomy, and defined legal powers including the right to search (see also Sleigh-Johnson 2007) and to acquire and possess real property. The use of the seal, which allowed an act to be identified as one performed by the whole body, had become common in the latter part of the thirteenth century and during the fourteenth century. Charters of perpetual existence were granted long before the legal concept of separate existence was recognized. A gild established at Abbotsburg before the Norman Conquest was granted property to "possess now and henceforth". Others were later founded "evermore to lasten," and still other gilds "to abyde, endure, and be maynteyned without end" (Walker 1931, p. 97). And if this had been forgotten, then rights to hold, purchase, and sell lands in perpetuity—and, critically, authority to limit or revoke those rights—were re-stated again in the early (1279) statutes of mortmain (Hein 1963). Limited liability, too, existed in practice long before the mid-nineteenth century. The principle that only the goods of the corporation could be taken in lieu of a settled debt was recognized in legal judgment in 1429, 1440 and again in 1442, and became firmly established during the reign of Edward IV (Walker op. cit.; Hein op. cit.). Clauses to this effect inserted into contracts were recognized and enforced by courts, and the principle was assumed to hold for incorporation by charter. Parliament took a deal of time to catch up with common practice. Limited liability for some overseas trading companies was not granted by Act of Parliament in 1662. It was another 200 years before limited liability for all companies who desired it was possible, and before it became mandatory for all bodies comprising 20 people or more to register as companies.

That entrepreneurship—often defined as innovation, risk-taking, and judgment—was also to be found as early as the thirteenth or fourteenth centuries is not surprising either. It was widespread, as was the enterprise itself. The basic unit of production was the immediate family (parents and children and, often, grandparents). Wives and daughters were often found alongside men in urban crafts as cap-makers, glovers, parchment-makers, dyers, bow-stringers, tanners and barber-surgeons, and, much to the chagrin of the gilds (Hilton 1984), in small-scale retail trade, especially of victuals, cloth, and ale. The Church, too, was an entrepreneur: it had long operated markets alongside its places of worship and offered hospitality on along the pilgrimage routes which it promoted (Casson and Casson 2014).

In Japan, the *za*—though neither as complex internally nor as influential as the European craft-guilds—were important to the development of commerce during the medieval period. They, too, had a clear identity and continued well beyond the lifetime of any one man. Their function was to link up, and to mediate between, groups of merchants, aristocrats, and temples; and to carve out and protect areas and trades. They restricted competition in markets of all kinds from, say, firewood, charcoal and needles to lamp oil, tangerines, silk, and dried fish (Yamamura 1973). As takings from agriculture fell away, they provided nobles and temples with revenue. And only once it became clear that the restrictions they brought meant commerce generated less revenue than it might without them did the *za* die out. Even then the commercial organizations which followed were modeled on the *za* in that they passed leadership down through the male bloodline and often achieved a commanding position in their trade.

The Kano workshop, for example, established by a family of painters in 1530, had, less than a century later, come to sit atop a pyramidal structure comprising three hereditary and two collateral branches; and it would go on to train the great majority of painters during the Edo period, whether they worked for Shogun or daimyo or as independent artists in small towns throughout Japan (Gerhart 2001). The stability, longevity and influence of Kano was ensured by putting the needs of the organization, not the individual, first. There was a clear hierarchy focused on the male head of the family and workshop (the master painter); projects were directed by him; he handled the most prestigious works in any project; and his name was recorded irrespective of who in fact worked on it. Well defined methods for training apprentices were developed to unify artistic production; composition, brushwork, and quality control were standardized; and techniques were passed through the generations and across branches. Vital here was the house's publication of books on art history and techniques; on training and its importance relative to talent; and on the structure of the organization and its future. At the same time, there was room for flexibility when and where this was required by the organization. Room for exceptionally talented employees to develop their own artistic vision was also created either through adoption or marriage into the family or by establishing a new branch in the House (ibid.). A particularly talented artist (if also a family member) could even take on the most important pieces, direct projects, and have his name recorded, while the head confined himself to administration and management.

Compendiums on method, technique, training, organizational structure, and future directions, were not unique to Kano. At about the same time (the early seventeenth century), merchant houses in other trades were producing their own sets of rules and instructions. These, too, were designed largely to ensure the stability of the house and its continuation beyond the lifetime of any one person. Family and non-family were asked to be industrious and frugal, obey the government, show restraint, treat subordinates (and especially non-family) fairly and compassionately, and eschew gambling, gluttony and late nights (Ramseyer 1979). Clerks and apprentices were brought deep into the business, shown the ins and outs of how it worked, and encouraged to speak out and make suggestions without fear. Those who proved themselves competent were promoted even if they were new employees; older staffs and those who became sick were treated kindly. At the same time, the difference in status between clerks and apprentices had to be observed; and everyone in the business was enjoined to separate private matters from official tasks (ibid.).

The division of the organization into three tiers or classes—managers, clerks and apprentices—was a common one, as was an attempt to secure a balance between the head of the business, family, managers, and clerks. In the larger businesses, a council of managers (and branch managers)—whose procedures and judgments were guided by elaborate regulations—determined policy. They also had a duty to ensure that the head did not act rashly; and, if they had no other way to bring an unruly head to heel or have him removed, they might use litigation to escalate disputes though Government preferred to keep out of the organization's internal affairs (Ramseyer op. cit.; Gerhart op. cit.; Gaens 2000).

Emotion

Deepening affect found expression not only through the qualities of organizations but also through art. Despite the strong influence of the Kano workshop and its willingness to meet the taste of the Shoguns, many artists—including its former pupils—turned away from its intellectual, idealistic, high-minded stylisms, and looked toward the natural world or the lives of the most ordinary and lowly men and women. Their work—light, unaffected, sensuous, and often surprising—was concerned above all with emotion and realism. Its ambition, or so the words of Hokusai (b. 1760) intimate, was to make 'every dot and every stroke … as if living' (cited in Paine and Soper 1974, p. 153). Ganku's (b. 1749) Deer, for instance, has remarkable texture and depth combined with an apparent lack of artifice; the animals seem to have been lifted out of a moment of time. No wonder, then, that art (most especially the wood prints) from this era would later have such an influence on the French impressionists.

There had been an earlier pulse of affect. During the Late Heian, artists in Japan also gave vent to emotion through unaffected realism and naturalism (Paine and Soper 1974). The best of it is quick-moving and rule-breaking: the animal caricatures from the eleventh or twelfth centuries—especially the Monkey Worshipping a Frog, and a Frog Throwing a Hare—are satirical, playful, and charming, and do not seem remotely to fit the word 'medieval' and all that it conjures up in the European mind. The same can be said of the Wasps of Hell and Hungry Demons (thirteenth and fourteenth centuries). The feeling that art and its subjects were important in themselves also permeated classical literature. It centered on themes of love and illicit affaires. Love and desire—unencumbered by considerations of career, politics, wealth, and power—were more likely either outside marriage in a relationship with a man from another household, or in marriage with a man of higher status; these were circumstances in which the man had little to gain except the woman and much to lose including his good name (Haruko and Phillips 1993; Haruko and Rowley 2010). 'True' love, though, was an ideal more easily indulged in books or on the stage than in everyday life; and longing was tempered by the security that came for a wife who bore children, ran the household and managed its subordinate members with compassion, and for whom more selfless conceptions of love had greater meaning.

The emotional content exhibited during both these pulses is all the more striking because both are preceded by bouts of Puritanism: the late Heian followed a time when art was more about iconography; the Edo a time when the Zen sect of Buddhism (which military leaders had initially flirted with during the Kamakura) came to the fore and Japan had fallen into division, instability, and uncertainty. Book learning was cast to aside. One's own nature, character-building, frugal living, decisive action, and the concentration of the will to eradicate selfness, were all that mattered. The disposal of self was to be achieved not gradually but suddenly, and the individual shocked out of rational thought (Paine and Soper op. cit.). This was the time of the priest-painter. Ink monochrome; quick, bold lines; large, unfilled spaces; the minimum of detail; and only the hint of form. Art was now about mastering techniques that were taken to embody aspects of religious teaching. Emptiness on a surface described the infinity of time and space and its part in man's life and his union with nature. Abbreviated painting—a severe economy of strokes which reduced forms to a few, bold, suggestive lines—represented abstract and ineffable thought. Splashed-ink—a technique said to require the utmost concentration because it allowed no second chances or revisions—embodied the belief that the Buddha's enlightenment was received through a momentary flash of inspiration (Gutiérrez 1961). The themes of paintings, too, were symbolic of those beliefs: for instance, the changing seasons of landscape denoted the union of man and nature. These techniques brought an emotional quality to this art in that so much was left to the mind of the observer. But whilst the means are reminiscent of the impressionist movement, its ends were those of the iconographer such that it was, argue write Paine and Soper (op. cit.), neither art nor iconography.

At about the same time the frogs and hares were being drawn in Japan, painting in Europe remained stiff. At the start of the twelfth century artists were concerned, as Gombrich (1991, p. 133) puts it, with the arrangement of traditional sacred symbols, not with an imitation of natural forms. Yet change had begun a century earlier at Cluny—the first and most austere of the monastic orders—on the pilgrimage route to the Middle East. The self-delight wrought into the stone figures seemed like a deliberate gibe at the po-faced. Sincerity and light won out at Chartres, too, and would later shine through Pissano (1250–1330) at Pisa and Pistoia, though Donatello and Brunaschelli, and through Giotto who translated this feeling of 'being' onto flat canvas.

Painting in northern Europe, meanwhile, remained distinctly mediaeval in its rigidity despite Italian influences and the Eyck brothers' innovations; and it would not be long before the legitimacy of any painting would be questioned by the Puritans. The written word could broadcast moods with greater ambiguity. Friendship, heterosexual and homosexual passion, and every other aspect of human relationships and emotion could be played out there and, in Shakespeare's (1564–1616) writing at least, without dogma. By 1640, however, as Puritanism neared its zenith and reached into every corner of life, Shakespeare's sonnets were either changed or excised as new editions sought to cut out the ungodly, unwholesome, and impure. It would take another generation or so for the pendulum to swing back and for pockets of affect to join together into a new movement—'the Enlightenment'.

6.4   Conclusions

The presence of Weberian features and market economies before they appear in Europe, and uncertainty over the distinction between economic, organizational, and social spheres, bring into question many assumptions about the origins of organizations in general and businesses in particular. The apparent distinction between social and organizational is just that—apparent. The organization is an immediate, observable, and applied solution to everyday problems, yet driven essentially and ultimately by a need to defend relationships. Trade and production for exchange is but one unremarkable problem in response to which organizations are formed. Trade is itself a necessary practical response to struggles among groups of patrons and their clients, especially as population densities increase and groups are unable to secure additional land. It is competition under these conditions, and a desire to avoid alienation, that encourages rival groups to share resources, to rotate power, and to industrialize. Industrialization, then, is not an end, but a means to an end whose emergence is very likely over the long term.

The speed with which industrialization has spread queers the pitch for any attempt to explore and explain it through comparison with other parts of the world. But in Japan—the first state outside Europe and America to experience modern industrialization—it took root with ease, judged at least against the long struggle and continuing poverty in so many other parts of the world. It centered on existing, older commercial and industrial centers, densely populated, and set within 300 km of each other (Tokyo, despite the construction of highways to speed up transport and communications between itself and the rest of the archipelago, lay outside that sphere and remained a center of consumption until after Japan's industrial revolution.). And it was long preceded by events which reflect changes in emotion and patterns of relationships and organizations which, in England, go some way to account for its industrial revolution.

These arguments lie some distance from Macfarlane's view that England and Japan islandhood formed a protective shell (against invasion and consequently civil strife and famine) within which preventative checks on population could evolve, Malthusian disasters were avoided, and sufficient wealth garnered, to enable industrialization to proceed. My argument is that being an island sharpened competition, encouraged population growth, spurred on commerce, and indirectly prompted changes in emotion, organizations, and organizational patterns that would erupt as modern industrialization. In this regard, 'overpopulation' was never a problem and no solution was needed. The point is highlighted by China. Parts of the Empire moved further along an imaginary 'industrial continuum' earlier than either the UK or Japan had done, only to be hampered by the sheer size of the state: there was always somewhere else to go. Population densities could always be relieved when life became too uncomfortable and competition too intense. China's size and its treatment as a single unitary state made it more difficult to secure its eventual industrialization.

Chapter 7
Big Societies: China and the Philippines

7.1 Introduction

The patterns into which relationships shape themselves as population increases reflect a gradual willingness to share resources and rotate power among competing groups, and to allow commerce to infiltrate the collective. Trade brings physical marketplaces and cash and encourages the creation of businesses and settlements. Over the long term, organizational life fosters more affective states of mind and may spark mechanization and industrialization. These features help to define any big society. Both China and the Philippines found ways to manage tensions amongst competing groups of patrons and clients. Both necessarily turned to commerce and industrialization. Both have seen large businesses—few in number but strong in influence, and often connected to political leaders—sitting atop layers of much smaller businesses. And both have seen the growth of backdoor markets and their associated risks. These traits are understood not as an explanatory context, but as a descriptive one in which the significance of small businesses and their everyday relationships is best appreciated.

7.2 Patterns of Government and Business

In China the facade behind which groups of patrons and their client compete is the party. It is the party that serves as parliament where leaders fight it out and decide who will govern for the time being, and who will collect what from where and redistribute to whom. The public forums, such as the NPC and the State Council, are idealized reflections of those gritty disputes. Gernet (1997) describes all this as opposition between different tendencies ending in factional struggles, 'with each faction seeking to exploit to its own advantage the irritation provoked in the

© Springer Nature Singapore Pte Ltd. 2018   99
R. Hodder, *Small Business, Big Society*,
https://doi.org/10.1007/978-981-10-8875-9_7

population by the authoritarianism and incompetence of party officials (pp. 663–664). Solinger (1984) describes and analyses these struggles in cyclical and somewhat mechanical terms, but conveys well enough the heated competition amongst these groups. She saw at work three ideal types. The radical, who viewed the world through the lens of class conflict; the marketer, determined to free up the economy and improve productivity; and the bureaucrat, concerned above all with state control. A moderating influence, the bureaucrat would put China back onto an even keel following the wild excursions on which it was taken by radicals and marketeers. The marketeers had the upper hand between 1953 and 1955; only to give way to bureaucrats and radicals between the late 1950s and mid 1960s when China was brought back from the brink after the Great Leap Forward; only to be launched by ascendant radicals into the long decade of the Cultural Revolution; only to swing back again to the bureaucrats and then the marketeers as China lurched to the right, temporarily in Solinger's view.

Whatever the value of these cycles as an explanatory device, the effort to squeeze out commerce was a hard-headed attempt to forget a lesson already learned. Each and every dynasty had sooner or later come to accept the necessity of commerce and industrialization. This was especially so as populations swelled, densities intensified, and competition grew both inside and outside China. Even Mao's determination to de-populate the cities, encourage self-sufficiency in both rural and urban areas, and effectively outlaw trade, could not reverse all that. Once the force of his personality was gone, and as the allegiances he once commanded began to wither, commerce resumed.

Factions evolved along with the market. The boundaries separating them are uncertain, shifting, blurred, overlapping, drawn in different ways, and open to different interpretation. There are the 'taizi' (太子) or princelings or elite (the children of former or current political leaders); the bureaucratic bourgeoisie; the 'tuanpai' (团派) or those who cut their teeth in the China Youth League; the new leftists, the Maoists, or populists; the rightists (who desire political liberalization); the Deng Xiaoping faction; and the Shanghai, Guangzhou, and Chongqing factions. Factions are also found in local (provincial and sub-provincial) politics, sometimes mirroring, sometimes adding to, an already complex national picture.

The essential split is between those who support China's middle class and big business; and those who sympathize with, and draw support from, the very large number of people who have been left behind in rural and urban areas and lost their share in China's wealth. As many commentators have noted, politicians on both sides of this split need to work together; both sides need each other. If social stability is to be maintained, then those who have not yet been absorbed into the ranks of the very self-conscious and self-regarding middle class must be brought along and provided for. This need to disperse power is recognized in a number of ways.

Most obvious is the distribution of posts amongst competing groups. Another is the slow but constant reform of the legal system since the early 1980s. The stated aim—to regulate government behavior by making all people equal before the law—was entirely understandable in the wake of the Cultural Revolution. The jolt from the Tiananmen Square and the fall of the Soviet Union piled on still more pressure to make government more effective, transparent, and participatory. By 1997, 'governing the country according to the law' had become the guiding principle. There is also growing interest in international law, especially in those aspects of it which have a bearing on commerce and China's concerns overseas. The courts remain under the Party's thumb. For instance, politically connected firms are more likely to resort to legal action in commercial disputes precisely because they can exert influence over the courts (Ang and Jia 2013). But while the Party is shielded, Party members involved in corruption are not especially if their political opponents have sufficient pull.

The dispersal of power also finds expression through fiscal decentralization and localism. True, Beijing confirms appointments of provincial leaders and key subordinate posts, and moves appointees around; books are audited in Beijing; allegations of corruption are investigated in Beijing; and the boundaries of military districts fall across provincial boundaries. But provincial leaders have the same bureaucratic rank as central government ministers. Some of them sit on the Party's Polit Bureau. Most importantly, provinces have their own revenue and are responsible for the lion's share of the country's public expenditure.

Another potent expression of the dispersal of power is the percolation of commerce throughout society and the rise of small businesses. During the fourteen years after 1978 the growth in the numbers and their share of retail sales was dramatic and often seemed to be spontaneous' (Economic Daily [经济日报], 22 December 1989, p. 3). The number of private trade organizations (business with less than eight employees) rose from about 100,000 in 1978 to over 14 million by the late 1980s. Over the same period their share of total retail sales increased from under 0.5% to around 25%. Meanwhile, state-run units of the state system of procurement and distribution became responsible for 39.4% of total retail sales (a fall of 15.2% over 1978), while collective-run units held a 34.4% share (Sui Xishan (ed.) 1988).

Private trade organizations also grew in size to become private enterprises (businesses with eight or more employees). Many were said to be joint-funded partnerships with funds of 50,000 yuan or less, employing between fifteen and thirty workers; but very large enterprises with funds of more than 10 million yuan and over a 1000 employees also appeared. The number of private enterprises was put at around 40,000 for the end of 1988 (Economic Daily [经济日报], 21 October 1989, p. 2); 66,500 for the end of June 1989 (Economic Daily [经济日报], 18 October 1989, p. 1); and 90 790 for the end of 1989—a fall of 14% over the end of 1988 (China Business Times [中华工商时报], 21 March 1990, p. 1). Other sources, though, gave a minimum figure of 115,000 for the end of 1987, to which could be added another 50,000 private enterprises registered as collectives, and a further 60,000 registered as cooperatives, making a grand total of 225,000.

Initially, the vast majority of these larger businesses operated in the countryside: about 20% were in the urban area, predominantly in the suburbs of the municipalities; and only a mere handful operated within the urban districts of the cities proper. Only a few thousand were found within the administrative jurisdiction of China's largest and most important cities. Tianjin contained around 9000 by the beginning of 1988 [Communist Party (Tianjin) 1990]; Guangzhou held barely 1700; Beijing had just 1300 by April 1988; Shenyang and Chongqing each held between 1000 and 2000; in Shanghai there were fewer than 1000 at the end of June 1987.

This rural or suburban bias partly reflected the specialization of households and the gradual concentration of land allowed for through the transfer of contracts under the responsibility system (ibid.). It also reflected the diminishing influence of administrative will. Restrictions (some formulated locally and others embellishments of national guidelines) governing the hiring of labor, the provision of welfare by enterprises for their workers, the availability of sites, and the issue of licenses, were more likely to be enforced near or in the city. There were also economic reasons, such as inflated rents, which forestalled attempts by private enterprises to operate at close quarters with subsidized, large-scale, state-run and collectively-run enterprises.

Despite these restrictions the remarkable growth of small businesses surprised many in government and bureaucracy. The all-weather and omnipresent state system of procurement was supposed to remain the primary flow channel and, therefore, the mainstay of China's new commercial development. In theory, changes in administrative organization and in the contracts governing the acquisition and movement of goods would result in a new system: one which imitated private trade in the sense that whilst economic units remained appendages of state administrative organs they would have greater freedom for independent action. It would be more responsive, flexible, and efficient. The role of small businesses was to remain supplementary, delivering agricultural goods (especially perishable commodities) and everyday industrial consumables, and providing catering, repair, construction, transport and other services. In this way they would help improve morale of the people (especially the urban population), keep state commerce on its toes, and stimulate the economy. In practice, however, small business did not just compete with state commerce: they began to infiltrate the lower echelons of the system. Outlets formerly managed by state-run and collectively-run enterprises were often released on contract to private traders and then subcontracted (JJRB [经济日报], 22 December 1989, p. 3).

Hostile commentary on small businesses soon followed. They challenged and weakened the state system of procurement and distribution—a system which binds together the components of the state and collective systems of ownership, which enables the economy to be coordinated, and which was therefore viewed and wielded as an instrument of economic and, far more importantly, of political regulation (Economic Daily [经济日报], 16 March 1990, p. 1). The system had long guaranteed civil and strategic (military and non-military) supplies (Economic Daily [经济日报], 16 March 1990, p. 1); it allowed tight control to be exercised over prices and the money supply (China Business Times中华工商时报, 28 March 1990, p. 6); and it eliminated usury and the disruption of the domestic market by private traders (Economic Daily [经济日报], 16 August 1989, p. 2). Thus it acted as a crucial stabilizing and unifying force, especially during the disturbances of 1989 and at other times of political upheaval over the last forty years. Its de facto privatization was now being witnessed with predictable consequences: parasitism, inertia, and disintegration (Economic Daily [经济日报], 1989: 22 August, p. 3; 3 September, p. 3; 11 November, p. 3). Trade meanwhile bred narcissism (ibid.), vice, and political corruption; it attracted the dregs of society; and it provided the means for dissent (Economic Daily [经济日报] 1989: 16 October, p. 1; 11 July, p. 1; 21 October, p. 2; 9 December, p. 2). The tensions it generated had already exploded into assaults on tax offices and on tax officials; and counter-revolutionary and illegal organizations were infused with the values of individualism and 'self' (Economic Daily [经济日报], 16 October 1989, p. 1; 11 July 1989, p. 1.). They charged full or excessive market prices while continuing to benefit from supplies of goods and materials bought at subsidized prices from state and collective units; and they sold goods at excessively high prices to an urban population whose direct subsidies from the state then had to be raised. They engaged in land and housing speculation, and they imposed excessive rents and evicted tenant unfairly. Tax evasion nettled the authorities even more. By the end of the 1980s at least three-quarters of all private trade organizations were believed to be evading taxes (Economic Daily [经济日报], 2 August 1989, p. 1). Often they simply would not register with the tax bureau or they would register as collective enterprises and take advantage of tax concessions and preferential treatment. Or they concealed their incomes, failed to report changes in income, doctored their accounts, bribed tax officials or drew them into a complex web of reciprocal obligations. Concern with tax evasion did not originate solely from it economic implications. It was an political act (Economic Daily [经济日报], 2 August 1989, p. 1; 3 September 1989, p. 2) which flouted and brought into question the will and competence of the administration. Indeed, there were rumors that private traders had helped to finance the pro-democracy movement and its occupation of Tian'anmen Square in 1989.

Even so, more upbeat views were also being expressed, at least within the Party. A party report published in 1988 presented the usual defenses—that private traders absorbed surplus labor, helped integrate town and countryside, and kept the state and collective enterprises on their toes—but then went much further. Private entrepreneurs were named and praised for their courage, insight, vision, adeptness in management and administration, sensitivity to policy changes, a willingness to take risks, and the strength to rise above and ignore gossip. Any failure on their part to move further towards the realization of their full potential reflected the administration's failure to provide an institutional framework within which private enterprises could work. Local officials and the general populace had to realize that the antagonism between 'socialism' and 'capitalism' and, therefore, between public ownership and private ownership, was arbitrary and misleading. A reasonable level of exploitation is quite acceptable at this evolutionary stage. Worries that the rapid development of private enterprises will undermine and topple the public-ownership system were misplaced. Private enterprises comprise only 1% of China's economy, and are never likely to capture a share of more than 10%. Moreover, private enterprises are, in the main, joint-funded organizations and therefore very similar to those of China's publicly owned enterprises which issue shares. The solution to any problems surrounding small businesses lay with the local and central authorities.

Private enterprises needed legal protection and their legal status clarified. The tax system should be improved. The size of loans and the conditions under which they are granted to private enterprises should be brought into line with those granted to state and collective enterprises. And a single specialized bureau should be established with responsibility to coordinate the development of private enterprises with the operations and plans of other administrative bureaux, and to provide training, legal advice and technical information.

The report was far off the mark in its estimation of the private sector's future share of the economy, but prescient in many other respects. A decade later government agencies were established or re-assigned to promote small businesses: the Department of SMEs, the State Administration for industry and Commerce, the Bureau of Township Industries, the Foreign Trade Centre doe SMEs, and another Department of SMEs under the State Economic and Trade Commission (Bennett 2014). In 2003 their legal status was defined. In 2007 state and private property were given equal status in law. Private merchants were even permitted to join the communist party. Access to finance would remain a problem: fewer than 0.5% were able to secure loans from banks. Nevertheless, by 2001 there were around 30 million, growing to nearly 40 million by 2004. By 2014 they numbered around 50 million and were responsible for around 60% of industrial output value, 75% of employment, and 70% of exports. By the start of 2018 they numbered a little over 65 million. As they grew in number, some continued to grow in size. More than 8 million were classified as corporate entities (see Fig. 7.1). A few have become very large indeed (measured by operating revenue [营业收入]), ranking alongside the China's state-owned leviathans (Fig. 7.2). On average, the five hundred largest private enterprises are about one third the size of the largest five hundred enterprises irrespective of ownership (Fig. 7.3a, b).

Patronage is also central to an understanding of the Philippines. Why, asked Landé, do the wealthier classes or their representatives so often lead political parties and benefit from government policy and action. How did they manage to win the

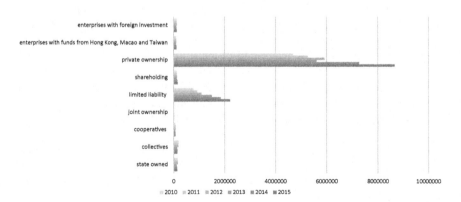

Fig. 7.1 Number of corporate enterprises by ownership type (China). *Source* 2016 年中国中小企业运行报告, 国家统计局

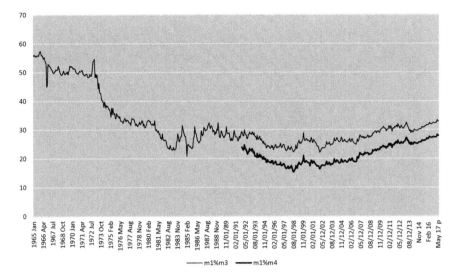

Fig. 7.2 Narrow money as percentage of broad money (Philippines). *Source* Bangko Sentral ng Pilipinas

votes of the poor? An important part of the answer, Landé argued, was the system of patron-client relationships or political clientelism: 'the upwards flow of votes from ordinary voters to wealthy candidates … and in return, the downward distribution of public and private funds and other favors to individual leaders and their followers among voters. Hoping to share in this distribution of benefits, poor voters could not afford to vote their class interests by supporting candidates of the left' (Landé 2002: 120) (Fig. 7.4).

During martial law under Marcos, the two-party system collapsed and was replaced by competing presidential candidates all of whom were heavily dependent on their home regions for support, and treated political parties as transitory electoral vehicles. Philippine politics had certainly changed over the years, but 'personalism and clientelism' remained for many an important element in electoral politics. It explained not just electoral politics but unreliable and unpredictable formal institutions, a poor regulatory environment, dysfunctional government, and the general weakness of the Philippines—all of which undermined entrepreneurial activities (Roxas et al. 2013).

For some writers the root cause of patronage was culture; for others it was structure. Hutchcroft argues that the Spanish failure to engage in state building provided room both for the emergence of strong British, American and Chinese trading houses, and for the entrenchment of a Chinese-mestizo landed élite. This decentralization of power was reinforced by the Philippines' American rulers, who concerned themselves mainly with the construction of representative institutions while leaving outside those institutions oligarchs with their own strong economic and social bases. After independence, these oligarchs, both directly or through their

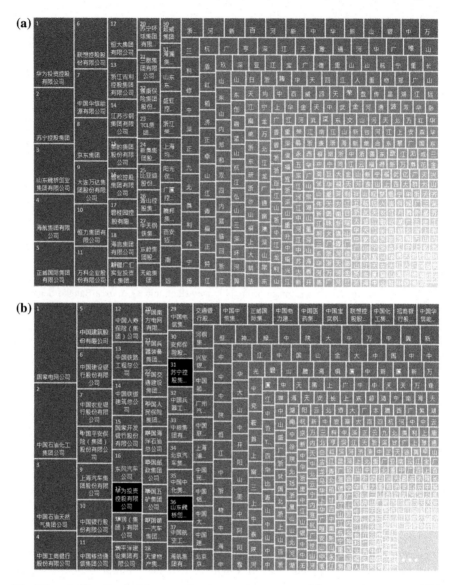

Fig. 7.3 a, b Five hundred largest private enterprises, measured by operating revenue 2017 (China). *Source* 2017 工商业联合会

proxies, moved in and out of those institutions at will and, as they did so, continued to maintain and build up their own external social and economic power bases. Local patrons in the provinces, through their personal relationships with the center, drew money, materials, and authority, towards themselves. Family businesses, faced with hostile and unpredictable circumstances, established complex and aggressive networks of relationships through which they could influence the political economy to

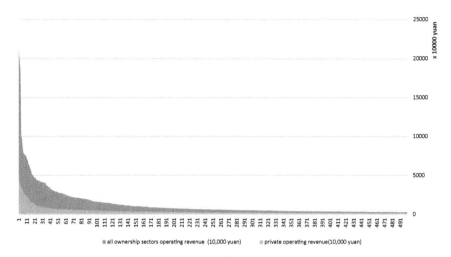

Fig. 7.4 Comparison of operating revenues by ownership sector (China). *Source* 2017 工商业联合会

their own advantage and to the disadvantage of their enemies and competitors. The center was rendered weak, and the state was left vulnerable to influence from powerful individuals and factionalized groups operating outside its institutions. Thus, the Philippines lies some distance from a strong, regularized, formal, impartial, legal-rational economy and polity of the kind described by Weber as a bureaucratic administration. In particular, argues Hutchcroft, the Philippines lacks calculation in the administrative and legal sphere; and family and business are not clearly separated. The essential question facing the Philippines is how it might transform itself from its present condition into a regularized, legal-rational, and bureaucratic state?

Sidel, too, concentrates on broad historical and structural conditions. He argues that local bosses—in municipalities, congressional districts and provinces—emerge and become entrenched under certain structural conditions. Widespread poverty and economic insecurity greatly accentuate the significance of state resources and provide those with control over those resources and state regulatory powers with the means to accumulate private capital. The actions of the Philippines' American rulers—who 'subordinated a weakly insulated state to officials elected locally and under … restricted suffrage' (2002: 133), and superimposed this system upon an economy at such an early stage of capitalist development—was bound to produce 'bossism'. Since access to resources is the overriding priority, and since that access is controlled by locally elected politicians, then the provision of public goods and services is very likely to be dependent upon the discretion of those local politicians (2002: 136–137).

As attractive as these kinds of explanations are, there is nothing especially different or Filipino or developing about patronage or its intertwining with commerce and politics in the Philippines. It is simply an aspect of relationships; and the circumstances that encourage trade in the Philippines are entirely familiar to many other parts of the world. An extensive and highly fragmented archipelago meant that, even with relatively low population densities, patrons quickly found themselves in competition with each other and devising strategies to attract and hold clients. In this, trade played an important role, supplying prestige goods and goods with ceremonial significance, as well as helping to raise the material standards for their followers (Junker 1999). The growth of population and population densities on the islands, and Chinese and Spanish involvement in trade and immigration, threw up small urban settlements by the sixteenth century together with kilns and textile manufacture.

By the middle of the twentieth century, competing units had been drawn together and a central government behind which these groups could compete. The organizations' design was imported from America; but once associations, ideas and sentiments which had become attached to it in Europe and America were stripped away, it was in its aims and methods entirely familiar and would be so in any large society. Indeed, at first, it seemed to American administrators that the Philippines provided a more ideal example of how it should work. It was only later that the Philippines would come to experience corruption and to all kinds of shenanigans that America had itself been prone to. And, in both countries, despite all the problems, the organizational arrangements were successful in that they did what they were supposed to do: disperse power and redistribute resources among competing groups of patrons and clients. A deep aversion to the centralization of power was part and parcel of this together with localism—features that were accentuated in the Philippines by its linguistic divisions and fragmented geography, and by the ambitions of Marcos.

The fact of commerce and the manner in which it developed is familiar, too. Across the Philippines a blanket of small businesses was laid down, an important source of income for local government. Above this, are much smaller numbers of very large businesses centered in Manila, with branches in smaller towns and cities. These larger business are not on especially well linked into networks of local, home-grown enterprises. They take by far the largest share of sales; a few have true monopolies; and many are arranged into oligopolies. Whatever the strength of cultural or structural accounts of Philippine economy and society there are other sound reasons for the concentration of economic power. The islands' population was, until fairly recently, small and thinly dispersed so that absolute numbers and densities were well below, say, levels on the eve of industrialization in Britain or Japan. Moreover, the archipelago lies just on the fringe of the trade thoroughfares amongst countries in East and southeast Asia and beyond. This, too, limited the intensity of commerce. Under these conditions, large businesses would need concessions—guaranteed markets—if they were to survive and flourish. These facts merely aggravated the concentration of wealth inherent in the practice of commerce.

7.3 Becoming Wealthy

It was argued in Chap. 4 that long-term growth rests on a willingness to make transfers (official and unofficial) from the financial sector to the real economy, and from rich to poor. Implied in that argument is a simple, imaginary closed community in which workers buy all the items they need from the company that employs them: there is no means to fund companies' profits. Workers could go without some items for a time and save. But the amount saved, when eventually spent, is nothing more than delayed expenditure. Or employees might invest the amount saved in the company. But the amount saved is derived from their wages and is now being returned to the company as a sum for investment rather than through purchase of it goods. Alternatively, workers from different companies may direct their spending at one particular company. This generates a profit but only at the expense of other companies (so that eventually some workers find themselves without job and without an income) and so only temporarily. Even if that successful company reemploys the jobless, their new income cannot be greater the price of the goods they produce.

This community is only imaginary; and for most people savings are very real, exactly quantifiable, and essential in everyday life. For many others, too, savings reflect virtue and reliability. But even though it is usually taken as given, there remains a problem with the notion of savings (the difference between income and expenditure). Why would the owners of capital pay workers an amount which, collectively, is greater than the income from the sale of the goods or services they produce? How then is it possible for the worker to save? By the same token, how can the owners of capital save (profit) if the workers do not have an income greater than the wages paid?

In practice, therefore, companies are compelled to find external communities; and they must take on loans to improve their techniques so that they can produce more items and better quality ones. But once those fresh, external communities have been absorbed, companies are back where they started—producing items for a population which cannot afford to fund their profits let alone their loans and interest payments. Businesses must once again search for new populations and new loans and repeat the exercise ad infinitum.

Meanwhile, the backstreet economy grows wealthy. It does so, partly through the interest payments generated by these rounds of expansion, and partly through the trade amongst backstreet players in financial products created to overcome the limitations imposed by the stop-start nature of the front street's expansionary rounds.

The logic of commercial activity, then, is degenerative. The desire to sell for profit is, at first, an affront to relationships and for this reason is often conducted only by or with outsiders. Commerce also requires external contact because the market has to expand if it is not to degenerate. And even after these avoidance measures (seeking loans and external communities) are taken, businesses find themselves back at square one where decay sets it once again. Without transfers, an economy will be still-born.

China has been highly effective in ensuring growth. Marked inequalities of wealth between east and west and urban and rural China, together with questions about levels of debt and toxic assets, suggesting comparisons with the west's economic conditions shortly before its financial crisis in 2008: these points alone might explain why China might be readier to make transfers (and in ways that are opaque) and nimbler in doing so. But there is also no question that China has not lost sight of its relationship with people. And whilst the generation that knew the make-do spontaneity of guerilla war is almost gone, and those who learnt its application in the thirty years after liberation are ageing, Puritanism has not yet rubbed out a willingness to experiment. Nor has the knowledge which accrued managing a centrally planned economy for thirty years or so been thrown away. State enterprises and collectives and their descendants have retained very important role, far greater than mere numbers of organizations suggest. Some of these are natural monopolies. Many others have formed oligopolies. The largest enterprises number no more than a few thousand and comprise no more than 2.5% of the total number of enterprises in China. The very largest 500 businesses (a fraction of one percent of the total number in China) have aggregate sales of around 60 trillion yuan—a figure a good deal larger than the gross disposable household income (Fig. 7.5).

It may be for these reasons as much as any other that China is willing and able to set aside economic rules and process and make vital transfers. These are made as subsidies to companies which provide goods and services to the populace as well as employ large numbers of workers. Or they are made by writing-off at debts at will,

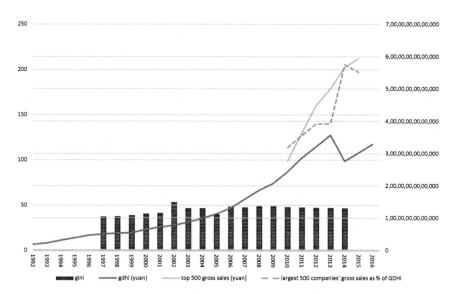

Fig. 7.5 Gross household disposable income and largest companies' gross sales (China). *Source* United Nations; 工商业联合会

or by loading debts into asset management companies, or by making loans through shadow banks to government projects that are not viable economically. In other words, large state-owned behemoths and collectives as well as private companies are being used to disguise transfers as inefficiencies and losses, made up for by subsidies which are in turn often recorded as sales and profits. It is, then, also quite possible that the huge inequalities in profits and sales witnessed amongst companies are in fact subventions about to be made to the general populace. A crisis is not off the cards, but it may be that China continues to grow while standing on what appears to be to the edge of a crisis that does not materialize at least partly because successful and unsuccessful companies are serving as channels for alternative forms of state welfare.

The complexity of this response is not only, nor even primarily, a consequence of making do, of spur-of-the-moment action, of relying on spontaneous intuition and experience rather than method. It is also an expression of an uncomplicated understanding of the essential patronal relationship between government and people. Despite what is, by international comparison, the formidable power which the Party can be bring into play (a police force of 1.5 million under the Ministry of Public Security, and an army of 2.5 million, as well as the apparatus of the courts and the prisons), this is small beer given China's huge population. Government and people know that any leadership which relied on sticks of this kind would already be looking for the door, hat in hand.

The Philippines has been less effective. Transfers have occurred, but in a far more haphazard way. The growth in narrow money—which remains at around twenty percent or more (Fig. 7.6)—has not been eroded by the rise of the backstreet market. The are many reasons for this: most businesses and people on the front

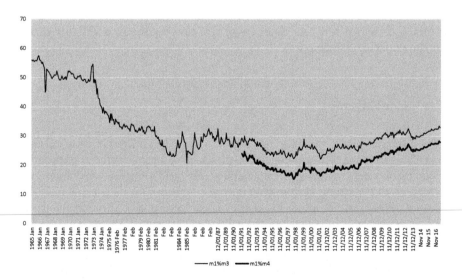

Fig. 7.6 Narrow and broad money (Philippines). *Source* Bangko Sentral ng Pilipinas

street only use currency; the backdoor market has until recently remained fairly rudimentary; tax collection by the bureau of internal revenue is inefficient; banks make it difficult for people with small incomes to open and maintain accounts, while their secrecy laws give account holders a good deal of protection; the switch in central bank policy from targeting the money supply to targeting inflation has meant looser policy; and transfers used to secure votes, to maintain supporters, to get things done in government and bureaucracy, and to avoid getting things done (and which often come under the rubric 'corruption') are commonplace. It would be easy to summarize much of this as an expression of poverty, inefficiency, and corruption; and, certainly, that would help explain why the World Bank regards informal business in any country as tantamount to criminal. But this ignores the role of narrow money and a very large community of 'criminal' businesses and markets whose existence and activities have to some extent buffered the archipelago from the IMF and other organizations whose actions would have otherwise caused even more damage. For example, in the early 1980s borrowing from overseas and government spending, combined with rises in the price of oil, and mixed with political crisis following the assassination of Aquino, sparked inflation, a moratorium on the repayment of overseas debt, and a run on the pesos. The solution, favoring backstreet markets overseas and demanded by the IMF, was a sharp tightening of monetary policy, triggering a collapse in GDP to −7% for two consecutive years in 1984 and 1985.

It may be that in China and the Philippines and in big societies like these—where relationships have not yet ossified conceptually into disembodied structures, rules, and laws—new ways are being found to make transfers, avoid the logic of commerce, and so generate growth. Encrusted with ideology and theory and morality, and transformed by Puritanism into the conventions of the market, the west balks at transfers, believing such actions to lack common sense and morality. Dependency versus initiative, a something-for-nothing culture versus industriousness, scroungers and deceivers versus the honest and hardworking, are just some of the easy, black-and-white caricatures used to excuse inadequate transfers made in a rigid and begrudging manner.

7.4   Conclusions

Both China and the Philippines imported models—the Philippines from America, and China from the Soviet Union—through which to manage political competition. Both models were quintessentially familiar: in the Philippines chiefdoms were amalgams of competing factions with interests in trade; China's imperial rulers had already devised various means to balance out competition among different interests, and knew the value of commerce and large state enterprises. The models took root not because they carefully and consciously took account of historical precedent, but because the logic of relationships and the patterns they lead to are always at work in any society. Big society and its essential patterns are constantly being created, lost and rediscovered as representations and practice alter, as the emotional atmosphere changes, and as economic growth ripples throughout the collective.

At the same time, it must be recognized that when sketching the patterns which comprise any society, it is easy and often necessary to ignore the fuzziness through which only roughly defined shapes or patterns can be glimpsed occasionally. Economic growth is one reason for the haze. It alters the details and scale of organizations and their patterning. Improvements in monitoring and communication can sharpen up organizational boundaries and practices and bring what appears to be an obvious sameness to them; or, by increasing the sheer volume and speed of ideas in circulation, make societies appear even fuzzier and even more chaotic. Or the success and fact of growth may justify, entrench, or undermine, particular understandings of existing patterns and practice. Or cities with perfect lines, perfect edges, and perfect corners, with precise movements precisely timed, may suggest a firmness and permanency that is in truth illusory. For it is, in truth, the quality and logic of relationships and emotion which are primarily responsible for big societies and their fundamental similarities and superficial differences. For instance, while the patron-client framework is deservedly influential, there is, writes Kerkvliet (1995), a need to move beyond it and develop a more textured view of the Philippine polity. It would be difficult to claim that the vision of all officials in all branches of the government and bureaucracy of the Philippines is limited by their personal ambitions. Even during the years 1961–86 there was a tendency for the Supreme Court to rule in favor of those people with less wealth and less influence from the poorer areas of the Philippines. By contrast in the UK and the USA, judicatures were more likely to rule in favor of the establishment. The return to democracy in the Philippines, the loss of patience with Estrada, the gradual pro-fessionalization of the armed forces of the Philippines and the civil service, the slow maturing of politicians, and attempts by the Church to cultivate institutional and personal probity among politicians and members of the armed forces, and the professionalization of business practices, have been accompanied by, or have allowed more open expression of, a strengthening interest in kinds of debates— such as those surrounding the rule of law, individual and institutional probity, business ethics, anti-trust legislation, and the morality of a market economy and mass representative democracy.

'Factionalism' in China also exhibits multiple dimensions. More than twenty years ago, Dittmer (1995) argued that informality tends to be dominant, while formal politics often provides no more than a façade; individuals establish formal bases more as fallbacks in the event their informal bases (and their patrons) should weaken or be removed; and while the formal members of the elite are supposed to be equal, there is among them an informal hierarchy of patron-client relationships. Yet, he noted, 'the historical trend it to formalization' (Dittmer, op. cit., p. 18). This is especially true since the death of Mao, for the 'overall thrust of development since the advent of political reform … has been towards increasing formalization, as measured by the frequency, length and regularity of meeting sessions, and the number of people or procedural stages involved in drafting legislation' (Dittmer, op. cit., p. 17). The secularization of Mao Zedong thought and Deng's pragmatic focus on growth, and 'the attendant dismissal of the specter of an elite "struggle between two lines" and "people in the party taking the capitalist road", have reduced the ideological barriers to the operation of factions (Dittmer, op. cit., pp. 30–31). The ebbing of ideology, combined with an easing of disciplinary measures against officials and attempts to legalize their tenure, and to restore popular respect for officialdom, have allowed factional behavior to become somewhat less clandestine. Elite factions have now begun to pursue and to represent the interests of their constituencies. Indeed, in the wake of reform, elite coalitions have even begun to move away from 'factions' towards 'policy groups', the next stage being the formal structures and formal alliances which make up a 'bureaucratic' polity. Of course, few things are certain: informal politics in China tends to 'reinforce traditional hierarchical relationships (including the "cult" of leadership inherited from the empire), and culturally embedded relationships more generally (for instance, time honored primordial "connections") at the expense of rational-legal and meritocratic arrangements' (Dittmer, op. cit., p. 33). Nevertheless, there is a growing institutionalization of various bureaucratic systems at all but the highest levels; the reliance on explicit rules and procedures is increasing; informal groups, now oriented more towards policies designed to enhance bureaucratic interests, are being transformed into professional, vocational, business and pressure groups—and even, as in the case of the reformists and conservatives, into quasi-parties. Moreover, as a political form, 'informal politics … tends to be progressive in terms of policy, as its flexibility facilitates more rapid change by offering short-cuts to standard bureaucratic procedures. This has helped make China an extraordinarily well-led country compared to others in the Third World (albeit not always wisely governed)' (ibid).

Fuzziness also means that any feedback which derives from existing patterns of relationships is uncertain and haphazard and this in turn contributes to their indistinctness. Every now and then, small businesses (as noted in part II of this book) cross paths with government, NGOs, and other aspects big society (such as schools or companies). Sometimes actors barely notice these intersections; sometimes lives are altered forever. Either way, it is only particular relationships which are affected by other particular relationships. In this way, changes and differences accumulate incrementally. Existing patterns do not stamp themselves on society and reproduce themselves, not least because they are in the first place vague and unsure.

Part II
Working Relationships

Chapter 8
Happenstance

8.1 Introduction

In part one it was argued that relationships occupy an indeterminate state. They take on meaning only when set within a mental context, and yet those meanings are rooted in, depend on, and inform practice and events in the social and natural worlds outside. Relationships harbor their own logic which leads to their arrangement as organizations and as states and markets. This logic reflects their uncertain state and, for example, the qualities of emotion, an indispensable drive for interaction, a need for food and shelter and water, the restrictions imposed by environment, or the demands created by high population densities.

The patterning that is China or the Philippines or any big society form descriptive contexts rather than explanatory ones. It is the particular instances of relationships—not any patterns they seem to be part of—that constrain and stimulate. Indeed, the mind's limited ability to envision accurately patterns of relationships, and its varied understandings of them, creates doubt over what is, in fact, 'out there'. Doubt and ambiguity leads to patterns of uncoordinated practice that are, in fact, indistinct, permeable, and shifting. There is, then, no coherent entity capable of exerting a coherent influence, of imprinting itself on actors, or of reproducing itself in some other way. It is particular instances—the particular sets of relationships which actors come up against—that lure and push; and it is variation in understanding and practice which demands that actors constantly adjust representations and practice so that an earthy, working fit can be realized here and now. Even the most complex society is constantly being generated, each moment of each day.

The previous six chapters established a context not to explain small businesses but to help appreciate the significance of relationships that comprise them and the rest of big society. Ordinary, everyday relationships and their constant adjustment are not wispish motes that take on substance only when compacted and formatted into structures that shape society; they *are* society in the making.

This chapter shows that piecing together the organization from common and garden relationships takes place gradually and often without much planning. It is through a kind of happenstance that existing relationships reveal new dimensions which lend themselves to the creation of the business, only later to be made a little more explicit and turned into a set of lessons, a rough formula, to make a business.

8.2 Dumplings and Flowers

The dumpling restaurant in Pingshan[1] is run by Mr. Li and his wife. They rent the building they work and live in together with their three-year old daughter and Mrs. Li's parents. Mr. Li is the head of the family and business. He is also the cook. Mrs. Li waits on the tables (Plate 8.1). They employ a washing aunt,[2] a waiter, an assistant cook, and a dumpling-maker. The year before, they rented a restaurant in Longhua and, before that, in Daya Bay and, before that, in Huizhou. They took on that first restaurant nearly five years ago. They had met there. She had been a waitress and he a cook. They had married there. When the owner retired, he let it out to them on favorable terms. Soon they had gathered enough capital to move on, looking for more opportunity, and for something better, though each had a different idea about what that meant.

Mrs. Li is eleven years younger than her husband. '*Before getting married the boss was really very nice to me. It was like being an empress.*[3] *He stopped gambling and drinking. He brought water to bathe me, and he gave me a massage every day. But after the marriage he was completely different. I could not accept it at first. I then asked my friends and it was the same for them. It is life, I think. No matter how much you complain, all you can do is accept it.... Sometimes he and I can't talk with each other nicely, because we think so differently. He is much more mature than me and thinks over things more than me.*[4] *We get bored if we stay together all day, and then we argue.... When we do he roars*[5] *at me; but he never hits me back even though I hit him. After that we make up*'.

Perhaps, she wondered, if it had been too easy for him to marry her? His family had paid nothing; she had not yet had a wedding ceremony; nor had she met either of his parents. Maybe fate had brought them together, though she was not altogether clear about why.[6] Perhaps, she thought, it was because of the child. What she found most disagreeable was his determination to play cards and slot machines and drink with his friends (Plate 8.2). That had been one of the reasons for leaving Daya Bay.

---

[1] 平山.
[2] 洗碗的阿姨.
[3] 我那简直就是女皇的日子.
[4] 考虑的多一些.
[5] 吵架时会吼.
[6] 这就是缘分吧,也说不上为什么.

Plate 8.1 Waiting on tables in a restaurant in Pingshan, Shenzhen

But a man in his twenties, she said, will be enticed by that; and she understood only too well that he needed some way to relieve the routine and boredom of work and family. She stayed in the restaurant all day with only an occasional rest in the afternoon before the evening sitting (Plate 8.3). She would have had to stay at home anyway to look after the child. She and her daughter had been to very few of the sites; only to the zoo about a mile to the north, and to Happy Valley, a theme park. She had friends but they were not true friends.[7] Their relationships with people in the neighboring shops and restaurants was good, she thought. *'They will take care of my child ordinarily, and come and help when we're especially busy. But they are not true friends.... A true friend is sincere to you.*[8] *When you have things that can't*

---

[7]真正的朋友.
[8]就是他是真心对你的.

Plate 8.2 Playing cards outside a restaurant, Nanshan

talk about with your parents, you can talk about those with your friends. I have some good friends. We can chat and go shopping together in Shenzhen; but I can't open up to them completely'. And so, while she enjoyed the occasional outing, such as a trip with the daughter of the owner of the dry-cleaning shop next door to buy the better quality counterfeit goods, he would go out with his friends and return sober and, he assured her, no longer gambled.

Her sense of isolation was not helped by her father. He was a short, stocky man who had been a laborer on construction sites. The work had been heavy and the hours long. The boss would say eight hours, but he would have to work nine; and he had to pay all kinds financial penalties for all kinds of mistakes and misde- meanors. Part of what was left would be released in dribs and drabs, enough for him to eat and drink until the building was finished when he was handed the rest of his wages. He was too old for that kind of work now, and tired of all that nonsense. He decided to work for his daughter and joined the couple when they moved to

Plate 8.3 An evening meal at a restaurant in Pingshan, Shenzhen

Nanshan. He got very little, just pocket money—ten thousand yuan last year, though it seemed less, he said. Had they stayed in Daya Bay, he said, it would have been more. The restaurant there was larger than this one, and the business was good. There were plenty of workers with money to spend and with nothing to do at night except eat and drink. '*Keep the restaurant open late into the night*' their landlord had advised. Yet his daughter and his son-in-law complained that the restaurant was too small and closed its doors before the evening got going. They had given up that restaurant, and now they were planning to give up this one, too. His daughter quickly countered. The restaurant at Daya Bay was small and polluted. The stench of coal gas hung in the air. She couldn't bear it. She nearly collapsed from the smell when she went to one of the plants to collect money from a Korean who owed them money for a meal she had served him the day before. Longhua was even smaller. The second floor was long and narrow, and the stairs to up to it were steep and winding. The first floor had room enough for only one table. The kitchen was so poorly ventilated that smoke either filled the restaurant and choked the guests or, if the back door and window were left open, poured out onto the neighbors who complained incessantly. She and her husband should have picked that problem up before they signed the contract, she said, but they lacked experience; and they could not afford to renovate the fans and pipework. As for Pingshan, there were only few restaurants when they moved there; but competition was tougher now; and they risked losing their capital if they stayed on. The fact of the matter, she said, was that the number of people coming to their restaurant had gone down while the family she and her husband now supported had grown. If her mother and father went out to work they would bring in more money than the restaurant.

In this fractious atmosphere, the little problems which everyday work threw up, and had to be dealt with one way or another, became an unwelcome distraction. Each person was living a life in which the business got caught up. From the perspective of a temporary waitress, uncertainty reigned.

When guests sit down, I serve the tea, take their order, give the order to the chef, serve the dishes, and urge the kitchen to cook for the impatient customers first. During busy periods, Xiao Lei will help me with the heavy plates and tell me which table the dish should go to. We get very tired running up and down the stairs. Xiao Lei doesn't always make clear which fillings the guests want in their dumplings. I will figure it out if I can. One guest comes in for dinner alone, and just orders a plate of dumplings. There are so many people tonight and we serve him very slowly. Eventually he leaves without having had his dumplings. Later, Mrs. Li notices it, and asks me if he's already gone? I tell her that he can't wait any more, that we seem to have forgotten him. Mrs. Li doesn't say anything. At another table, three girls are in a hurry. With angry faces[9] they remind me again and again to serve the food quickly. They say they've ordered cold dishes which don't need cooking and should be served now. But the kitchen is unable to keep pace with the orders. I can't do anything except shout at the kitchen loudly. Xiao Lei is urging the chef to cook for another table. Sometimes we are not clear about which table the dish belongs to. The chef won't tell us which table the dish is for; he just leaves the food at the kitchen window. We need to ask each other to make sure which is which. Generally, Mrs. Li knows, but the waiters will also check the dishes with the guests. Another table of guests is in a hurry and, just as the food is ready, they get up to go. They are determined to leave without paying. Mrs. Li says it doesn't matter; we will eat it ourselves. She is used to this and doesn't seem unhappy.

Until now, Mrs. Li has forgotten about her daughter. She asks Xiao Lei to look for her. Then she, too, joins the search. She can't find her next door. Eventually she finds her washing shoes in their flat on the third floor. She comes down the stairs holding Xin Ru's arm. The little girl soaked to the skin. Mrs. Li shouts loudly at the boss: "Look what your daughter did! She washed my shoes. There's water everywhere and she's used up a whole bottle of shampoo." The flat is at sixes and sevens, but Xin Ru's mother doesn't fly into a rage and her father just smiles.

I carry on clearing the tables and take the dirty plates to the sink and help the washing aunt. We clean the plates and bowls and send them back to the kitchen. When she has nothing else to do the washing aunt will help the dumplings cook if he is overwhelmed with orders. As I go back upstairs to the second floor clear away some tables, a box full of cups and plates which Mrs. Li's mother has left on the edge of the mahjong table slips to the ground.

---

[9]很气愤的样子.

Many of the cups and plates inside break. Mrs. Li's father is angry. "What are you doing? Can't you be more careful? You should put it on the ground! If you put the box on the table of course it's going to fall and break. That table is being used every day by someone or other." When he's angry you can hear his thick, Sichuan accent. Mrs. Li's mother says nothing and picks up the pieces. As I help her she says to me very quietly "It's okay'.

Shortly afterwards, I hear the boss ask Mrs. Li: "Where's Xin Ru? Can't you take care of her?" Mrs. Li is unhappy and snaps back: 'She is next door. I'm working just as hard as you are. Why can't you figure out where she is?" At that moment their daughter appears and everyone asks her 'What's wrong?' The sudden attention startles her and she cries. Her grandmother, rather than aggravate the situation, quickly gathers her up and distracts her: "You smell lovely! Are you wearing perfume? What's the matter? Did someone bully you?" Xin Ru's mother is less sympathetic. "All she knows is how to complain about other people. She's the one hitting the neighbor's children when she's playing with them. She's pretty stubborn and competitive."[10]

A few minutes later, as everyone is busy clearing up the tables, Mrs. Li cries out: "That box of bowls is ours! What's it doing outside?" Hearing this, Xiao Lei looks up, runs outside grabs the box, and brings it back in. He's got the plates mixed up. Some bowls, cups, glasses and chopsticks belong to a tableware company. It collects them from the pavement just outside the restaurant's front door, washes them, disinfects them, seals them with plastic film, and returns them to the restaurant. But the larger plates and bowls used to serve the food belong to the restaurant. Xiao Lei only narrowly avoids the plates being taken away. "I was too busy and got muddled. It won't happen again", he says.'

The employees did not complain about the imprecision of their duties and did not mind swapping tasks. The atmosphere was familiar and human (Plate 8.3). The washing aunt empathized with Mrs. Li's parents. They were in an invidious position. This was especially true of Mrs. Li's mother who, as well as looking after Xin Ru, worked unpaid sweeping floors, clearing tables, and serving food. The washing aunt and her husband had arrived in Shenzhen five years earlier when her daughter-in-law got pregnant for the first time. In Hubei, she and her husband grew vegetables in a greenhouse made from large plastic awnings. It was very hard work. To keep the insects from biting, they dressed in long trousers, socks, and long-sleeved shirts, and wrapped a scarf around their heads. It was very hot work, and within a few minutes every layer of clothing would be soaked through with sweat. They hired temporary labor during the harvests; otherwise they worked alone. None of their children helped. Their daughter, a high-school teacher with a child of her own, kept in touch as much as she could. But she was busy and had her mother-in-law to help bring up the child. They rented out the greenhouse when they moved to Shenzhen where they continued to work around their grandson. She took him to the kindergarten in the morning. She joined in the classes to help him settle down but now she spent much of the morning on household chores. In the afternoon and evening she worked at the restaurant. Her husband worked as a sweeper in a large building. He was, she said, too old for anything else. In the afternoon he picked up the child and cared for him at home or took him for a walk and an ice cream. Her son and daughter-in-law worked during the week and sometimes at the

---

[10]性子可要强了.

weekends, too. It wasn't easy: there were bound to be conflicts living together, usually over the child. *'A daughter-in-law should have self-respect and not be too willful. It's difficult for us old people, too. On one occasion, I was feeding my grandson and because of that my daughter-in-law got angry and said "do you want to feed him after he goes to university?" We weren't happy about that, but for the sake of our son's happiness, we didn't say anything.'* She was hurt, but, she said, *'it's okay just to get along'.*

This readiness to work around the tensions and disputes, to just 'get along', went without saying in many businesses. Mr. Cui, the owner of another restaurant a short walk to the south, found that *'relatives, on the whole, work hard...they will do their best....for the restaurant, like going to the market to buy food* (Plates 8.4, 8.5, 8.6 and 8.7) *or washing dishes or the vegetables ...The tableware and the food will be cleaner if they do it.'* Relatives who were paid regularly were even more likely to do a good job *'as they feel embarrassed if they don't get things done'.* But his responsibilities to them did not end with money. *'You know my cousin is here working in this restaurant. In addition to paying him a normal salary, I will buy some clothes or whatever for him – to help improve our relationship'.* His cousin was young and, like Mr. Cui, had dropped out of school early because he didn't enjoy it and because his parents had no money. He had come to Mr. Cui to learn a trade and learn about 'life'.[11] When differences or refusals did arise, Mr. Cui felt he couldn't push it too far because he was family. *'I can't say too much. So I will have to do the work myself.'* Workers he hired 'off the street' might want to finish a task as quickly as possible, but at least he didn't need to worry about family.[12]

If 'getting along' helped to insulate relationships which made up the business, then by definition it helped to protect relationships 'outside' the business. He was the middle of three of brothers. His elder brother had a business in Hangzhou; his younger brother was an itinerant decorator. After dropping out of school, Mr. Cui left Henan for Shenzhen where he spent three years working in factories. He also married; and because the pay was low he returned home with his new wife to Henan. He spent eight years there, working in a hotel restaurant, learning how to cook and how to manage staff. In the last year or two before returning to Shenzhen, he and his wife had had a difficult time. They fought more often and more fiercely and for reasons memorable only for their pettiness. Once back in Shenzhen he set up a business and did so quickly. With little hesitation he decided on Pingshan and took over a restaurant without changing its name or suppliers. His wife settled down and a child came soon after. Her parents then followed, giving up their factory jobs to open their own small businesses: her mother set up a newsagents and her brother a clothes store, both a few minutes' walk from the restaurant. Mr. Cui also installed his own mother to help with the baby. Domestic life still had its problems: mother and wife had their differences. *'Sometimes it is really difficult to deal with. If I say my wife is wrong, she will unhappy. If I say my mother is wrong, my mother is*

---

[11] 见见世面.
[12] 不需要考虑亲情的问题.

Plate 8.4 Preparing fish for the restaurant, Shenzhen (*Source* **R.E. Hodder**)

unhappy. So sometimes I choose to turn a blind eye. First, I will comfort my wife. Then I will comfort my mom.' But he believed that if his wife can learn to understand his mother then she will not always be angry.

None of this meant that workers unrelated to the family are treated more harshly. When Xiao Lei ran outside to rescue the crockery he had left on the pavement, Mrs.

Plate 8.5 Selling fish at market, Shenzhen (*Source* **J. Hodder**)

Plate 8.6 A meat stall in Nanshan (*Source* **J. Hodder**)

Plate 8.7 Selling fruit on a cold evening in January, Nanshan (*Source* **The author**)

Li did not blame him. '*I've been a waitress for a long time, so I know what he is experiencing. It doesn't make sense to me why some employers don't allow employees to make a little mistake. Some are so rigorous that you are fined five RMB if you break a bowl or a cup – and that is a lot as a proportion of your wages. I don't want to be as heavy-handed as that*'. And he was what they wanted at the moment: *When he came here, he told me he wanted to be temporary. That's good. I asked if he has done this kind of work before. He said yes. So I hired him. I don't want to hire a novice. I am afraid he might quit after he's learnt what he wants. It is not easy to teach someone, and when its busy and he asks you something, you really don't have the time to tell him.*'

Customers were allowed even more rope. Long after they finished eating, groups of men would often stay on into the night, talking and drinking. If they drank there was money to be made. But they could also make trouble. '*The worst thing for me is when a gusts spits on the floor. We had one who spat everywhere. He could have gone to the toilet but he chose to spit on the floor. Another vomited. One time our young waitress went upstairs to serve the food. She was so busy she didn't notice that a guest had vomited on the step and she slipped on it and fell down. It was disgusting. We got sand and covered it and cleaned it up quickly. But we can't be angry with them. We tell them to go to the toilet.'* Some became aggressive. *'We were taking time getting to one guest who began to bang the table and swear terribly. The waiter asked him to stop and the guest slapped his face. Most people can understand that it takes time to wash and clean and prepare and cook the food when its fresh. It's the same at home. Other guests just leave without paying. I had to chase a group the other day and argue with them: they must pay for the food they have eaten. One man ran up a large tab and the just stopped coming to the restaurant. I see him sometimes walk past, but I don't have the nerve to call him. I don't think he can have forgotten because he used to come to dinner all the time.'* Another guest was determined to argue. *'Yesterday he ordered either dumplings or noodles. He spoke so fast that I didn't hear clearly. Then he criticized me for it. It is his character. He is very picky. He will talk at you and if you miss one word he will criticize you and if you dispute anything he says, he won't let it go.'* The solution, she discovered, was to ignore whatever he said and to never answer back. *'In fact'*, she said, *'the man doesn't have a bad heart. He is that sort of person by nature.'*

In drawing boundaries (no drinking or gambling) around her husband's behavior, Mrs. Li was protecting the social aspects of the relationship—an emphasis reinforced by her view that his need to let off steam was good for him, good for their relationship, and so good for the child and the family. When she delivered the *coup de grâce* to her father in response to his criticisms of decisions which she and her husband had made—and yet remained tolerant of his presence and sympathetic to a life spent on building sites—she was again protecting her relationships with him. When she put aside the waiter's mistakes, she was introducing a degree of compassion and flexibility to rules which, if applied rigidly, would damage her relationship with him, leave him and her family on tenterhooks, and do the company little good. When Mrs. Li introduced 'rules' about how customers ought to behave she was establishing a distinction between the 'customers' (and their behavior) and the person she served, making allowances for personalities and circumstances, and protecting her relationships with them. She was, again, just 'getting along' (treating 'rules' not as absolutes but *as if* significant in their own right) just as her washing aunt 'got along', and just as Mr. Cui 'got along', in order to protect relationships—relationships which also happened to be good for the company.

The emergence of this conceptual distinction between relationships and organization is an immediate, visceral and practical response to the problems that actors face. It is rarely thought out and planned.

Sumei married her boyfriend shortly after the fruit store they set up together ran into trouble. Another large fruit shop had opened about 400 m away, robbing them of customers. The solution, they believed, was to give up fruit and to specialize in flowers. The fickleness of their customers was not the only problem they faced. Her husband was the eldest of four children. *'His parents didn't want him to open a flower shop. They thought there are too many risks. He has two little sisters and a little brother. They were all born in countryside, and his little brother is still at school. His father is a construction worker. One sister got married with a guy from Hunan and they have a two-year-old daughter. The other sister is still single and she's been working in Shenzhen since 2009. She never gives any money to their parents and just spends it all on herself.'* But her husband insisted on the venture whatever the risks and the implied responsibilities to his parents and siblings. *'We have discussed it: he thought we should depend on ourselves and.... I agree with my husband. I want us to run this flower shop properly. All the money in it is his; none of it belongs to his parents.'* Friends, too, were creating problems, asking to borrow 5000RMB here and another 4000RMB there.

Yet, as Sumei saw it, her relationship with her husband lay at the heart of their difficulties—difficulties which, had she more confidence in that relationship, would quickly melt away. Both she and her husband left school early. Both were determined. Both worked for a number of years in other people's companies. Both drew hope from classmates who had dropped out of school and gone on to 'become very rich bosses'.[13] And it was vital that the two worked together to make the business work. But in doing so their relationship became functional, sterile and focused solely on the business and money. The quarrels that blew up were, she said, often instigated by her. *Sometimes I want to fight with him, because I want to feel that he cares – I want him to care for me more. And if couples don't argue and if they keep it all in, that doesn't strengthen their relationship.* They were, in other words, a deliberate attempt to remind herself (and her husband too) that they cared about each other. This aspect of their relationship had to be maintained not only for its own sake but also to protect and nurture their family. Neither of them wanted to be a burden on the children they hoped for. *'I love both a boy and girl. You know, if you raise a boy today its expensive because when he grows up you have to pay for his marriage. But if you raise a girl you don't have to spend so much. My father-in-law and mother-in-law both prefer a boy. I think they are rather old-fashioned.... Me and my husband hope that our children will study hard....go to college and get a bachelor's degree. We would be very proud of that. But if they don't want to go to university we won't force them to. They should be allowed to make decisions for themselves and learn to take responsibility for their decisions. I think this is more important than anything else because this is the basis of any truly good person.*[14]

---

[13]变成了很有钱的大老板.
[14]一个厉害的人.

8.3 Creating Neighbors

The relationships protected while forming the organization extend beyond immediate kin and close friends. Sumei and her husband had to contend with more than
just the desertion of their customers. As they began to switch from fruits to flowers,
they were inundated with troubles. Everyone, it seemed, was after their money.
Customers were passing on counterfeit money. They were also visited by two men
selling advertising space on the internet and claiming to represent a company
affiliated to Baidu. '*They promised to put our information in an attractive part of
Baidu and gave us a 70% discount if we paid in cash. The price after the discount
was 5000 yuan. That's not a small amount to me and I told them that, and that I
can't pay so much at that moment. Then the two men got out their IDs, kept
showing them, and kept saying that they really are staff from the company. Then
they told us that if we did not buy at once we would have to be the most stupid
people ever, and they beat their hands on the desk. We both felt that there was
something wrong, that they might be fraudsters, so we refused to pay the money.
The next day my husband called the Baidu Headquarters Customer Service and he
was told that there was no such affiliated company. We were nearly cheated*'.

Nevertheless, by turning the cheating, the manipulation, the lies, and the loss of
customers into something else—the market—all this could be distanced from their
relationships with the outside world that remained affective and might deepen and
even, perhaps, become as close as kin. '*You know, there are lots of people in
Shenzhen who are from other parts of China. You face all kinds of problems going
somewhere new and different. So helping each other out is necessary. When I come
across difficulties, they will give me a hand. When they have problems, I will give
them a hand, too. A lot of shop owners around here have children about four or five
years old. They have to take them to kindergarten in the morning and bring them
back home in the afternoon. So before they go they will often ask me for help. At
first, when a customer wanted to buy something, I just said the owner would be
back soon and asked them to wait. But as we talked more with the owners and got
to know them better, we learnt more about what they sold and the prices and so on.
So now, if a customer turns up and the owner is out, I will sell the goods immediately and give the owners the money when they get home. They do the same for
me. The other day we went to the hospital to see a doctor, leaving the shop in the
care of our neighbor. He is a very nice person and when we got back from hospital,
he gave me the money he got from selling flowers. We do have differences. We are
all from different parts of China and have different backgrounds. At first, when I
discovered some people have very different outlooks and opinions from me I felt a
little uncomfortable. But they have a right to their views just as I do. It's not a big
deal. We all have to learn to tolerate other people. As they say, 'a good neigh-
borhood relationship is better than relatives far away.*'[15]

---

[15]好远亲不如近邻.

The sense of alienation which ultimately spurs on the protection of relationships was unmistakable in the case of Mr. Lu. In 2013 after he completed his postgraduate studies by working as an intern for the Port of Dalian, he moved to Shenzhen to sell property. He had been approached through his family by a distant relative who co-managed a small branch of a large real estate company. The branch was short of staffs and there would be no difficulty in securing for him a position, though he would be paid on commission only. Lu accepted the offer: the commissions, he was told, were generous; and he felt he needed wider experience. Experience is exactly what he got: the job lasted three months every moment of which he detested.

The company had branches littered all over Shenzhen. The one he joined was split into two sections (sales and rentals) each with around ten workers or so, each led by a director. His relative led rentals. Mr. Lu was placed in sales. Every day when he arrived to start work he would find waiting for him a list of telephone numbers to call. The calls would usually be made in the late afternoon or evening. During the morning he and his colleagues would go out in groups of three or four. They held a large advertising board, struck up conversations with passers-by, and stood at the entrance of supermarkets handing out leaflets. An introvert by nature he found this work awkward; and he found his colleagues trying. A few swung between complete lethargy and fanatical, but directionless, excitement. The majority were content merely to find a shady spot and crack melon seeds.[16] He grew scornful of them. They were, he felt, all fundamentally lazy and uneducated. His own performance was not, he admitted, outstanding but he was reluctant to drift aimlessly. His superiors, meanwhile, were unreasonable and petty. They paid him nothing and yet constantly he risked being fined for breaching trivialities. *'For example, if you don't wear a tie when you arrive in the morning, or if you don't upload your work report every two hours (they ask you to upload your report onto their system every two hours), you will be fined. Every night, too, you must file a daily report. You also have to take part in meetings – a morning meeting, a noon meeting, and an evening meeting. I am sick to death of all these. When I worked at Dalian I never come across this sort of thing and it's hard to adapt. If you don't upload your report on time a superintendent will turn up and say you're not working and you should pay 20 yuan as a fine and so on. In fact, it doesn't matter whether you are working or not or if you make your report up, just so long you file it.'* And then there were any number of corporate slogans to learn. *'But I never put my heart into this…. I can't remember the slogans even though I was shouting them for three months. I just made shapes with my mouth. Before each meeting we will yell out the slogans. And in the morning we will stand outside the front door to take an oath, dressed in suits and ties and leather shoes. People can tell you are an estate agent from just one look at you'.*

He left the company two days after the resignation of his relative (who he saw very little of) and went to stay with his aunt and her husband who was, to Lu, something of a hero. His uncle's family had been very poor, and he had been very

---

[16]嗑瓜子.

rebellious. When he decided to drop out of school, a row with his father ensued. So he left home to become the boss of his own company. Lu also got on well with their son who was five years older than he.

His cousin, Yang, had just returned from Xinjiang where he had had a successful career as a real estate agent. He had saved enough money to start a business with Zhu, a classmate from high school. Zhu, who had already set up one hotel two years earlier, opened a second in October 2013 and asked Yang to buy into both. Zhu and Yang each put in half the necessary capital and shared the profits equally. But the relationship between the two men quickly deteriorated. Zhu thought himself a seasoned old-hand in the industry; Yang felt that Zhu saw him as his deputy (or worse) rather than as an equal partner. He received lists of vague instructions— apply for this or that certificate, buy this or negotiate that—from someone who in every other respect did very little. *'Every day that boy comes here to sit at the counter, wears headphones and just plays games and surfs online. He just sits there until ten at night when he returns to his own hotel, just in front of this one. The next day he does the same thing all over again. Apart from taking a break to eat he is playing games at the counter. I just can't bear his idleness.'*

They also had very different approaches to their guests. Zhu refused to supply toiletries and towels on the third floor, arguing that the price of the rooms there was very low and costs had to be kept down. If guests wanted towels and toiletries they would have to pay for them and take them up themselves. *'Sometimes the guests forget to take towels and toothpaste and so on with them when they go upstairs. But the boy will still say "No way, we do not supply these things in third floor. If you want those items you're going to have to pay me for it."* In marked contrast, Yang saw it as just a towel, a convenience, which kept the guests happy and cost very little to provide. Before long, the two men could not sit down together without arguing. Matters finally came to a head at dinner one evening when the two exchanged blows with each other suddenly. The following day, Zhu proposed to break the partnership.

It was at this point that Lu was invited to step in. Neither Lu nor Yang had enough cash, but Lu did have a family who, it turned out, was prepared to support his venture. His mother put in 50,000 yuan of her own savings, and both she and his father parents borrowed money on his behalf from others—both family and friends. Some of these loans bore interest, some did not. Either way he was responsible for paying the entire sum back. In this way he raised more than 700,000 yuan for his part in the business. Together he and his cousin bought out Zhu. Lu received a twenty-year contract on the second hotel for which he became responsible while his cousin took on the first hotel.

Learning the ropes was not easy. There were problems with cleaning staff. *'Last year, one cleaner we hired was very recalcitrant. I asked her to clean the public toilet in yard. She answered "You didn't ask me to do that when I first came to work here" and refused. And she began to shirk other jobs.'* So they hired another on a trial basis, and then another. There were problems with companies contracted to clean the bed linen. They would pick-up and deliver to the hotel. During the high seasons they collected linen every day. *'The company's owner told me that for the first few days they will clean the linen for free—as a trial. At first it was fine; but later, to save costs, he would mix our linen up with his other customers' bedsheets; and then it took longer and longer for him to return the washed linen and soon we didn't have enough fresh linen. We had to complain; then we had to change companies; and then change again.'* The internet companies, too, were a constant source of grief. '*Most of guests book rooms on Internet. For example, you have three empty rooms and you advertise these through Qunar, Elong and Ctrip. Then, suddenly, these rooms are sold through Qunar. Then someone else wants to book the same rooms through on Ctrip. I have no choice but to refuse the booking. Then Ctrip will call and complain. They will shout you: "why do you refuse to sell your rooms?" The guys working for these websites company try to scare you: "you **must** agree to this booking". They get very fierce and threaten you: "we'll make sure you can't sell rooms anymore."'* In the face of intimidation he had no choice but to stand his ground.

Despite it all, he felt he was the better for it. He was, he said, learning to put aside his self-regarding introversions. The challenges—the clumsy management at the real estate office and his rough entry into the hotel trade—were 'the market'. Unfairness, manipulation, greed, incompetence, selfishness, and a willingness to take advantage of the inexperienced were just part of that. Most importantly, and most satisfying from his perspective, was that he now helped others to navigate their way through it all; and, in doing so, he was helping to establish a community of genuine relationships. '*I have made quite a few friends since I came here. I have two fellow-townsmen from Henan who were guests at the hotel. They stayed with me for six months and I gave them a good discount. They started out in the matsutake business and now they are also managing a hotel. Now we often help with each other. For instance, if we are full we will send guests to them and vice versa. They will often ask me for advice. how do we deal with the websites? What if the websites refuse to pay? They will call be about all manner of things and I will help. When we have time we will often drive into the mountains to roast a sheep or a pig and relax.'*

8.4 Conclusions

An observation of some consequence is that the psychological 'distancing' or separation of relationships from the organization and its rules and processes, is not just about the protection of relationships and the good of the organization. Sometimes it can be about dissipating, overcoming, or even *avoiding* some emotional 'trauma' or, less melodramatically, an especially acute sense of alienation. That is to say, formulating a kind of emotional salve is an important motive in the establishment of an organization in the first place.

Chapter 9
Looking for Solace

9.1 Introduction

The company is a coming together of relationships. The spark is utilitarian and, at another level, psychological. It describes the protection of relationships in the pursuit of utilitarian objectives. It is also the case, as noted in the last chapter, that a desire to salve, or even avoid, emotional 'turmoil' can play the greater part in initiating the organization. Sometimes, the defense of relationships is the first and foremost consideration. This chapter elaborates on that point.

9.2 Resentments and Reconciliations

As an educated youth and 'rightest',[1] Liu's paternal grandfather had been compelled during the 'ten-year catastrophe'[2] (or Cultural Revolution) to move from Henan, where he was born and brought up, to Xinjiang, where he was involved in the western development strategy.[3] His maternal grandfather, a teacher, also relocated to Xinjiang from Henan. Liu's parents made the trip to Henan shortly after the reforms began in the late 1970s, only to return to Xinjiang in 1993 when Liu and his elder sister were young children. A decade later, his paternal grandfather, having lost his wife, returned to Henan, to be joined later by the remainder of his children. Not until 2012 did his maternal grandparents, following three of their six children, eventually move back to Henan where, shortly after, his grandmother died. The geographical distance separating the two branches of the family was complicated by one of blood: Liu's father was the product his father's extra-marital affaire. For all these reasons, Liu felt much closer to his mother's side of the family (especially her

---

[1]右派.
[2]十年浩劫.
[3]西部大开发.

© Springer Nature Singapore Pte Ltd. 2018
R. Hodder, *Small Business, Big Society*,
https://doi.org/10.1007/978-981-10-8875-9_9

eldest sister and her youngest brother, both of whom still lived in Xinjiang). He had met his father's half-brothers and half-sisters but very rarely; and his paternal grandfather, though still living, was only a childhood memory.

When he reached the age of nineteen, Liu attended Sichuan University in Chengdu, from which he graduated in 2013. He had chosen the University largely because of the weather; and he had done so without consulting his parents. '*I like the rain...I like rain very much. It [often] rains at night. When the first raindrop falls I will suddenly wake up. Then I will tear the curtain aside and look out. I am in a better mood when the rain is heavier. Maybe it is because before in Xinjiang, as soon as it rains, my parents wouldn't go to work, and stayed at home. Rainy days are warm and cozy. So I like rainy days very much. In Chengdu I never bought even one umbrella. I always let the rain drench me.*' His decision not to consult his parents, nor give them the reasons for his choice, was fixed in bitter resentment at the favoritism which, he believed, they had shown his elder sister. It was not, he said, subconscious behavior. His family was '*deliberately slanted [in her favor] because I was badly behaved and I am a boy. So every time there was trouble, the first thing my parents would do is blame me and protect my sister. If I had a fight with my sister, my parents will beat me first even before bothering to find out what it was about. My elder sister got better school reports than me and was better than me in every other way. She studied really very hard and very well. At high school she was held up as an example to me all the time.*' Moreover, he had been born 'outside the plan'[4] and his birth punished by a two-thousand yuan fine. His mother tried unsuccessfully to avoid the penalty by lying about his date of birth; and, since then, no one could be entirely sure about his true age.

Dogged by these resentments, and afraid of failure, his national college exams[5] were a miserable experience. As he revised during the build-up to the exams, and in the days after, he kept thinking about how his parents had treated his sister during her exams. They had rented a house for her next to the school; stayed there with her day and night; and cooked for her. All his classmates were cared for in similar ways by their parents. But *he* was put in an apartment by himself; his mother turned up to cook only every now and then. Liu spoke very little during that time, did not thank his mother or father, and resolved not to ask them for advice on where he should study.

A sense of detachment followed him to university. He formed what he regarded at the time as his one true friendship. '*We got to know with each other in freshman year. I just wanted this one –at first sight. He was riding a BMX bicycle - very cool. I just took to him as soon as I saw him.*' Together they set up the university's first society for extreme sports[6]; and in their first year spent whatever time they had outside class occupied with this. '*We were really very happy at that time... We are not in the same class, but at the same school. He lived in the east dormitory and I in*

---

[4]是超生的.
[5]高考.
[6]极限运动协会.

the west. There was a big door in the middle. It was like we had to look at each other across the magpie bridge.[7] *I was truly, truly excited to find such a temperamentally compatible friend.*' Each had the sense that the other knew and understood what the other thought and felt, so that little explanation had to be given when asking for advice and help. Liu spent far more time with him than with any other roommate or classmate. To make just one such friend in life was enough.[8]

The significance of that friendship became more important as Liu's relationships with his classmates—a group of four or so—cooled. He was on their team in a robot match. Early on during the competition they were joined by a new team member who Liu could not stand. '*I didn't like him, and he didn't like me. It is mutual. He spent all his time creating opportunities to get close to leaders and teachers but did not work and didn't do anything properly. He talked a lot but did very little. I prefer someone who works more and talks less*'. And yet this new member got on well with the rest of the team who '*became close to a person I hate. Well, gradually, I wouldn't walk up to them.*'

He left Chengdu to work for TPLink where, again, he quickly slipped into isolation. He did not like the company. He was frustrated at the ban it imposed on visits home during his first year, and disappointed at the nature of his work. He had had no clear idea about day-to-day tasks and responsibilities before he joined the company, and quickly found '*there was a huge psychological gap between imagination and reality. The company was in the Guangming district. The title of my post was IE -Industrial Engineer. My function was to manage the production lines, heighten production efficiency, and ensure quality. It also meant I had to manage the people working on the production line. Everyone says that industrial engineering is the soul of industry*'. If so, he said, then it was the '*hell soul.*'[9]

Nevertheless, he worked hard, driven by what he took to be a promise from his director to move him into research and development, provided he performed well. Liu knew that he had his work cut out. His major had been mechanical design, not industrial engineering. He would have to make up for this and other shortcomings, and do so in only four months. '*I just kept my eyes firmly fixed on this goal. If I couldn't reach it, then the job would become meaningless to me. I don't like industrial engineering and I'm not fit for it. My expectation was that as long as I demonstrated my ability, I will be moved to R&D.*' He met his part of the deal, or so he thought. He was awarded first place in the company's internal exams. His verbal presentation during the final oral exam '*was very good, and so was my speech. I think they were all shocked and impressed*'. And yet, when he met with his director to discuss his transfer, he was told '*this thing would have to wait for another time and you must continue to work in this post for the moment. I then realized I had been cheated. There is no question that he gave me his word that I*

---

[7]鹊桥. An allusion to the legend of the marriage between a mortal (a cowherd) and the daughter of a goddess.
[8]一个人要是能交一个这样的朋友, 够了.
[9]灵魂个鸟蛋.

would be transferred and get a higher salary; and I believed him.' It was now clear, he said, that all along his director had been evasive and secretive. *'I felt I had been duped and I felt completely disgusted with this director. So I wanted to resign. I wouldn't tell him I intended to resign. I would just look for another job privately.'* But word got out and when confronted by his director he admitted his intentions. *'His face at once changed, suddenly turning hostile. Then he became very angry and cried, "OK. Go! Go through the formalities." Subsequently I found out that the annual bonuses were distributed three days after I left. If I had worked for just three more days, I would have received the year-end bonus. At the time I thought so what? I was new to the company and I had made little contribution to company; I don't deserve the year-end bonus. But now I think I was very foolish. I worked for the company so I deserved the bonus'.*

In the weeks before he left Shenzhen to spend the New year break at home, he looked for his preferred job, *'and for that job only. So I attended just one interview at DJI –only this company and no other'.* He could not tell how the interview went. *'I was told by HR to wait for the result – sometime around the end of the year. I had to wait without much hope because I had nothing but a few months 'experience at TPLink. I was little better than a new graduate and so I had very little confidence in myself'.* The days spent in Shenzhen after his interview and before his journey home were *'the most painful of my life. I suddenly realized that I had become a layabout[10] and only then I knew the importance and necessity of a job. It enriches you; it is fulfilling; it gives you a purpose; and it brings in money'.*

His time at home was no better. *'I felt embarrassed because I had not yet found a job. So I lied to them. I told them I had a job waiting for me. I felt very depressed, awkward, intimidated, and worried about what I would do if I hadn't passed the interview. I lied to my parents, saying that I had asked for several days off. In fact, I had no idea when I could leave home. I hadn't bought any train tickets to go back. I didn't tell my parents the truth because I didn't want them to worry about me. My mother often thinks that I'm not eating properly or short on clothes. So, when I have a meal or cook, I will take some pictures to send to my mother, so she can see I'm okay. Every day I was well-behaved and understated. I didn't dare to be noisy. When I finally got the offer I felt very happy and bought a ticket for Shenzhen, leaving the very next day. Then I told my mother that my holiday is over and I'll be going back tomorrow. She had no idea what was going on and couldn't understand why I left so suddenly.'*

Liu returned to Shenzhen elated, grateful, and chastened; and over the next two years he came to view organizational life rather differently. *'I think everyone becomes utilitarian when they enter the workforce. You can have friendships in office but they are not the same; they are more superficial.... Because we are in a competitive situation, we take precautions against each other.... Making friends is a two-way thing, you can't do it unilaterally.... Friendships take a lot of time and energy, and holding on to a friendship is not easy. Sometimes I prefer to remain*

---

[10]一个无工作状态.

alone rather than spend time with people I'm not that close to. So, often, I won't keep the dinner appointment with ordinary friends.[11] *It's a waste of time just sitting there, my mouth open. It is too boring.'* On the other hand, the fact that everyone was in the same boat, that each knew there were limitations, that there was a distance amongst them, made it easier to get on with his colleagues. *'We often make fun of each other and joke around. In our department there are over forty people. The department is divided into several groups and I am in the mechanical group. We work on different floors and in different offices; it depends on the project. So we are not always together. There are six or seven of us who are quite close. We often go out together, either just as a group or when the department organizes an event. Last year, we climbed Wutong Mountain; we spent a couple days and a night at Changlong; last week we visited a colleague who lives in Huizhou; and every month, as soon as we get our salary, we will go out for a big meal. This time it's my treat, next time it's your turn.'* It was also easier, amongst these friends and other colleagues, to argue without fear of the consequences. *'The arguments at work are incredible. But argument is argument - we are still good friends. For example, we will have many different schemes to develop a new product. You like this one, and I like that one. It's very easy to quarrel: I think your scheme is no good, and you think my scheme won't work. We both have our own reasons. We will argue, we will disagree; and sometimes we will go to our leader to solve it. Often he will let us put both schemes into effect because he doesn't know which one is better either. Actually, the leader is very happy to see us argue and experiment. The better one will be adopted. Work is work. It's best if we don't mx up work and personal emotions.'*[12]

Liu found this openness very attractive, though the hours were long and there was no overtime pay. *'I usually wake up at seven and then cook. I walk out the door at about at eight and reach the company at nine. We start work at ten, but I want to read books first thing in the morning because there are few people at the office then and it is very quiet. We start at 10 and work until at least ten at night, with an hour-and-a-half for lunch and then again for supper. I'm usually in bed by midnight. At first I felt very tired and I wondered what the point of working so late was. But that was foolish of me. I like research and development. It is interesting. It is good. Love is love. Every day I am busy. If we have a good idea, and as long as it is a good idea, the boss will help us to realize it, whether it's an idea about the product, the corporation, or company activities—anything is okay.'*

Meanwhile, as he distanced his relationships and focused his energies, he moved closer to his family. *'I've gradually got more connected to my family and I will call my family regularly every week. I think this is very necessary. At university I was young and ignorant and, often, I didn't get in touch with my parents for long periods.* 'He began to appreciate his sister and take an interest in her life. *This year my sister founds a boyfriend. I was amazed. My sister never goes out with anyone.*

---

[11]普通朋友.
[12]大家最好不要把工作上的情绪带到生活中, 我们都会把他们分开的.

I went home for National Day holiday. She said "Let my boyfriend pick up you at the station." I said, "No, it's ok. I don't need it." In fact I was surprised and I felt a little hurt at the thought that a strange man was stepping into my family. If she had offered to pick me up alone, I would have said yes. But with a strange man—I felt very awkward. But when I met him I thought he was ok. He doesn't look wretched... Actually he looks very honest and he treats my sister very well. He stayed with us for three days.... He's an honest, simple and frank man. I think he's good. They work in a same research school, so he's able to help her work for her doctorate. So I admitted defeat—"Only you can take good care of my sister, and I accept you." Now it's her turn to make fun of me.'

His parents, too, seemed to be more caring and interested in him, and he now valued them more than before. *'Recently my mother has started calling me often. She starts off by asking, "have you had dinner? What dishes have you eaten?" And then she'll ask "When will you find a girlfriend? When will you bring her back? I will cook delicious dishes for you both when you bring her home." Hearing this, sometimes, I will hang up the 'phone, because I'm not going to talk about this with them. Probably they think it's time for me to get married. But I think there is nothing that should be or should not be. Let nature takes its course. But after I hang up, I will call my sister and tell her that I just hung up on our mother, and ask her to ring her and console her and explain. Every time my sister will help me and she always understands me. Sometimes I think that humans are a very peculiar kind of animal, treating their close ones harshly and treating strangers very kindly. It is really odd.'* Behind this, was the guilt he felt about the way he had treated his mother during his college entrance exam. He had been looking for something at home and come across her diary in which she wrote: *'My son has been feeling very low for several days. I dare not say anything to him. All I can do is cook well and make sure he is fed properly.'* He was touched by her words, and reproached himself for all those grievances about her he had bottled up. He was, despite it all, really very grateful to his parents. *'I feel that no matter what I decide to do, they will always support me. As long as I am eager to do it, they will stand up for me.'*

As for his friend from college, he still heard from him. *'After I left Chengdu, he drifted through two girlfriends. In college he often jumped from one girlfriend to the next. Every time he would run to me and ask "What do I do now? I now don't like this girl and I've fallen in love with another girl." My reply was always: "What the hell are you doing? You want to shift girlfriend again? How many times?" And every time he would say: "I really don't like this one and I have found another one who is better." I would sigh and say, "Well, do it if you like. That is just like you. I think you'll end up getting divorced! I will go to your second wedding." We have come to know each other very well. He has a good character but he has some emotional problems as a man.... We are different in many aspects. If not, we couldn't be friends for such a long time. We all have qualities that someone else wants but doesn't possess. He likes my honesty, and I like his chutzpah. We all are changed by each other.'*

9.3 Emotion as a Stimulus

It is only a small step from understanding how the organization can begin to soothe emotional trauma to understanding why a desire—probably unformulated and subconscious—to avoid hurt, can help to stimulate the organization. It is, then, not just practical requirements that lead to the organization, but a need for emotional change stirred up by other events.

Probably nowhere more than in the slums of Manila does the need to make a living drive the establishment of small businesses. Liberty grew up with her father, mother, two brothers and six sisters on a small farm in Negros Occidental. She finished high school and worked first at Robinson's Plaza in Bacolod as a cashier before she made the trip to Manila '*as a game of chance*'. There she moved through a series of contracts, starting as a sales lady at Landmark, Makati; then at SM Mega Mall, again as a sales lady; then as a cashier at a Japanese restaurant; and then as a secretary at a hardware store in Sampaloc. Then, in 2003, '*I got pregnant, I stopped working, and I stayed at home. The father didn't know that I was pregnant. I didn't tell him. I took on all his responsibilities. He was studying and I was afraid that if I told him he might break-off from his studies, and I didn't want that.*' Three months after giving birth she went back to work, supported by her sister who cared for the child, a girl, who they named Bea.

For more than five years Liberty worked as a personal secretary at the Claret School Cafeteria before it closed; and then as a sales lady once more at a branch of Philam Life Homes in Quezon before that, too, shut down. At around that time, her sister married. The timing was fortunate in some respects as Bea, now seven, was to start school. But school costs would have to be met; and who would look after Bea when the school day ended, usually around mid-day? Liberty was already worried that Bea might be influenced by the "*Tambay*". '*They don't go to school; they are noisy especially at night; they bring in strangers; they drink wine or Red Horse; and when they are drunk they make even more noise even in the middle of the night and don't care if they disturb us and wake us up. Some of them use drugs; they get high; they try to push the drugs on others; and they fight.*' The sense of disorder they brought was aggravated by the *barangay's* failure to clear garbage from the streets. Both problems she laid squarely at the feet of the *barangay* captain who, she said, spent all his time overseas attending seminars. Then there was the gossip that went with being a single mother. This, more than anything, concerned Liberty most. If neighbors wanted to talk about her behind her back, that was up to them. '*I am the one who made the decision to raise my daughter by myself, I want this kind of life*'. But '*I don't want my daughter see that I have a problem with the neighbors. She's young and she might be affected and feel that she is the problem. To be an unwed mother isn't at all easy—I can say that for sure. But I know that I can handle it. As long as my daughter is with me, my life is full of joy. She gives me all my happiness, and I do everything for her. And the most important thing is she and I are happy.*' Making sure Bea *felt* this, however, would be impossible if Liberty was not there for most of the day.

The solution, she believed, was to put up her own business. The idea was a re-working of a pancake stall she ran while pregnant. It required very little capital and gave her an income for her daily needs. Her new venture offered a greater variety of cooked food. '*I started to cook a few dishes. They were sold-out every day. I thought to myself this business is good. I use only a little capital but if everything is eaten the profit is double, and our food is also free every day. So I cooked more dishes and cooked more food, and always they were finished. Lots of people now buy my food. I already have regular customers who buy from me every day. At 10 am I have to be sure their orders are ready so they can pick them up. Now, all our expenses are met by the business. It pays the rent for our house, the electricity, water, and my daughter's schooling. I can also save a little money— in case of emergencies and for her future studies. Our life isn't luxurious. It's very simple. What's on the table is enough for us. This kind of business is hard work, but we are happy.*'

The business was not only their bread and butter; it also nurtured the relationship between mother and child. Liberty could work from home. She could be there when Bea left for school in the morning and got back in the early afternoon; she could be there at the weekends; and she could be there during school holidays. The succession of humdrum tasks which comprised the business fostered in mother and daughter a sense of mutual trust, responsibility, and dependency. '*I wake up early morning around 4:00 AM. I need to prepare Bea's food. I want to be sure that before she goes to school she eats her breakfast. Then, after that, I prepare my ingredients and start cooking, because I need to put the food outside in the morning. My clients come to me every morning. Some eat breakfast. Some take the food with them to eat at work. By midday I am sold out. Then I rest for a while, before Bea's comes back from school. Then, when she arrives, I prepare her lunch. Once she's finished her lunch, we both take a nap. Then Bea helps me to look after the business. She helps me wash all the plates and cooking utensils, and helps me with all the other household chores. Then, later in the afternoon, we will go to market; and, when we get back home, I start cooking dinner. After dinner I help her with her homework and, after we've done her assignments, we pray together. At 11 pm, as long as I've done everything, I sleep*' (Plates 9.1, 9.2 and 9.3). Once separated from the utilitarian practicalities of 'the business', the faith in one another which these routines demanded sealed a relationship that was deeply affective and probably unbreakable.

The distancing and focusing of relationships required by the business also encompassed Liberty's relationships with her parents and siblings, and her neighbors and friends. '*I didn't ask for any help from my family. It's not nice to go there and ask for help, especially when they already have their own problems; and I need to show them that I can stand on my own*'. Nor did her parents and siblings ask much of her. If she could save and still have money left over, she would send that, but it was never a large amount. '*I also tell my daughter that we can only spend money on what we need, and she understands. I thank God that my daughter isn't spoiled, that she understands my situation.*' Friendships, too, had to be distanced if they were to be nurtured. '*Friends are part of our lives. Not all my friends ask me*

Plate 9.1 Helping out before school, Manila (*Source* **J. Hodder**)

Plate 9.2 Breakfast is ready, Manila (*Source* **J. Hodder**)

Plate 9.3 Keeping the fish fresh at market, Manila (*Source* **J. Hodder**)

for help. Some of them have a better income than me. Some of them, though poor, are content with what they have. Some come to me to borrow money. If I have anything spare I will give it to them; but if I don't have anything I will tell them straight—I only have enough for me and Bea. They understand and that's why they are not insistent. Anyway, they are more likely to come to me for advice on other kinds of problems. Sometimes we go out together and eat, or take a walk with our children'. For these reasons, the capital to establish the business was scraped together from her own savings and from a moneylender—someone quite separate from her circle of family and friends. And now that the business provided a revenue over and above that needed to keep the business ticking over and supply her and Bea with an adequate income, she wanted it to expand. She took out a loan. The loan was short-term and, she said, low-interest. Every day for two months the lender would appear to collect a payment on the principal and interest. She could then take out another loan if she wished. It was necessary and far better than the alternative: *'If you go to a bank to borrow money there's a lot of papers to produce and processes to go through before they lend you the money. The moneylender is easy – there are no documents that you need to submit. Only the rich become very rich, but the poor are always poor.'*

Life was hard but they survived and found contentment. Through her business, even the community was no longer one of the *tambay* and chaos; it had become warmer, more familiar, even friendly. Perhaps it was the fact that the business had brought financial stability and had encouraged a more affective view on life that it became possible for Bea to establish a relationship with her father. *'In 2013 I was shocked when the father of my daughter called me. He wanted to see Bea. Can I bring Bea to him? He's been looking for us for years, but he didn't know where to start until he saw us on Facebook. He didn't have the courage to send us a message until my friend gave him my number. Bea wouldn't talk to him at first, because she was angry with him, and because she thought he wanted to take her away from me. I told him to give her time; and, eventually, I took her to SM North and we ate together in a restaurant there. When he arrived, my daughter had a very long face and began to cry. She wanted to go home. It took time. I explained to Bea that he didn't want to, and couldn't, take her away from me; and that he just wanted to see her. He now had his own family and was an SPO3 policeman. Now they are talking to each other over the 'phone. If Bea needs money for her school project and we don't have enough, she will call her father and he helps out. His wife doesn't know about me and Bea; but his mother and brothers know, and they have accepted her into their lives. I am very happy for her.'*

Just a short walk away, Zenaida was having to juggle her husband and in-laws. She was one of eight children—four brothers and four sisters. Her father and mother were still living. As the eldest, she was very aware of the difficulties her parents had faced; and she had had to take on heavy responsibilities early in life. Her father, a taxi driver, gambled and drank. Partly to make up for those periods when he stopped working or lost money, she would help her mother sell food. She left school at sixteen, married at nineteen, and had her first child that same year. Neither she nor her husband had finished secondary school, and neither had money. He worked as a room boy at a hotel in Quiapo. At the end of each six-months contract he would have to wait several weeks or months before the hotel would consider him for another term. So she, too, found work at the hotel, washing and ironing clothes. Life became a little easier when her husband was given permanent work as a waiter. The salary, though small, was regular, and tips could make a big difference. But when the restaurant closed, they were back where they had started only this time with no work and three children.

Her parents suggested that, to help ends meet, she take over the sari-sari stall her father had opened after he gave up driving altogether (Plate 9.4). She felt uncomfortable depending on them but accepted *'because at least we had income to feed ourselves.'* She was also determined to ensure that her children would not have to experience the continuing unease, uncertainty, and fear that poverty brought. It was those same feelings that pushed her to set up a tricycle business for husband (Plate 9.5). She bought the motorcycle over three years. The repayments were calculated according to a fixed 'boundary': a set amount of income, determined by the distance covered each day. This sum was handed to the lender every night. She left the remainder of the earnings with her husband. She also set up a hamburger stall (Plate 9.6), the income from which was used to cover daily expenses and to fund her own money-lending business. The burger stall did not require much capital, and the burgers were sold quickly. Even in its early days the stall was bringing in five hundred pesos above costs.

The routine was relentless. *'I wash my face in the morning, drink coffee, and open my sari-sari store. After that I start washing clothes. When I've finished I start cooking lunch for when the children get back from school. Then I take a rest while*

Plate 9.4 Taking a break from the sari-sari stall, Manila (*Source* **J. Hodder**)

Plate 9.5 Fixing the tricycle, Manila (*Source* **J. Hodder**)

Plate 9.6 A hotdog and hamburger stall at night, Manila (*Source* **J. Hodder**)

they look after the store. Then I prepare food for dinner and attend the store. The evenings are the busiest time and most nights I will not close until 3 am' (Plates 9.7 and 9.8).

The pleasure of having a secure roof over her family and three meals a day in their stomachs drove her on. So did the satisfaction of being her own boss. But the prime mover was the protection of her relationships—relationships which the business consumed and maneuvered with its utilitarian demands. For the family to survive they had to distance their relationships. In particular, she and her husband taught their children independence and self-respect, and they refused to make any claims over their lives. *'I want my children to finish their education, because I didn't finish mine, because I want them to have a better future and better life, and in that way give them what they want. They are young now and what they want will change as they get older. But when they grow up I will let them decide. If they want to put up a business, it's up to them, that's their decision. If they don't want to, that's fine, because they have right to choose, and that's their own decision. That's one of my dreams—for my children to finish their education'*. Friendships and relationships with neighbors were also shielded in that she did not lend to her friends nor allow the hamburger or *sari-sari* stores to extend credit. The focus and discipline required by the businesses also nurtured her relationship with her

Plate 9.7 Early morning at a sari-sari stall, Manila (*Source* **J. Hodder**)

Plate 9.8 Back from school for lunch, Manila (*Source* **J. Hodder**)

husband. '*We used to argue with each other. He didn't have work, we didn't have money, and our children didn't have food. Yet I could see him with his friends drinking wine.*' The absence of food on the table and the smell of alcohol on his breath ignited in her suspicions of another woman; and this in turn sparked in him doubts about her and his own inadequacies; and so it went, around and around. '*But*

Plate 9.9 A barber's shop, Nanshan (*Source* **The author**)

now we have stopped arguing. We have matured, and our children are growing
up. It's not good for them if they hear us arguing and fighting. My husband sees
how hard I work to pursue these businesses; and he sees how our life has improved.
We support each other; we each support the businesses; and so our relationship
has strengthened.'

Jiang's business, a barber's shop (Plate 9.9), was from the start as much a refuge
from childhood and an emotional salve as a way of moneymaking. His parents
divorced following his mother's infidelity, committed in retribution for his father's
adultery; and both had gone on to take other partners. His family was, he said,
'special' and 'bad' and, since dropping out of school in Hubei and then leaving
home, he spoke to them by phone only once a year, usually during the spring
festival. He had returned to his hometown only once—for his own wedding. He was
now thirty-three.

He entered his trade just after leaving school. He became an apprentice and then
a barber in Hunan, before moving to Luohu in Shenzhen where he directed a branch

of a large chain store. He ran the shop for ten years, thinking all the time about how *'to open my own barbershop. But you know, running a business takes a lot of experience, so I did my best to learn as much as I could to develop a rounded understanding of how it works'*. The routine and discipline was punishing. Work started at *'about ten in the morning and did not stop until around ten-thirty in the evening. Basically, there was no leisure time. Work in the shop <u>was</u> daily life.'* With this regimented life came a need to distance relationships centered on the friend-ships which substituted for the family he felt his parents denied him. For him, friendship was by definition free of utilitarianism. With *'those who just want to secure small advantages at other people's expense, no friendship was going to develop'*. In fact, he said, it was only on the basis of sincerity that he was able to raise the capital he needed to start his business—*'more than one hundred thousand yuan. It was very hard for me to find that kind of money. I had some, but nowhere near that amount. My friends helped me a lot. When they knew that I needed money to run a barbershop, they each lent me about ten thousand yuan. Without their help, I wouldn't have started this shop.'*

That was four years ago and, since then, he had married. The couple met when he worked in Hunan. *'We were just colleagues. After working in that shop for about two years, I came to Shenzhen. When I found a job managing the shop in Luohu, I asked her to come here: we were recruiting more staff and the salary here is much higher than in Hunan. She joined our staff; we fell in love with each other; and, after I set up my own shop, we got married'*. But as far as the business was concerned, she remained staff. *'How to run this shop is up to me. She just helps— washing hair and other trivial things.*[13] *And when we close the doors at the end of the day, she will help to clean the shop'*. She had a say in business planning, but the final decisions lay with him. *'I want to run a bigger shop. She refused; she said that we don't have enough money to expand. She wants a stable life after marriage. She doesn't care how big the shop is, she doesn't care about being wealthy. As long as our life is stable and there are no major problems she will be content. But we talked it over it together and estimated how much money we need to expand. We're saving now and we're accumulating the experience we'll need'*. The new shop will be twice as big as this one in size and in a better area. *'We'll need about 300,000 yuan. One of my friends started something very similar in 2008. His business is now bringing in about 10,000,000 a year.'*

As with his friendships, Jiang's relationships with his in-laws were premised on the fact that *'I come from a bad family. I promised myself that I would make my wife and her family happy. There are four people in her family. She has an elder brother who is running a clothing shop. He got married two years ago. Their parents worked in a car factory when they were young, but are now retired. They exercise, play Mahjong, and so on. We keep in contact with them mainly by 'phone. We call them once a week to tell them our life in Shenzhen is good. We don't want them to worry about us. When we make a call to them, we always report only the good, and*

---

[13]处理一下琐事.

conceal anything they might worry about. They are old and they shouldn't have to worry about us anymore.'

Employees, and the apprentices he retained, were neither friends nor family, but the distancing of relationships which allowed the technical aspects of the business to work effectively also required the social aspect of their relationships to take on a strongly affective quality regardless of their status in the shop. *'I will only tell them how to improve their techniques. A good boss will think how to solve a problem, rather than blindly assigning fault.'* This—and selecting people in the first place for their moral quality and their willingness to do their best for others—was, he believed, far more effective than any regulatory system (Plate 9.9).

The distancing of relationships demanded by the operation of the businesses meant that he was now in a position to provide for his wife and their future children what his parents had failed to provide for him—an emotional refuge, a family. *'We have not decided to have a baby yet. I want to spend more time with my child when he or she comes to the world. Once you have a child, you have to take the responsibility for its happiness. This is extremely important, especially between the ages of 1 to 6 years old, because this is a key period if they are going to develop properly as a person. During this time, parents should provide them with the space to grow. I want my child to study in school, but exactly what they want to focus on will depend. It's best for them to decide when they grow up. I don't want to do what a lot of parents are doing—forcing their children onto the starting line,[14] worrying that otherwise their child will lose out. I won't do that. When my child is very young, I will give him enough time and space to play. I read an article on the meaning of play for kids. It said that the development of the cerebrum is related to play. Generally speaking, the child's instinct is to play, and that this enriches their cognition. So I'm going to give my child a lot of time to play. I think when I have the bigger shop up and running, then I'll have the time to spend with my child. How children develop their understanding of the world and their personalities is entirely up to a child's parents and people around them'.*

9.4 Conclusions

The emotional changes encouraged by the organization (and, indeed, required if the organization is going to function and survive) quickly percolate outside it. The prospect of creating an emotional refuge, a salve, can also drive the establishment of the organization. This suggests that prior experience of organizational life or sufficient imagination or both are at work, too. Thus, the emotional atmosphere throughout large tracts of society can shift remarkably quickly.

---

[14]起跑线.

Chapter 10
Being Direct

10.1 Introduction

Mrs. Li might have come to realize the ambiguity of her relationship with her husband even if they had never run a business. The washing aunt might have been hurt just as much by her daughter-in-law's comments, and yet just as diplomatic in her reaction, even if both had not been part of the same family in which each adult had to earn money. Cooperation and being in a group of any kind makes demands; relationships are used and adjusted whether society is commercialized or not. While actors initially find ways to deal with the ensuing alienation (a state that Mrs. Li explained by 'life' and 'fate'), these are not enough. There remains a strong desire to recover from that sense of impotency and detachment. This is realized by opening a conceptual divide such that, simultaneously, relationships are treated *as if* entirely genuine and important in their own right and *as if* something different—a functional technique or mechanism or structure. This psychological 'distancing' of relationships, and the creation of 'processes', 'rules', and 'procedures' occurs through a kind of happenstance. The practices which emerge happen to carry certain advantages in particular circumstances and, for this reason, are made routine. But distancing and the creation of 'structures' can also take place in a more deliberate and explicit manner.

10.2 'Distancing' Family

In the precarious hand-to-mouth existence of Manila, the need to distance relationships was a lesson which Leah took from her parents' marriage. Her father had worked as a postman, and her mother as a street-sweeper for the city. Her mother put her to sell chocolate at her school to learn about money and how to save. When the school day ended at noon, she and her friend would sell *banana cue*, *turon*, and

© Springer Nature Singapore Pte Ltd. 2018
R. Hodder, *Small Business, Big Society*,
https://doi.org/10.1007/978-981-10-8875-9_10

sticky rice just outside the school gates. In 1982 her mother went to work as a domestic helper in Hong Kong where she remained for the next eight years, sending back cash every month. The remittances were made to Leah's father, until her mother got word that he was using the money to stray outside the marriage. Leah then took over responsibility for managing their finances. Denied this source, her father began to open the letters he was supposed to deliver, helping himself to the dollar notes inside. She remembered him sitting at the kitchen tables going through the post, especially the registered mail, collecting the money earned by countless other workers overseas. His generosity to his *kerida* and a growing number of complaints over missing post eventually gave him away. He was suspended from work for six months while the police investigated the matter. Luck seemed to be with him: evidence was deemed to be insufficient, his case was dismissed, and he returned to work, though now he was trusted only with the local post. But damage to the family had been done, and it disintegrated; Leah's parents separated; and her brother dropped out of school and turned to drugs. Looking for stability in her own life she married at nineteen and at the age of twenty gave birth to her first child. By this time her father and mother each had a new family to support.

It did not take long for Leah to see in her own husband her father's unwillingness to take on responsibility; but she had made up her mind that she would not let her own children suffer a broken home. When her father died, her mother received three hundred thousand pesos from the post office for death in service. A large part of the sum was used by her mother to start up a money-lending business. Ten thousand was given to Leah to set up a *sari-sari* stall. This would, both hoped, give Leah and her children a steady income which her husband failed to provide. Business was good at first; but profits were steadily eaten away as she found herself extending more and more small loans (a pack of cigarettes here, and a beer there) that were never recovered, while the cost of feeding her family grew. When she could no longer re-stock the business she closed it, and applied to work at a local slaughterhouse, packing chicken for supermarkets. Each contract was for six months and could be picked up again only after a compulsory furlough of weeks or months.

Towards the end of her final contract Leah's husband complained that her wages and his joblessness undermined his 'dignity as a man'. An argument followed—one they had many times before. *'It's hard to budget...If he gets 1600 pesos in one week, he would give me only 1000 and keep 600. If he gets two thousand he gives me only 1500, and keeps 500. He always keeps back a good part of it for wine and shabu.*[1] *One time we had an argument and in front of my mother he hit me. My mother told him that the next time you beat my daughter, that'll be the end of the marriage.* 'On this next occasion, to avoid further confrontation, she gave way and hoped for the best. *'He got work, and it was fine for several months; the money wasn't quite enough but he gave me all his wages. Then he went back to the same routine - he drank and ended up not going to work at all. I was pregnant at that*

---

[1]Methamphetamine.

time with our third child'; and the rent could not be paid. This time Leah's mother-in-law stepped in and brought the family into her house. Both she and Leah's parents chipped into buy milk, rice, and other basic necessities for the children. Leah accepted the help. Under no circumstances, she insisted *'do I want my children to see their parents separate like I had to see mine.'* Yet neither did she want her family to suffer this continuing dependency.

A way to end it seemed to offer itself when her mother-in-law retired and gifted Leah with enough capital to set up her own, modest, catering businesses. Early in the mornings, Leah boiled corn, sweet potato, banana, and *tsampurado*,[2] to sell as breakfast to children on their way to school. She and her family moved out of her mother-in-law's house and back into a rented house; and her husband returned to work. Again, though, her husband fell back into his old ways, and payments to cover water, electricity, gas, food, school (from clothes and shoes to books and bags) and old loans drained her business of cash. Compelled to look for another source of income she found work at a launderette, washing and ironing neighbors' clothes. She also worked as a saleslady at the store which her mother-in-law had owned and, on her retirement, sold to her own daughter who, for the moment, remained uninvolved in its management. (It was this transaction which had generated the money gifted to Leah to start up her catering business). This job proved to be crucial for Leah's eldest child's education. Unable to afford the tuition fees, Leah agreed to forfeit her wages as a saleslady in return for her mother-in-law's offer to pay for his education. The arrangement continued for eighteen months or so, until her sister-in-law took over the running of the shop.

It was at this point that a series of events came together which allowed Leah finally to exert sufficient pressure on her husband to keep him out of her business and financial affairs once and for all. First, a number of scholarships (funded by local factories) was made available to give children from the barangay a university education. The average score required was 85% which her eldest son had achieved in his final year. Now that his fees were taken care of, she could concentrate on finding the money to send his younger brother to university as well even if his scores fell below those needed to win a scholarship. (Her daughter [her youngest child] would also go on to win a scholarship from the program, enough to take her through university). Secondly, Leah's brother who had been affected badly when their parents separated was now in a position to help a little. He had married, fathered two children and, through his wife, secured a job at a large store in Greenbelt 2—an upmarket shopping mall in Makati. His salary was, from Leah's perspective, very respectable, though her sister-in-law was reluctant to see any of it go her way. She saw no reason to subsidize Leah's husband. Nevertheless, a donation from her brother, together with a loan of 15,000 from a money-lender (to be paid back at 300 a day over sixty days) gave her enough capital to set up a covered stall selling fried chicken skin.

---

[2]Chocolate rice porridge.

She was, she said, determined to make this business work. Free of any dependency on her husband's family and, therefore, from any claims her husband might try to make, she centered the business and all income and expenditure on herself. Her husband had no say or influence on these matters. The business was popular and grew. It brought her into contact with a greater range of people who were willing to advise or help if only by making regular orders. By the time her daughter was at university, it was making enough money to cover all Leah's expenses. She could even save enough to add chicken spring rolls and iced candies to her range of products.

Focusing authority (especially over finances) was a lesson that Susan brought to her marriage from the start. Her mother was single, and her father, a security guard, had five children with another woman to whom he was married. They had little money from him, though from time to time he did help her mother, a laundry-woman, to collect, wash and iron uniforms for staff and students (in midwifery) at Fabella Hospital. The income was irregular as it depended on customers who often had to wait until the middle or end of the month when they received their wages before they could pay. Susan and her mother sometimes went for a day or two or longer without food to eat and soap to wash. *'I promised myself'*, she said, *'that I would study very hard so that if I had a family they would not have to live like this'*.

After graduating from the Technological Institute of the Philippines with a degree in Commerce, Susan was introduced by her father to his cousin who owned a small art gallery. He appointed her as its accountant. The gallery, which sold paintings, books, antiques, and general bric-a-brac, was small and so was her salary. But if she sold a painting or collected money from customers who had bought on credit she took a commission. She could earn enough to live on. Moreover, her boss trusted her; and during her father's illness, and after his death, he helped with the medical bills, taking some of the strain off her mother who was still washing clothes. Not long after this she found herself the de facto manager of the gallery. She oversaw sales and collections; she prepared salaries and assigned duties; and she had a say on who was to be hired and fired.

The business grew and so did her savings. When she married she was entirely clear that *'I am the decision maker in the family, about financial or any other matter. When it comes to my family I am the decision maker. My husband gives his salary to me. As a wife it's my right to know where he put his money – every single cent. If he sends money to his family without telling me, I will be angry because I don't like him keeping any secrets'*. Shortly after the birth of their first child, her mother gave up her work as a washerwoman and came to live with them and look after her grandchild. Susan also began to lend money commercially. These were short-term, high-interest loans. A loan of 1000 pesos would earn her 200 pesos over thirty days. She also used her credit card to buy goods—such as fridges or jewelry —on behalf of her customers who would pay her back over an agreed term, usually between 6 and 12 months. After their second child in 1998, the business her husband worked for collapsed. He received a payout of 80,000 pesos. Some of this went into extending and improving their house (which now towered above their neighbors). The rest he used to set up a carpentry, welding, and driving business

Plate 10.1 A jeepney driver, Manila (*Source* **J.Hodder**)

under his wife's firm control. After their third child, Susan bought a jeepney. The income earned from this was split between herself and the driver. The 'boundary' (the minimum income remitted to the owner each day) was 500 pesos, though she also took on responsibility for the jitney's maintenance. A year later they bought a second jeepney, and a third the year after that, all operating on the same terms (Plate 10.1).

The couple were now prosperous, especially in comparison to the rest of the community. They had various sources of income: the gallery; money-lending; carpentry and welding; and the jeepneys. She controlled them entirely and they operated as one, each supporting the other, each contributing to the family's expenses which she tightly regulated. Any money that her husband had, whether he used it to drink or play cards or mahjong, came from the allowance she gave to him. Occasionally he tried to earn a little money on the side by lending a part of his allowance to his friends; but unlike his wife he found it difficult to recover the debts and he never succeeded in making the enterprise work.

Their children's education accounted for the greater part of the family's expenses. She rotated her two sons between private and public schools, so that one or the other son was at the private school at any one time. This continued until her second son asked to remain at public school (which he found easier and where he had a set of friends) allowing his sister to take his place and to flourish.

In 2010, they ran into trouble. Susan was de facto manager of the Gallery, but not the owner. When the owner (her father's cousin) died, his two sons took over and the atmosphere changed. Neither man seem prepared to cede control over the business to the other. She was in an invidious position: if she was asked by one son to buy in stock or make a collection, or to remit the sale of a painting, the other would be offended and become suspicious. She took the decision to resign, ploughing her retirement trust from the gallery back into moneylending and into her children's education. Then she fell ill and required a series of operations on her gall-bladder and continuing treatment. The effect on their finances was ruinous. Their savings and cash were eaten up, and their businesses collapsed. And with her businesses, she felt, went her reputation and her relationships in the community. *'Because I can't lend them money any more, some of my friends became cold. It seemed that nobody knew me anymore. The politicians, including the barangay captain, didn't want to know me either. It's very hard to find real friends though at least now I can balance them with my family because we all understand each other and support each other.*

But she remained determined that her children would finish school: *'if they have a good education they won't have to go through the poverty I suffered. If all my children finish their school I can say I have fulfilled my duty as a parent and my dreams will have come true.'* She set up a small food store, a *carinderia*, with the remainder of her savings. Her husband went back to working as an employee in someone else's business; and it was Susan who now borrowed (from her husband's cousin) for her children's schooling. Their days were long. She woke up at *'four in the morning to prepare the food for the store and for the children before they set off for school. After that I start cooking. My mother helps me. Then, when we've finished cooking, we take the food outside to sell. It's usually all sold by midday. If so, I take a nap and then I prepare for the next day. If I have spare time I'll play bingo and then go back to my house and prepare food for our dinner. I'll usually be in bed by 8 pm.'* The business, the decision-making, the control over expenses, all remained centralized; the distinction between family and business remained clear. But there was change in two important respects. First, whereas she had been less careful about separating out friendships from her business dealings before the collapse, she was now fastidious in doing so. Secondly, whereas she had executed the separation of family and business so completely that she alone took on the burden of responsibility, she was now more inclusive and more trusting in that she assumed that other family members could also make a distinction between family and business just as she did. Her mother was involved in the cooking, her husband would help in other aspects of the business as would her children. Indeed, she wanted them to know how to manage a business. *'Who knows?'* she said, *'Someday one of my children will decide to put-up one for themselves.'* This last comment was not about succession. It is noteworthy that so often the business—despite its practical importance and its significance as an emotional refuge (or, rather, in the creation of one)—is not seen as something to pass on. The emotional deepening which the business fosters often leaves parents unwilling to see their children as instruments for advertising their own achievements or perpetuating their own ambitions.

In Lucy's case there had been little choice but to take on the business, though only because she had been part of it from the very start when she and her mother put up a small, open-air stall and laid out half-a-dozen kinds of food. Over the years, throughout Lucy's school and college days., the business flowered slowly into a restaurant with its own branch, and a livestock division which bought and sold live pigs and cattle in Davao, Cebu and Manila. The practices and techniques which her mother had used as the businesses grew, Lucy adopted and continued. Profits were kept small but the turnover was high. Most importantly they worked hard at their reputation for cleanliness, good food and good service—a reputation which spread by word of mouth through their customers, through Lucy's networks and those of her mother, her brothers and her sister. In this way they established a sound core of patrons who returned again and again. Of particular value were the civil servants. If they liked the food and the atmosphere they would return most days, and sometimes in the evenings and during the weekends too. And if they were throwing a party at home they would be certain to ask Lucy to cook the lechon and other dishes. In return she lavished them with discounts and credit (anything from ten or twenty days to eighteen months) and even a free meal every now and then. She would sometimes extend the same courtesy to her other customers, though if she did not know them well or if she thought that they had come to expect a discount and were taking advantage of her, then she would first raise the price before offering to reduce it, and she would be hesitant to offer them credit. Her refusals were made with humor and affected exasperation: she did not want to offend but she could not ask her friends to keep her in poverty.

She dissuaded her own children from entering the family business. Her eldest son was, with a kind of inevitability, encouraged to read medicine; the others studied agri-business and marketing. She, too, wanted her children to be independent, though lent her eldest son money to set up his clinic; and she was saving to give her other children the same advantage once they had qualified in their chosen professions. There was also a desire on her part to broaden the family's base: resting her future and that of her children upon the vicissitudes of the catering business was not in her view a wise strategy, and would not provide them with the status that she wished for them.

Above all, perhaps, was the concern that her relationships with her children, and their relationships with each other, might be tainted—much as her relationships with her brothers had been—by arguments over the business. As Lucy's mother aged, she let the livestock division fall into the hands of Lucy's brothers, and gave Lucy authority over the core of the business—the restaurants. The two parts of the company remained under one business license (registered in Lucy's name) but were run independently. To her brothers the arrangements seemed unjust. As if to add insult to injury Lucy would not favor their supplies of live pigs over those of their competitors: she would only buy what she thought to be the best meat at the best prices. And whilst she had, to begin with, lent them money, she had not received the return she had expected and was reticent to lend them anymore. The livestock trade may well suffer from the difficulty of late payments, she had said, but the catering trade was also risky. She would not add to her risks at a time when she had, for the first time, borrowed a large sum of money to set up a new branch that was only just beginning to break even. All this caused bad feeling.

Then her brothers acted clumsily. Lucy had been careful to renew her business license and pay her taxes. After 30 years she had learnt that rather than play them for fools, it was always better to cultivate relationships with officers of the Bureau of Internal Revenue who, in any case, with their strong corps d' esprit and deep pockets, made good customers. She and her mother built up an understanding with them. They would take into account the vagaries of her trade, the loans she now carried, and the news that she had until recently been subsidizing her brothers. They appreciated that she was only trying to make a living in an uncertain world; and she knew that they needed to bring in a reasonably convincing stream of revenue. They would negotiate with her in a calm, friendly, informal manner, and reach a settlement in which she would be allowed to under-declare her sales, and stagger her tax payments. Her brothers, however, under-declared their sales, and tried to hide it from an official who lay outside her community. When the official examined the port authority's records of shipments, and found that the volume of trade was far greater than her brothers had made out, the lie was discovered. As holder of the business license under which her brothers operated, Lucy was liable to pay their back tax and penalties. There was also the possibility that it might seem as if she had gone behind the back of those officials with whom she normally dealt. So she paid for her brothers' cack-handedness and explained to her friends in the Bureau what had happened. She then turned on her brothers: she had lent them money and received nothing in return; now she had paid their taxes and their fines; and she had to patch up relationships which she and her mother had worked hard at over many years. She instructed them to apply for their own permits, and she made arrangements to turn her side of the company into a corporation. She would hold fifty per cent of the shares. Of the other half, her sister was given the majority and the remainder was divided equally among her brothers, who were thus left with a small stake in a business from which they were effectively insulated and would find difficult to tear at after their mother's death. In return for this reprieve (Lucy had toyed with the idea of giving them nothing) they could expect no help in their own business affairs.

There was much bitterness now, and much sorrow. Lucy had seen her mother struggle all her life to give her family something, and she had struggled with her. Lucy was now repaying that debt and affection and carrying on her mother's work; and with a light humor she and her children and her new bouncy grandchildren had accepted the inconveniences which her mother's failing mind and body caused them. Her brothers, she thought, had been remarkably selfish in their actions and had threatened to undo all that had been done. By distancing her own children from the business and by encouraging their independence, she hoped to spare them from the heartaches of her past. She had not ruled out a successor. If there was to be one it would be her eldest daughter. But her daughter was interested in other things at the moment and Lucy would not press her into a business which guaranteed nothing.

10.3   Loosening Control

The willingness of the parent to prepare the child for greater autonomy is one reflection of emotional deepening brought about through organizational life. This has a crucial role in the gradual weakening of authoritarianism. But there are other immediate and practical considerations at work, too. The ageing of those in whom authority is vested is one. Song, a first-generation migrant from Fujian, China, owned a wholesale company dealing in agricultural commodities in Davao's Chinatown. The company was an important source of agricultural products for traders in the city's marketplaces. It diversified from rice to cocoa, coffee, and corn, and to ceramic tiles imported directly from Fujian. Song had lived in the Philippines for more than thirty years. Both daughters were married, and their husbands' families had their own business interests: his eldest daughter's in-laws owned an insurance firm; his other daughter's in-laws owned a hardware company. Song and the fathers of both son-in-laws had been friends long before their children were born. All three companies bought goods and services from each other, or will point customers to each other's company. But risks amongst these companies were not pooled: there were no cross-subsidies, loans or investments. And within Song's company, the various interests were, to an extent, insulated against each other such that the mistakes or ill-fortune of the one could not bring down the other. Flour was kept separate from rice and corn; both these divisions were kept separate from tiles. His wife and daughters were each assigned one division, and the costs and income for each were drawn up independently. At the end of the year, wife and children provided him with a summary of accounts, and each received a modest proportion of the profits. They kept this for themselves or re-invested it in their division. The evolution of these divisions had been gradual. As they got older, he could not simply rule by fiat over his children with their own cross-cutting loyalties, especially when he was so dependent on them and given his desire that they should continue in business when he was too old or no longer around. A degree of freedom and opportunities to develop experience and confidence had to be devolved.

Complexity also makes authoritarianism difficult to sustain. Even if the leader is fit and at the height of their abilities he will find himself unable to handle the demand for increasingly sophisticated and quick decisions as the organization grows. Pan (who, like Song, is a first generation migrant from Fujian) owned a company supplying fertilizers in the southern Philippines. In addition to a permanent staff of about 20, his nephew worked for him as the business's comptroller; his brother was the company's vice-president and ran port operations; and his wife administered both permanent staff and hundreds of piece-time workers and drivers, exercising considerable authority over pay-rolls, contracts, work allocation, welfare, disputes, and discipline. The company's logistics were complex. Large quantities of agricultural chemicals were imported from Indonesia, Malaysia, Singapore, China, the United States, and elsewhere. Each shipment was administered and paid for separately; and supplies were funneled to a myriad of small farmers throughout Mindanao, as well as to many agricultural enterprises in Davao. Estimating, ordering, and delivering materials of the right quality and at the right times was no easy matter, even though the company kept large stocks in reserve which it drew on if shipments were late. So closely integrated was it, that divisions made in any one part of the company were likely to affect its entire operations. Thus, while the owner focused responsibilities for overseas orders on himself, most decisions, including those concerning the type and timing of orders and shipments, were necessarily made in consultation in the field. It was only in field, and in consultation, that the intricacies of the operation and the ramifications of any decisions became apparent.

At some point, then, as people age, as complexity grows, and as the affective deepens, authority must be surrendered conceptually to rules, procedure and process which, having evolved as part of everyday relationships and practice, are now elaborated upon and added to. Take, for instance, the Davao branch of a company that processed and exported copra. Competence and ability were amongst the most important qualities for anyone who wanted to join the company, or was looking for promotion. These qualities, almost Calvinistic, were specified, measured, and regularized through exams held in Manila (where the company was centered) and took on a life of their own. The company was owned by a Chinese family, though less than five per cent of its managers were Chinese. The rest were Filipinos, and it was they who held key positions including those of auditor and heads of station in the outer provinces. The branch manager at Davao was one of the few Chinese. He was also linked to the owners through the marriage of his cousin, though he was not particularly close with them. He met the owners infrequently, and ritually, once a year in Manila on the occasion of the company president's birthday. He had worked his way up from warehouseman over twenty-two years, proving his trustworthiness, reliability, loyalty, and competence again and again before reaching his present rank. He was very proud of this. Kinship, he believed, might have opened the doors for him; but it was the trust which the owners had in him to follow process which propelled him upwards. He was the personification of the company's animate qualities; and it was this that allowed him to run operations in Davao and to oversee the buying and processing of copra by his stations in Cotabato, General Santos and Padada. The upper prices at which he could buy were fixed by the central office in Manila where a better view of price movements nationally and internationally was to be had. Otherwise he was his own man. Appointments in Mindanao were in his hands. His wife served as his secretary: she received no salary but was privy to his decisions. The Filipinos who held positions of authority and who ran the provincial stations had been appointed on his recommendation. He, after all, knew their character; and the criteria according to which his judgments were made were those of the company - righteous, alive, and autonomous. Punctuality and competence mattered; sobriety, chastity, faithfulness, thrift and abstinence from gambling, mattered even more. Did their wives complain about their drinking in private? Did they drink too much in public? Were they womanizers and gamblers? Or did they drink in moderation, eschew gambling and fast women, and keep only to their wives? Were they good family men? Did their thrift manifest itself in the smallest nuances of behavior? Would they turn off the air-conditioning when they left the office or when it was already cool enough for them to work? He was careful in his selection, for just as their successes would be an extension of him so would their failures. To instill in all his workers the proper values, and to guarantee the success of his appointments, bible studies and prayers were made a regular part of company life. He had freedom, too, in forming external relationships so important to the company's success. Many of his suppliers were Chinese, but only prices and profits mattered. When buying or selling, merchants in his business would tout for the best deals in different parts of the country. And when a deal was struck there would be no reliance on trust. Contracts were drawn up, then faxed, and then sent by post just as fast as the post office would allow. It was not that each merchant could not expect the other the show common decency. But with so many deals being made so quickly, mistakes would be made, and misunderstandings would arise, unless agreements reached after much haggling were written down formally.

10.4   Official Winds, Invisible Castes

Once the affective becomes commonplace, and an obedience to rules and procedure and process becomes an everyday occurrence, there is a risk that these constructs will come to be seen not as a means to protect relationships, but as disembodied absolutes. Alienation quickly intensifies and leads either to outright dissent and instability or to the readmission of an affective mood and a softening of practice.

Ma spent fifteen years working as a chef and manager of restaurants and canteens for a number of large organizations in Beijing before taking up a management post in a new catering company in Ningxia with its own interests around the country, including a large restaurant in Xi'an with a floor space of around 1000 square meters. It was this restaurant he was asked to manage. It was a long way from his wife and their young daughter in Beijing where both his parents and those of his wife also lived. *'My wife was just angry though gradually she came to understand me'*; though when he returned home after his first stint away to find that his child did not recognize him he was deeply hurt. Yet there was no solution. *'I told my boss my problem but he doesn't care: The motto of this company is "implement all orders"*[3] *so I must to go to Xi'an.'* More frequent visits home were also out of the question given the practical difficulties of travelling back and forth between the two cities, his long and uncertain hours, and the rigid and punitive nature of the rules which he was expected to uphold. *'Everyone has his or her responsibility which means that if something goes wrong the boss will assign blame according to his or her rank. For instance, a chef's responsibility is to manage the dishes. If there is something wrong with the dishes, he is the person who takes responsibility.'*

---

[3]其一执行, 其二执行, 其三执行. Or, literally, *first, carry out orders; secondly, carry out orders; thirdly, carry out orders.*

'He must report this to the manager; the manager must report it to the safety manager; the safety manager must report it to the boss of the Career Development Center in Ningxia; and if there are documents that need signing or related financial issues [most commonly a fine deducted from a worker's pay], *the incident must be reported to the boss of our company. The whole procedure must be completed and the problem solved within twenty-four hours.'* Employees understandably concentrated their minds on avoiding fault, blame, and fines. There were few positive incentives. There were no obvious rewards not even if a cook might win one the many competitions to demonstrate their best dishes. There were training courses, but none offered anything new to anyone who already had a few years' experience under his belt.

But whilst the lines of authority were clear and rigid, and the rules sharp and punitive, employees, including managers, often took it upon themselves not to behave like machines. As a manager, Ma said, he had learned *'what kinds of faults should attract blame, and what kinds of faults just need a reminder, and how blame and reminders should be delivered. For example, a cook makes the same dishes over and over again and often will not notice gradual changes in its taste. For instance, he might not notice the dish getting saltier and saltier. It's not his fault. So I will just let him know and ask him not to put so much seasoning in it next time.'* A breakdown in the method of payment—such as the use of cash instead of a pre-paid card at certain times of the day in certain parts of the restaurant—would mean blame and a fine. There were many other practices which might attract blame, many very similar to those experienced by Liu during his time as an estate agent (see Chap. 8): arriving late, leaving early; infringements of dress codes; non-attendance of frequent and compulsory meetings and pep-talks; slow service; forgetting orders; getting orders wrong; laying a table improperly; not clearing away quickly enough. Creating space between employees and the numerous actions or omissions which triggered a fine and led to marks on files in personnel at headquarters in Ningxia was, in Ma's view, crucial to successful management. *'I can understand their pain because I have been in the business for years. They are exhausted trying to make money.... Cooks get up at 4am or 5am every day and end the work at about 11 pm, and are lucky to get four or five hours rest during the day; and have no weekends. ... I want to help them if it doesn't go against the rules. I don't mind mistakes which are minor. I don't think there is any use in looking down on my workers and treating them according to their rank. There's no point in ordering them to do something and expecting them to do it immediately. Even if your demands are good for them, they won't understand your reasoning and perspective. It makes no sense. You have to talk to them and treat them like family'.* The key to working effectively in these harsh conditions, he believed, was 'persistence', 'attentiveness to detail', and 'morality'. And it was on his assessment of these qualities (and first and foremost morality) that he recruited new staffs. *'If you don't have morality you are not honest and if you are not honest you are opportunistic.... If you have ability but don't have morality, I won't hire you. If you have morality but don't have ability, we may hire you.'*

For a younger, less experienced manager—Ms. Zhou—in the bowels of a large tire factory, the sense of alienation was palpable. '*When I joined the factory, we had two weeks military training on one little island. Then we spent three months being rotated through different parts of the factory to learn about the processes of production. Many of the jobs we would end up in were supporting roles, such as finance and legal work; but it's necessary to know about production and the industrial art of tires.*' They did not know and they had no choice over the posts they would eventually be allotted. '*The leaders of human resources made these decisions based on our performance, background and abilities. I was put into the engineering laboratory to work as equipment manager. I am not sure why. It might be my performance at the report-back meetings. At the end of every month during the rotation we had a meeting. The leaders praised me.... I was the only one using a notebook and speaking to my notebook. Everyone else just read from PPTs. Also, I had lots of ideas and asked about all the problems I came across. I said whatever I thought. As they say: "new-born calves are not afraid of tigers"* '[4]

The laboratory was a relatively independent unit, and physically separated from the rest of the factory. It stored over a hundred different kinds of instruments and machines. She was placed as its Equipment Technician with responsibility for storing and maintaining items kept in the laboratory, and for maintaining and repairing machinery in use in the rest of the factory. This required her to prepare schemes of work for repairs and upkeep, and for making, buying-in, testing, and installing new parts. She was one of ten leaders who included: '*the director and the deputy director of the laboratory; Mrs. Ni, in charge of the chemistry group. Miss. Li and Miss. Liu who develop new instruments and devise new experiments. Miss Ren is in charge of measurements and test standards. Mr. Zhang is in charge of the experiment reports. The finished product group is run by Mr Li and Mr. Hou who is also my mentor. In total there are more than one hundred workers below us.*' She had ten workers answering to her.

She had little difficulty falling into the routine. They arrived at 7.30 am to punch the clock. They began by cleaning the office—wiping the tables, sweeping and mopping the floor, and taking out the trash. The most recent employees took turns at this since the veterans were exempted. They would check the timetable for key events or designated tasks—such as a leadership meeting or delivering wheel rims. After that much of her time was spent with her staffs checking with operators the condition of machinery on the factory floor. Any problems were usually resolved with the operators who had a good knowledge of their machines, what the problem was, and where the solution lay.

She found the work occasionally challenging but mostly undemanding. The pace of work was slow and most days she had time for a shower at 4.30 before clocking off at 5 pm. But there were difficulties which seemed to arise from nowhere and assumed an importance which, in her eyes, they did not deserve. '*The laboratory bought a new magnetic resonating imaging machine. I borrowed the instruction*

---

[4]初生牛犊不怕虎.

manual from the operator so I could read it over a few days. The operator forgot that I had it. And I didn't know that Mrs Ni wanted it and was looking for it everywhere. In fact I saw her looking for something and I asked her what she was looking for and she ignored me. Maybe this is because we all have our own responsibilities and the machine belonged to her division and so it didn't occur to her that I would have it even though as the equipment technician I need to be familiar with all kinds of machinery. Later, when the operator remembered I had it and told Mrs Ni, she rushed up to me and yelled at me. I was baffled. I didn't talk back to her. After all, she is a veteran and senior to me. Everyone witnessed the scene, so I went to the deputy director to explain. I felt wronged when I had to go to her unwillingly and apologize.'

Another dispute sprang up between her staff, the 'fettlers', and an operator whose machine they were repairing. With the job finished, they asked the operator to clean up their workshop. The operator was unhappy with this: they had made it dirty and it was their workshop. The fettlers replied that the mess had been made repairing his machine and it was accepted practice, and only fair, that the operator should clean up. So they *'argued for self-esteem or face, nobody knows, and neither side gave up'*. At last an older worker, an operator from their division, came along sent both parties away, and cleaned up the workshop by himself. *'I talked to him later and we agreed that it was only common sense that the fettlers had sole responsibility for the condition of their workshop. This was to be the practice for now and evermore'*.

Then came an incident with another colleague in the leadership team who lived next door to her in the factory's living quarters they occupied during the week. Miss. Ren, who ran measurements and test standards, also had access to a number of instruments for which Ms Zhou was accountable; and there was a number of other tasks and responsibilities that overlapped. *'Miss. Ren thinks she is busier than me recently, and that certain tasks which she started I should therefore finish. My view was that if you can do it, you just do it. There is no point in trying to divide up work like this. Sometimes we are both unhappy with each other; and after work we will continue to be unhappy faced with each other. It's awful. I think it is better to separate work and life.'*

It was another incident—one involving a screwdriver—that stuck in her mind. *'It is my responsibility to manage tools, wrench, pliers, screwdrivers and so on. I distribute the tools to workers who need tools. It is not said that I will give the tools to whoever just because he wants one. I won't meet unreasonable requests. For example, I gave a worker a new screwdriver and then after two days he came here to ask another new one. I told him I just gave him a new one. He tells me that he lost it and he wants another one. I said no - such a request is unreasonable. I won't give him the new screwdriver. I say that you lost it and you should buy a new one to replace the lost one. Then he says why should I pay for my work tools? He won't buy one and I can't do anything about it. In fact a screwdriver isn't worth much. My real purpose is not to impose a fine, but to teach him a lesson. Eventually I gave him a new screwdriver; and because this time it is not easy for him to get it, he will value it much more and not lose it so easily. I thought it is impossible to put an end to disobedience; one can only try to reduce it.'*

This last matter stuck in her mind because it was then that she felt she was becoming like the leadership, running *'endless errands for them... I was wasting my time and life. There could be no life worse than this'*. An atmosphere in which such trifles as these emerged so frequently, she thought, could only be created at the top: the leadership provided a muddled view of responsibilities and practices and, at the same time, insisted on all kinds of petty observances. When the director spoke at their frequent meetings, everyone was quiet and dared not to make a sound. *'Everyone is afraid of the director. Although I have ideas I don't say anything. I'm young and I won't be taken seriously. There is a kind of official wind,[5] an invisible caste system,[6] in state-owned enterprises. The company is not state-owned anymore, but it used to be and it is not easy to change.'* Moreover, she could not understand what he was asking for during his weekly performance. The director would give just a general orientation, a 'blurred vision', and leave the interpretation up to them. *'He told me that I should build an equipment archive. He used a lot of words, but never said anything concrete. I had no idea what he meant or what to do. So I guessed. I used excel to build up comprehensive information on our equipment and its history and condition – when had it been bought, when repaired, why, and so on – and updated it. But it was crude and clumsy. So we then bought the latest laboratory management software to organize not just our equipment but just about every other aspect of our work. It's very good. It's very quick and you can update it in real time. I still don't know if this is what the director meant. But if he did, why not say that in the first place? So much time and effort would have been saved. He's been working here for more than twenty years and yet I can't work out his meaning or purpose. I have to guess at what he wants. Many times I get it wrong. It's exhausting trying to guess, and inefficient. I can't criticize. He has spoken like this for twenty years and it's impossible to change him. The only way is for you to adjust to him. He won't adapt to you: "When you can't change the environment, you must adjust yourself to it"'.[7]*

As with the boss, so with the mid-level ranks of the leadership team. Mrs Ni was vexatious; and she restricted her new apprentices unnecessarily by declaring a series of tasks and responsibilities out of bounds. This was understandable, Zhou thought. The basic pay was determined by education, length of service and performance. Mrs Ni was older, more experienced, and responsible for mentoring new staff; and she was a leader; and yet, because she had no postgraduate qualifications, younger staffs would be earning a good deal more than she in no time at all. They had tried to deal with this and other grievances in the most diplomatic way possible. *'When we encounter a problem, first we will talk about amongst ourselves. If we can't work out how to deal with it, we will go to the mid-level leaders, but only*

---

[5] 官风.
[6] 隐形的等级制度划分.
[7] 当你改变不了环境的时候, 就只能调整自己去适应环境来.

when we have thought carefully about what to say. Many times the way you speak is more important than the content. If mid-level leaders can't deal with it, then we will go to the director'. They quickly found that the leadership backed each other up. This had been expected as the mid and top level leaders had been working together for many years. But at least they had tried.

The overall effect of the relationships amongst the leadership, the observances they demanded, and their apparent inability to communicate any vision they had, encouraged subordinates *'to use their ingenuity and energy to curry favor with the leadership'*, and made it *'very difficult to make true friends at work'*.[8] The oppressive and petty atmosphere was not peculiar to her department. Reaching across the various divisions of the factory was often impossible without making requests through the hierarchy, so that in effect she had to work indirectly through two sets of leaders—her own and those of the other department. *'When we needed to use software to deal with experimental data, none of us was able to use it. But the workers in the Quality Management Department know how to use it. So we asked them to come and give a lesson to us. They delayed and delayed, and didn't come. When we reached out to them again, they shirked and said that they are very busy. Maybe they never took it seriously; and they stalled again and again. We got in contact with them again and this time there was no response at all. Later, our vice-president got to know about it. He was very angry and directly pushed the leader of the Quality Management Department into action. So the problem disappeared. The very next day one of them from that department came to our office to offer service training. The conflict between two departments could not be settled by us; it had to be handed over to our superiors.'*

The helplessness, the detachment from colleagues, and the pointlessness of life in the factory, meant that her relationships outside the factory with her friends, with her family, and with the wider world took on far greater importance. True friends, she believed, could only be made outside work. *'With them'*, she said, *'I won't be lonely and helpless'*. She was also more understanding of her parents and their misgivings about her plan to leave her job. *'I can understand their point of view. My parents think it is hard to find a job; and it's pretty good - especially for a girl - to have an easy and well paid job. All they worry about now is that I'll marry a good man with a car and a house and live happily ever after. Their generation suffered from hunger and starvation; so it doesn't take much to satisfy them; a comparatively well-off life is more than enough. But later they came to agree with me. My mother supports me full-heartedly and I appreciate her trust very much. My father took a little more persuasion; but my uncle, who he admires, managed to convince him. So my father too is very much behind me. It is time for me to think about what kind of life I want, what I want to do.'*

---

[8]我觉得工作中也很难交到真心的朋友.

10.5   Conclusions

The serial failures that Leah's businesses suffered before she finally excluded her husband and in-laws; the troubles that led to the collapse of Susan's businesses; and the solutions devised in response to the difficulties which Lucy, Song and Pan faced: all these instances help illustrate the need to establish a psychological distinction between relationships and process, procedure, and rules. Representations and practice come to be treated *as if* they exist beyond and apart from every actor: it is this belief in rule, hierarchy, process, and system that exacts obedience. But once this affective mood is normalized, the constructs that guide and shape practice into rules, process, and hierarchy degenerate into disembodied absolutes and immutable routines; and a new danger emerges. As it slips into a state of rigidity and intolerance, the organization becomes increasingly unstable and ineffective. Unless pools of affective relationships are given space, and once again begin to suffuse the entire organization, the risk of collapse becomes very real.

Chapter 11
Opportunities and Obstacles

11.1 Introduction

Relationships come together as a business often through a kind of happenstance, guided by little more than a wish to bring in a little money or create an emotional refuge. Sometimes, right from the start, there is an understanding of the need to distance relationships or to soften the Puritanism that has set in.

This behavior reflects the logic of relationships, but it is not automatic. That logic must be discovered and worked through. Sometimes this can take a lifetime; and sometimes those efforts will never be rewarded. To illustrate this point, the history of a family in Davao is presented, beginning with the marriage of Eduardo and Inday.

Eduardo's parents had been small farmers in Ilocos. Inday had been a governess in the service of the Morazza—a prominent merchant family—in whose company her father, a tall Chinese, worked in Cebu as an engineer. Both Eduardo and Inday had earned degrees; he from the University of the Philippines, and she from the University of the Visayas. He was a serving officer in the navy when they married shortly after the Second World War. There were no children during their first five years together. During that time he left the navy, worked as a forester, and then joined the BIR.

Their first child came in 1951. Nine more children would follow. They brought them up firmly. They taught them to respect their parents, God, and each other, and to defend the honor the family. They inculcated in them the belief that those who appeared conscious of their superiority or inferiority could never win the respect of others. They trusted to their common sense, tolerated their friendships even with those families of whom they were dubious, and they strongly encouraged their friendships with those families of which they approved. Parties were always given and had to be attended; the children were rotated among their friends as house guests; extra-curricular activities, such as ballet and music, were paid for; and they entwined their children's expanding networks of relationships with their own more

© Springer Nature Singapore Pte Ltd. 2018
R. Hodder, *Small Business, Big Society*,
https://doi.org/10.1007/978-981-10-8875-9_11

established networks. They carefully selected the right private schools for their children. And, with an imperious hand, they determined the profession that each child would enter.

Eduardo and Inday both had the means to establish a business. Over the years they saved money and bought land in Mindanao, the Visaya's, and Luzon; and both separately inherited small plots of land and property from their families. Eduardo received a few hectares in Abra, Ilocos, and a house in Manila; and Inday took on her parent's house and the land it stood on near Cebu. The couple also had the opportunities to start a business, and plenty of examples for them to follow. As part of his job Eduardo was in daily contact with businesses of all shapes and sizes. Inday, through her religious and charitable activities, came to know many of the great and the good in Davao. The family came to be linked by the marriage of their eldest son to the eldest daughter of the Castagna who had built up a large real estate company and owned a collection of petrol stations and other businesses all over the city. And yet the closest Inday and Eduardo came to crafting a business was the farm at Binugao, some two-hours' drive from the house in Davao city. The land was owned by three of the children—Angela, David, and Robert—but cultivated as a unit by Eduardo, David, and one other son, Ernesto. It produced rich harvests in mangoes and durian which the family enjoyed themselves. The rest was either given away to friends and neighbors (both the rich and the poor) or sold commercially. The income was irregular and mostly ploughed back into the farm part of which Ernesto gave over to trees for lumber that would take another fifteen years or so to mature. Both Ernesto and David saw an opportunity to turn it into something more, with ideas ranging from a commercial farm to a hotel with views onto unspoiled and empty beaches just a short walk away.

Why, then, did the couple and their children not establish a business? Some of their children were interested in such a venture; they had the capital to do so; they were surrounded by examples of how it could be done; they had ready access to some of the best advice obtainable; and they had networks in place that would have made it plain sailing. Why did the wave of commercialization that swept over the Philippines during their lifetime leave the family unmoved?

11.2   Parents

Eduardo and Inday viewed land and property as marks of status and, more importantly, as a form of security. With status and security came the means for an education and a profession for their children and grandchildren. They knew many families who had turned their hand to business; they also knew many, including some of the oldest and most respected, who had not.

They became especially close to Noy, the son of one of these dynasties. Their friendship grew around Inday's energy and her enthusiasm in helping Noy manage retreats and various other religious get-togethers and charitable events. It also turned out that Noy's sister taught Angela, their eldest daughter, at Assumption and later became the school's headmistress. Noy even arranged for his relatives' friends in the United States to look after Inday on her one and only visit there. Noy's family were landed and true Dabaweyneans—migrants who arrived in Davao long before the second world war, and who either bought land from the indigenes or married into their families. From the sprawling verandah, positioned to welcome the cooling breeze which swept in from the sea, turning the leaves and long grass pale, he remembered his grandfather gazing on the abaca that once dominated the estate. Even at that time their way of life and their standing was being challenged, though they did not know it. Their land had been worked by Japanese emigrants from Kyushu, Okinawa and western Honshu who had first come to the Philippines to help the Americans to construct roads. The Japanese were not merely good workers; they also proved themselves adept at managing large estates and acquiring land despite legislation introduced in 1919 to limit their growing wealth. More importantly, they came to dominate commerce and it was they, rather than the Chinese, who controlled retailing and industries such as hemp, fishing and lumber. After the war, with the decline of the abaca and the disappearance of the Japanese, commerce began to thrive more than ever as new merchants from the north moved in. It was not that Noy's grandfather had missed an opportunity; it was simply that he was not prepared to borrow money or dirty his hands in business. And so, little by little, they sold off their land and property to keep themselves in comfort, and to pay for the education of their children and grandchildren who would be expected to secure the family's name in the professions. For Noy, law had been chosen. Although it required him to undertake menial tasks (as would any profession) it was more than a cut above trade. So it was with great disappointment and shame that he failed the bar exam. His choices were now limited. Take the exam again, knowing that even if he should pass he would be tainted with that failure always. Or try his hand at business. It was not what he wanted: the merchants, though in the ascendancy, were still immigrants who were merely buying up symbols of prestige and worth. Yet he had no option; and perhaps there was more to being a merchant than met the eye. His wife, who he had met at high school, and her family were, after all, of this new breed from the north. He borrowed money from her relatives, and from the sale of a few remaining parcels of his land and property, he generated some cash of his own. With this they set up a small restaurant which flourished into an empire and would eventually lead to positions in government. Commerce was the route that Noy had thrust on him, but the professions would have been his preference. He very much sympathized with Eduardo's deeply moral antipathy to the payment of interest on loans, and with his and Inday's determination to ensure that all of children became professionals.

11.3   Children

Another obstacle was tension amongst the children. This was rooted in a hierarchy of sorts. David, the eldest child, had always been favored because he was the first and a boy; and, because he was favored, he was given authority and responsibility. Even now his brothers and sisters treated his advice more like instructions. But much was also expected of him. After he graduated from school he had, under his mother's influence, entered a seminary in Cebu. He found temptation and his father's opposition too great, and so was pushed with great ruthlessness into medicine. He obeyed because he was the eldest; and he succeeded because his father and mother and his brothers and sisters and, it seemed, the rest of the world, expected him to succeed.

Angela's life was also mapped out for her and, in return for her compliance and success, she too was accorded responsibility, authority, and favor. She was younger than many of her brothers and this drew out her parents' and especially her father's, protective impulses. When a child, they dressed her prettily as they saw it (in rough, itchy, hot, and uncomfortable outfits as she remembered it) and circulated her among good families with a preponderance of daughters, and send her to the best schools for girls. And it was only she who Inday and Eduardo chose to take with them to the theatre on Saturday evenings to watch a film. When Angela was sent to study in Cebu, it was she who was made responsible for managing the income from their lands and properties in the city and on its outskirts; for returning a portion of that income to her parents; for sternly metering the rest to pay for tuition, transport, books and food; and for the general upkeep of her parents' house where she lived with a number of her brothers, all of whom were at various stages of their studies. The sense amongst her brothers that she was favored, that she had it easy, and that she was spoiled, was felt deep into adult life though they appreciated that, just as their parents demanded much from David, much was expected from her too. She remembered vividly the moment her parents faces when her name did not appear in the newspapers' lists of successful candidates in the government board examinations, and the glorious feeling of relief which swept over her when her name was discovered in the paper's errata.

Disputes amongst siblings in later adult life were more often than not remnants of childhood, revived to give weight to some new indignation. The strains created by Angela's favored position in her parents' affections were felt especially by her younger sister. Francesca had studied in Manila where she had lived in her parents' house, keeping it in order much as Angela had done. Now that only she lived there permanently, her parents let part of the house, and asked her to collect the rent from the tenants there and at their other properties in Luzon, again much like Angela had done. But unlike Angela, she had not yet passed her board exams; unlike Angela she had siphoned off much of the rent and lavished it upon her own friends in Manila; unlike Angela she lived with a woman; and unlike Angela she would not accept any supervision. Through her parents' eyes, she believed, she was seen as stubborn, and argumentative and a distant second to her elder sister with whom she was always being compared.

Tensions amongst their brothers were of a different order. When Eduardo bought a new four-wheel drive pick-up truck and made it over to David for use in his work as a surgeon, Ernesto was told explicitly by his father that he could not drive it. Ernesto saw this as unfair and unreasonable: he had greater need of it since he was the one managing the farm. Eduardo replied that Ernesto was a careless driver who would tinker with machines about which he knew very little. The run-down jeep (the same jeep from which Robert was banned a year later) was in its sorry state largely because Ernesto, rather than take it to a proper mechanic, was always trying to fix it. This dispute came on top of another. Ernesto and David both wanted to put the farm on a proper business footing, but they could not agree on how to do so. Ernesto's attempt to register the farm as a corporation was blocked by David who feared it would end up all in Ernesto's hands after their parents' deaths.

Ernesto's frustrations were difficult for him to bear. He was a professional: a graduate in agriculture, much like his father. He had joined the army (twice) as an officer, and during his second term of service he was elevated to the rank of captain. In the army he was responsible for the lives of hundreds of men (regulars and militia) and charged with the peace and order of large areas of western and southwestern Mindanao where communist and, more recently, Muslim guerrillas operated. He was decorated twice for his bravery and presence of mind in combat. He had married, resigned honorably from the army, and fathered a child. He was widely respected for his generosity, for his gentle, shy, and self-effacing manner, and for his valor. Yet still his father and older brother treated him this way.

It was partly for this reason that he came to blows with Robert. The two men were drinking one evening in the nipa hut in the compound of their parents' house in Davao when Ernesto asked Robert why he objected to his friends entering the grounds? And why, still more, did their father seem more prepared to let Robert's friends in? Robert had replied that both he and Ernesto already knew the answer to the second question. Their father had said that many of Ernesto's friends were thieves and cut-throats. Ernesto cared nothing for this exaggeration: they were rough-hewn, certainly, but there was nothing wrong in that; and he and Robert shared many of the same friends. Robert replied that Ernesto had no right to question whether or not his friends came into the compound, especially after everything he did for their parents. And in a demonstration of his firmness in his belief he slammed a glass on to the table, breaking it. Ernesto, fearing that this was a prelude to an attack, had struck first with his fists, and Robert had counter-attacked in kind. Their mother ran out and threw herself between the two, throwing her arms round Robert, shielding him with her body and a stream of platitudes about family, children and filial piety. Angela followed, placing herself between Ernesto and her mother. With tempers fired by alcohol, and with broken glass scattered about, this was a brave thing for mother and daughter to do; and gave time enough to bring into the field Jojo, a compadre of Henry, and a policeman. He separated the two men, placing one inside the bungalow and leaving the other lying on a bench under a mosquito net by the nipa hut. The next morning

Inday made it clear through her silence and her funereal, but artful, mien how upset and disappointed she was at their behavior. Without saying a word she shamed them into sheepish apologies to everyone. There is no doubt Inday had saved one or the other from serious harm.

David, too, suffered his share of frustration. His position as a surgeon, his charity work to which he devoted most of his time, his personality, and his parents' and in-laws' names, gave him the opportunity to meet businessmen and politicians and build valuable relationships. He was asked to run as vice-governor of South Cotabato. Maria objected, and so did his father who was adamant he should concentrate on his profession and forget his fanciful business projects and political ambitions. Then came the opportunity for David, together with a handful of young surgeons from Davao, to set up a private hospital in Kidapawan in South Cotabato, some two-hours' drive from Davao. He jumped at it. His father did not speak against it, but he did face opposition from his mother-in-law who brought up the impending move in every conversation. What sort of life could Maria hope to have in such a small town? Then he was asked to invest in a gold mine in Davao del Norte. His partner owned a large security company and a luxurious hotel in Davao, and was well-connected with a number of rising political stars in both local and national governments. David turned to Maria, his wife, for money. She refused him: the mine was in an area where banditry and guerrilla actions were commonplace; finding gold in large enough quantities was always a risk, especially for small operators; and selling gold profitably in a market ostensibly controlled and monopolized by the state was a corrupt and uncertain business. But he would not to be stopped and he took out a loan from a bank opposite the hospital in Kidapawan. Collateral was needed; so he signed over land which, though titled in his name, was still the de facto property of Inday and Eduardo. It was only when the mine folded (Maria had been right) that Inday and Eduardo were told their land might soon belong to the bank. To mollify her when he told his mother the news and asked her for money, David said that he had arranged for Bing, the wife of one of his former employees at the mine, to work as a maid in his parent's house. She accepted the help, but she was not placated in the least. David was ordered to ensure that he made his payments to the bank: she would not bail him out.

The soft spot which Inday had for Robert showed itself again when he came under criticism from Tommy. Within a few days of his return from the Middle East, laden with gifts, and with his wife and children in train, he asked Robert in an off-hand, throw-away fashion what he intended to do with his life. Why had he not made provisions for the future? Robert at first ignored the jibe, and merely replied that he gave those kind of matters only such thought as they deserved. Tommy kept on over a period of some days with the odd comment here and there, gnawing away, comparing his own material success and his bright shiny family with Robert's lot. To silence him without a direct confrontation, Robert put it around to his friends (some of whom were also part of Tommy's old friendship groups) that he would strike. Tommy wisely left for Manila, only to be summoned back by his mother. He returned to find that news of the rift between himself and Robert had reached Inday. She had words with Tommy whose remarks, she said loudly and for all to hear, were unfair and misconceived. Did he, Tommy, think that they really cared for the baubles he brought them? Look at her house, look at her simple furniture, look at the way she dressed! She and Eduardo had done everything for their children: all of their money had gone into land and their children's education; and they had done everything to show their children how to live. Where had Tommy been when Eduardo had been ill? Who was there, at home, caring for them? Which of her children was generous to a fault? What kind of person was it that cared only for trinkets and money?

There was a certain amount of pose in the phrases which poured from her lips. Inday and Eduardo were not completely indifferent to their surroundings; and Tommy's display of material wealth would have been no fault had he been generous with it, and had he not implied, let alone said outright, that he was a better sort. But as far as his parents were concerned, the cheaper, the more practical, and the fewer luxuries which they and their children possessed, the better. Even such extravagance as their parents allowed themselves—a television set, a gleaming stove, a washing machine, the cutlery and linen in the sideboard, some good shoes, and jewelry—were transient and superficial when set against land and concrete and, above all, the education of their children.

There was, from this time on, always a distance between Robert and Tommy. And in Tommy there was a growing feeling that he would not be recognized for what he was and what he had achieved—a feeling made more intense by his desire to show that he, no less than his wife, a doctor, could provide equally well for his family. It was not just Tommy's callous one-upmanship that annoyed Inday. He was thought by a number of his brothers and sisters to be parsimonious and judgmental, and obsessed with keeping everything spotlessly clean and just so. His wife, too, they found rather affected and neurotic; and under her influence his children seemed remote.

Robert was close to his mother but had a fractious relationship with his father. Both men thoroughly enjoyed raising and training cockerels and betting on them at the pit. Yet Eduardo saw in Robert wasted opportunities. Robert had, for many weeks, been driving his father to the farm and back each day in an old and battered jeep so that they could prepare the birds for their fights. And each day, there and back, his father would instruct Robert how to drive safely and correctly, and how to change gear without wearing the machinery. Robert had grown tired and had asked his father if he would like to drive. Eduardo was silent until they reached the compound. He then declared that until such time as he saw fit, Robert could no longer drive the jeep. Robert retorted that he did not in any case want to drive what was no more than a pile of junk. His father then swore that Robert would never drive the jeep again. Robert left the bungalow, vowing that he would never return; and, as he left with his small daughter in tow, Eduardo ordered him never to enter the compound or eat his food again. Inday cried symbolically, asking why he treated her children in this way? During the first five years of their marriage she had been without child. She had then borne nine. Where was his gratitude for this blessing? Eduardo said nothing. He was resolute. His decision stood. There was more to this than just Robert's driving. He had given Robert every opportunity. He had sent him and all his other children to the best schools in Davao; and then to universities in Cebu or Manila. Robert had met all his efforts with ingratitude and recalcitrance; and though he had won a degree, he had stubbornly resisted entry into any of the professions. Eduardo had then arranged positions for him in his friends' businesses. All Robert had to do was turn up for work on the first day; but he had not done so. And Robert had, on no less than nine occasions (Eduardo had counted), answered him back. Had any of his other children ever been so disrespectful? There was no hope that either man would apologize and make amends; and so it remained for more than a year.

11.4   In-Laws

The presence of in-laws occasionally provided a distraction from arguments within the family but, on the whole, merely aggravated them. Her sons' wives, Inday believed, were concerned primarily with the interests of their own parents and siblings; and had nothing to lose if they set her sons against each other, encouraging them to compare themselves, to wonder who among them would, in the end, inherit land and property, and who would, in the meantime, benefit from their parents' favors.

Alfred's marriage to Fenilda lasted nearly a decade. But no children came out of it, and there were other problems which strained the relationship. Eduardo lent much of the money paid to him on retirement from the Bureau of Internal Revenue to Alfred and Fenilda who used it to buy a house in an expensive subdivision in Davao. Alfred, who worked overseas, agreed to pay his father back from the salary which he sent home to Fenilda each month. Fenilda, however, channeled much of the money to her brother who lived a few doors away on the same estate. He used this to set up a jeepney firm and a money-lending business. Fenilda secured a license and a route for the jeepney; her brother and his wife drove it; and all three of them shared in the costs and profits. Fenilda also took over Robert and Linda's food store outside the Gaisano's department store to whose salesgirls Fenilda's sister-in-law lent money.

Fenilda's food store collapsed when she was abandoned by her cook. She had paid him only a domestic's salary and this he often received several months late. Yet it was he who prepared food for the store as well as for Fenilda and her maid, for her brother's family, and occasionally for Angela, Inday and Eduardo. When that business ended, Fenilda bought three trucks, hoping to gain a foothold in the construction trade, hauling sand and gravel. This business also failed: she struggled to handle the drivers and the larger trucking companies kept undercutting her. Another unsuccessful venture—a mahjong parlor—followed.

By this time, her marriage to Alfred had been annulled on the grounds that no children had been produced. To end things quickly, Alfred gave Fenilda the house, provided she released him from all other ties and obligations. She agreed and turned the house into a workshop producing *nata de coco* for Dole. In the bedroom which she and Alfred had once shared, she put a small fridge and microwave oven. The rest of the house was ripped out to make way for noisy machinery, tangled hose-pipes, and barrels of rancid water. The business proved more successful than her earlier attempts, but it was technically illegal and soon she was paying out money to officials who monitored business licenses and land use.

Meanwhile, Eduardo—who had watched her businesses rise and fall, who thoroughly disapproved of charging interest on loans, who felt she treated him coldly, and who now had to watch the destruction of the very house in which he had sunk a large part of his government pension—had not yet been repaid in full. But worse was to come. He learnt through Robert that Alfred, during his last period of leave, had taken up with a woman who worked in a bar in the city. The next Robert knew of it, Alfred had married this woman and she was now expecting their first child. And it was to them, and her parents, that his salary was now being remitted. Eduardo refused to see Alfred and would not recognize or meet with his new wife.

Some months later after the news reached his parents, Alfred turned up on their doorstep with suitcases full of whisky, tobacco, and other luxuries, hoping that his father might be in better humor and more willing to accept his new family. He was met with a stony face and steely intransigence. Eduardo said that he would not even recognize Alfred's child. Inday was more sympathetic. Their grandchild was entirely innocent, and of this she and Angela tried, unsuccessfully, to convince Eduardo. Still, she would not allow the child's innocence to influence her belief that her new daughter-in-law's fast clothes and finery were exactly what a cheap gold-digger would wear. As if to emphasize her disapproval, she and Angela continued to see Fenilda and treat her with respect. Fenilda, they felt, was socially awkward but loyal. Inday understood Alfred's desire for children but his duty was to his wife; and since it was he who had borrowed money from Eduardo, it was his loan to repay. Whereas Alfred had, in Inday's view, behaved improperly, Fenilda was merely clumsy.

The cooling of relationships with the Castagna family began with what David took to be an easy and straightforward deal with the son of one his wife's nephews, Renato, who, following his parents' footsteps, ran a garage and gas station—a possibility that David also wanted to explore. David had decided to renovate and then sell an old Toyota jeep which Eduardo had given to him many years earlier. A share of the proceeds was to be used as a down payment on a new car; and part would go to help pay off his mother's debts to the Credit Union. Andrew would renovate the Toyota; the estimate for the job was P80,000. Once the work had been completed, a buyer was found who agreed to pay P270,000—some P70,000 more than David had expected. Renato then presented David with a bill for P110,000. This not only exceeded the original estimate but also included charges for parts which David had supplied. Renato's creative billing was motivated by the opportunity which this deal opened up to pay back a debt to his mother whose own business was supported by Audrey—David's mother-in-law. At this point Maria learnt by chance that Audrey had received P25,000 for the ring which she had asked her mother to sell. Maria requested that Audrey give the sum to Renato's mother. By repaying Renato's debt to his mother, Maria and David would only have to pay the amount originally agreed for the jeep's renovation. Audrey, however, chose this moment to recall an old loan which she had made to Renato's mother and kept the proceeds from the sale of the ring for herself.

The distrust which Audrey and David felt towards each other deepened when she bought several large plots of land and, to mitigate her own tax burden, asked him to register these in his name. He agreed until he was advised by his father that his own tax burden would rise. David pulled out of the arrangement at the last moment, much to Audrey's chagrin. It annoyed her even more when, sometime later, David sold a plot of land for more than three times the amount he had paid when he bought it from her eighteen months earlier. Audrey requested him to make up the difference: David would not have been able to make such a profit, reasoned Audrey, if she had not agreed to sell the land to him at the time and at the price that she did. David refused to make any money over to her.

11.5   Pyrrhic Victories

Eduardo and Inday's family and their relationships with their in-laws survived these and many other conflicts; but establishing a business was nigh impossible. Tensions flared up again after their deaths.

In 1999, the head of the Castagna family died, followed not long after by his wife. Before her death in 2001 she sold off large tracts of land and a collection of small businesses accumulated over a lifetime. A part of the proceeds she divided equally among her children. She consolidated the remainder in a real estate company, their core business. Positions in the company were distributed amongst her children, with sole authority to issue cheques vested in Maria. Both Eduardo and Inday were advised by family and friends to note how the Castagna had arranged their affairs. The couple listened and watched, but whatever they thought they kept to themselves.

In 2003, Eduardo died and Inday took absolute control of land, property, income, and expenditure. A year later, tragedy struck: David suffered a fatal heart-attack. What happened next reflected the two families' very different attitudes to relationships. David's in-laws took on the planning and costs for his burial. They arranged a plot for David in the same cemetery as his father and where the Castagnas were also buried. They built a palisade and placed a large sarcophagus under it. But, as the weeks and months and years passed it was left unfinished, while the Castagnas' tomb grew ever-more splendid. It was a two-storied house, replete with kitchen, bathroom, bedrooms (each with its own balcony), *objets d'art*, furniture, and air-conditioning, all to accommodate family and guests during All Soul's and anniversaries. And in the living room they put their parents' first car—a bright red mustang trimmed with chrome. A stone's throw away in the opposite direction, a small plaque could be found in the grass where Eduardo lay.

Over the next eight years, David's younger brothers and sisters approached the question of inheritance with their mother only indirectly if at all. She became more introspective and contented herself with a shrinking circle of old and ageing friends, playing mahjong. She was looked after by Vivian (who had been with the family since 1962) and by her children and grand-children, with Ernesto's daughter and Robert taking on most of the work. Then tragedy struck again. Robert's diabetes worsened and his kidney's failed. Money was raised from the sale of land; but he, too, died in 2012.

She retained her mental faculties for the most part but as her heart slowly gave out and her breathing became more labored, she suffered a little confusion. She did not complain though she could not lie flat for long and she must have been extremely uncomfortable at night when, so often, she would prefer to sit in a rocking chair watching soap operas on television.

After her death in 2014, she left no instructions about the inheritance of properties and land. The children came to easy settlements at first. The main plot and house in Davao was divided up equally and apportioned by a raffle, but kept as a single unit. They agreed to let Alfred and his third wife stay here with their young children. Another, still larger house in Davao was dealt with in a similar way. There was no agreement on a house and lot in Manila which Inday had contemplated selling if she received a good offer, but in the end decided not to sell. The children agreed simply to divide the rent equitably amongst them.

Trouble began with a second house and lot in Manila which their father had inherited from his sister. Francesca claimed it because she had looked after their aunt during her final years. It then transpired that Tommy had transferred to his name their mother's land and house in Cebu while she was still living and as Robert was being cared for in that very same house. His explanation was that tax on the property had been left unpaid and, given the death of father and their mother's weakness, action was needed. He had paid the outstanding tax and bore the cost of the transfer, and so it was now his. He also took the large, shiny SUV that had belonged to their mother. After all, he said, he had paid the deposit on it. Within eighteen months, his marriage broke down and his wife and children had a restraining order issued against him. He lost both the house he and his wife had shared and the small hotel he had built nearby; and he was reduced to sleeping in the office of the small internet café he had set up. He got no sympathy or aid from any of his brothers or sisters.

Ernesto hired his own lawyer and discovered that this had not been the only hidden transaction. Alfred had forged his mother's signature on the sale of a large ranch in Malaga. And, as if to add insult to injury, he allowed his new wife to eject Vivien from the house in which she had cared for their mother, and to demand that his brothers sisters 'book' rooms rather than turn up unannounced if they should happen to find themselves in Davao. Alfred undoubtedly felt extremely bitter. He had lost count of the number of times he had remitted money to his parents or returned from overseas to shower all and sundry with gifts and dollars. And he had fathered six children who had been unfairly spurned. He, too, hired a lawyer.

Ernesto contested the transfers, sales, and claims; and made his own demands on the farm in Binugao. He worked the farm and managed it and deserved it. Robert and David and their parents were gone. Robert's share had reverted to their mother who had not made her wishes clear. David's share had gone to his wife who, he thought, did not need it. And what good was it to Angela? Why should she benefit from his labor? In fact, why should she benefit from the shares in San Miguel which their father gave her in the 1980s? Ernesto's daughter had earned those by caring for their mother. Maria refused to sign over the land: it had been David's and he wanted his own daughters to have it. Angela had no objection to Ernesto keeping all the revenue from the farm. But their father had given her part of the farm, and he had wanted her to keep the shares. These were gifts—expression of his wishes, his personality, and her relationship with him. Was her brother and his daughter really demanding financial rewards for helping their mother? They would not talk again.

11.6   Conclusions

Relationships do not *have* to come together as a business, no matter how strong the drive for commerce in the wider community. Some are happy to take up, adjust, work on, and shape relationships into a viable business entity. Others are unwilling to do so. Noy's grandfather and Inday and Eduardo thought the instrumentalism which commerce required tawdry. This was not the main reason why they resisted turning to business. Such an attitude should not be thought of as a luxury which only those with land, status, and education could afford. There was any number of reasons, each of which by itself was enough to block that route. What these difficulties show is that the logic of relationships and their link with commerce is not expressed automatically. It has to be discovered and this involves a struggle. This struggle is felt just as keenly amongst those on whom the pressure to commercialize is probably at its most intense.

Filomina's early life was Dickensian. She was the fourth of five children. Her father, a small farmer, slipped from a coconut tree while collecting its wine and broke his back. Unable to work and support his children he sent Felomina to live with his sister. At the age of fourteen she worked at a fruit stall. Her days began at 3 am when she carried bananas and mangoes from her aunt's car to the fruit stall in a market. Then she was put to work as a housemaid for her aunt and uncle and for their landlady. Two years later, she was persuaded by her aunt to marry a neighbor's son, a sweeper at city hall. She learnt to make dresses at a beauty and fashion school in Cubao. She graduated and, shortly after, gave birth to her first child. Then she and her husband were told that, as part of a nation-wide scheme to help squatters, the land on which their house stood would be awarded to them should they wish to apply for it. They did so and found that their monthly income was not enough to cover the monthly payments. It was this that nudged her into setting up her first business—a piggery. The idea had occurred to her after her husband's transfer to a better paid job as a garbage collector for the city. Three years later, the lot had been paid for in full. The couple erected a fence around their land and asked those whose houses had begun to encroach on their lot to move. Their demand was met with threats and a lengthy court case. The action ended in their favor; but in the meantime their neighbors had grown in number and more vocal about the smell and pollution from the piggery. They shut it down and, in an attempt to recoup the lost income, she agreed to host a *jueteng* for which she was paid up to 450 pesos a day. This business lasted for only a few months before it ended with a police raid and seizure of the moveable contents of their house.

She decided next to put her dressmaking to use only to find the returns were minimal. So she gave this up favor of working overseas in Saudi Arabia. She built up capital successfully at first, until her husband suffered a stroke, and a fire razed their house to the ground. The set-back kept her in Saudi Arabia for a few more years, rebuilding her capital. Her husband added to this in 2006 when he took early retirement and a payout, only to suffer another stroke. Five years later, just before her youngest son was due to fly to Saudi Arabia to take up work so that she could return to the Philippines for good, he was killed in a motorcycle crash. The bike—owned by the company he had worked for—had been faulty; and in recognition of this she received 350,000 pesos. She planned to use this money, together with her own savings, to build a large bording house with twelve bedrooms. The idea was her late son's. She spent more than a year after his death collecting the documentation for a loan from the Land Bank to match her own capital for the project. All that remained was for her to put the title to the family home into the pot. But when she talked to her remaining children (both of whom were named on the title along with their parents) *'they refused. My children were worried that if my husband, who is already sick, were to die, then we might lose our existing house'*. Had they agreed, the boarding house would have been finished by now, and the income from the lodgers would have more than covered the monthly repayments. As it was, she said, still mourning and still hurt by her children's rejection, she would not be able to put food on the table for Christmas and New Year: she had yet to pay the business license for her stall in the local market. Here she sold pyjamas, sheets, pillow cases, school uniforms, shorts, and anything else she could buy wholesale at Divisoria.

Felomina was left exhausted and alienated. Each morning she would *'pray to the Lord… to save us all from danger and from gossip'*. Each morning she would make her way to her stall through a community in which *'people always gossip and destroy the lives of their neighbors'*. If she was asked to lend money, she did so carefully. Her policy was to see, hear, speak, and do no evil. Some were in genuine need; others were happy to go without food just as long as they had cash to gamble with. To the former she lent what she could when she could and always without interest; to the latter she said she had nothing even for herself. And each afternoon she would make her way back through that same community to what was, for her, a house rather than a home. She was, she said, unhappy with her husband. *'We don't go out; we don't have any happy moments; there is no love between us. The only reason we stayed together was the children'*. Perhaps this was so, though mutual financial dependency—she on his pension, he on her savings and on the money which her stall drew in, and both of them on the rent from a spare room—was better than independent destitution. Her children helped her occasionally just as she would buy a few groceries, if she had any money, to put in her daughter-in-law's sari-sari stall. But loans in either direction would have to be repaid. She lived, she made do, she accommodated; and, she hoped to leave her children a place of their own when she and her husband were gone.

Chapter 12
Conclusions

The transformation of largely agricultural societies outside Europe and America into industrial ones is a moment in the history of humanity as pivotal as the industrial revolution, or the rise of science, or the spread of the great mendicant religions, or the appearance of the first cities, or the shift to a sedentary life that took place some ten thousand years ago. It has been amongst the most pressing global concerns for more than seventy years, and has attracted corresponding interest in academia where it evolved into a distinct specialism – development studies.

This book works towards an understanding of development at a somewhat oblique angle and through a somewhat different (though equally diverse) literature. Its central theme is that to understand the social world is to see what is done, to listen to what is said, and to posit explanations rooted in social relationships: *nihil ultra requiratis*. The qualities of relationships, the working through of their logic, and the practical circumstances created by the natural world, are sufficient to explain development. Similar patterns are constantly being rediscovered again and again across time and geography; this is so even in the most complex and modern societies.

'Develop', in other words, is what people do. The mind is engaged in relationships from the moment life starts, excited by movement and smell, tastes and sounds, colors, shapes and textures, and by the making and exchange of things. Thus, representations emerge, practice evolves, and consciousness is stirred. Relationships shade into groups, groups into organizations, organizations into patterns, patterns into markets, settlements, and states. The group is a necessary psychological and practical response to being; so, too, is the protection of relationships by their 'distancing' from the 'organization'. The market, commerce, state and the mechanization of activity are all practical solutions to growing and competitive populations on finite land. And while the logic of relationships leads to these broad arrangements, the dimensional quality of representations and practice introduces layer upon layer of detail, uncertainty, and difference.

Big society, then, comprises organizations and their patterning. Organizations and their patterns are manifestations of a drive to protect social relationships. And

© Springer Nature Singapore Pte Ltd. 2018
R. Hodder, *Small Business, Big Society*,
https://doi.org/10.1007/978-981-10-8875-9_12

relationships describe mental states that arise from, are informed by, and inform practice: they do not reflect, nor are they arranged into structures, nor can they be composites of individuals. Yet people who are *of* the relationships that comprise organizations do not share a single mental context; their representations are not perfectly aligned; their emotional states are shifting; their practices vary. Organizations and their patterning are fuzzy; and the larger and more complex they are, the more nebulous and inconstant they become. It is only to the extent that those uncertain patterns are integrated into representations roughly shared amongst the populace that they inform practice. And it is only *particular* relationships which people come up against (not the organization and patterns in their entirety) that directly constrains, encourages, or influences in some other way. Organizations and their patterning are as much in need of being explained (by the play of relationships) as they are capable of explaining.

There is, therefore, about big society, a powerlessness. Two ways in which this finds expression are of some consequence. One is through the management of tensions amongst competing groups, substituting greater stability for power. Another is through the emergence of commerce, often in spite of government and its agencies. These qualities are true of any big society. They are true of China, however surprising this may seem given its reputation for authoritarianism; and true of the Philippines, despite its tendency to welcome the 'strong man' into office. A third manifestation of powerlessness, and one that is no less important, is the difficulties governments have in permitting transfers from the financial (backstreet) economy to the front street especially during times of Puritanism. This, however, is more true of the West today and helps to explain why, so long as this remains so, the balance of economic power and creativity is likely to continue its shift towards the 'developing' world.

This broad view of relationships, their play, and the patterns formed, is related in more detail at various points throughout the last ten chapters; but it is helpful to draw these together as follows.

(i) Emotion—an aspect of relationships which describes conclusions or representations freely reached and signals the mind's integration with other minds—has a vital role in the creation and patterning of organizations. It supplies a need to cooperate and a means to organize.

(ii) To protect them from the alienation that ensues as they are arranged into functional groups, relationships are 'distanced' psychologically from the group and the emerging organization. Outside the organization, a mental sanctuary is created in which relationships (and so constructs of "self," "you," "they," "community," and "society") are treated *as if* important in their own right and, therefore, should not be manipulated for particular ends. A contemplation of these matters finds voice through sophisticated modes of indirect communication, not least as art, sculpture, literature, music, and dance.

(iii) The treatment of relationships *as if* important in themselves implies the *choice* and, therefore, the admission that relationships are not necessarily important in themselves in all circumstances. Choice, then, is vital to the protection of relationships in two respects. First, without it, relationships are transformed, conceptually, into facts or absolutes which *must* be thought of and treated as important in their own right. An intimate or felt appreciation of their significance is now lost; and, as appeals are made to these absolutes, relationships may be turned more easily into instruments. Secondly, choice allows for the possibility that there may be circumstances in which, in order to preserve relationships, it is necessary to treat relationships as instruments or absolutes.

(iv) The deepening of the affective sphere *outside* the organization (that is, the treatment of relationships as if important in their own right) is paralleled by changes *within* the organization. The sense that relationships should not be manipulated is flatly contradicted by experience: within the organization, relationships are plainly re-shaped, re-directed and used for ulterior purposes. It is, therefore, essential: that rules, roles, procedures, hierarchies, and divisions of authority are treated *as if* absolute or, in other words, *as if* important in themselves and, therefore, distanced *conceptually* from their true social quality; and that choice is sustained.

(v) The treatment of the organization's rules, roles, hierarchies, routines, discipline, divisions of authority, and its functions and objectives, *as if* absolute (and their conceptual "distancing" from relationships) is necessary to protect the affective sphere. Were the true social nature of the organization to be recognized explicitly and openly, then the use of relationships for ulterior purposes in the form of the organization would have been exposed. That is, in open and general recognition both of the use of relationships and, therefore, of the instrumental potential of relationships, it is now easy to conceive of their use for whatever purpose and more likely that their instrumental potential will be realized. The affective sphere is now compromised and its quality as a distinct sphere and sanctuary is lost.

(vi) Whilst relatively authoritarian, the organization is not impersonal nor is it dehumanized. Authoritarianism may compel a reshaping of relationships, but these remain the substance of the organization. To eradicate social relationships would be to eradicate the organization. However, the reshaping of relationships, and the instrumentalism which first prompted that reshaping, create a sense of alienation. Constructs of "self," "you" and "they," and their place in "community" and "society," are no longer what they were, and behavior has altered. The crucible of relationships is now being re-ordered dramatically; and as the organization is driven towards a particular objective, its members find that their own understandings and sense of self are shaken, and that they are drawn into a gyre of instrumentalism and authoritarianism.

(vii) As emotion deepens outside the organization, along with growing alienation within the organization, it becomes necessary to permit within the organization: the emergence of relationships which are explicitly social (and treated *as if* important in their own right); and, therefore, compassion. That is, the affective sphere begins to intrude into the organization but in ways that are beneficial for the organization. This is so in two respects. First, the admission of explicitly social relationships within the organization helps emphasize the conceptual distinction between those relationships and organization's frameworks, and thereby ensures that the true social quality of the organization's frameworks remains unspoken. Secondly, with the admission of social relationships and compassion, comes recognition that competency, abilities, contributions, and failings are changeable, ambiguous, intimately entangled, and often dependent upon context. In this way, greater tolerance and, therefore, more room for creativity and flexibility are brought to the organization. There is less need for supervision and policing; and the organization becomes less authoritarian. There is also growing technical professionalism. That is, the treatment of the organization and its frameworks *as if* absolute (and their conceptual distancing from relationships) brings regularity, predictability, focus and reliability to practice. In short, the deepening of the affect outside the organization, and increasing professionalism within the organization, prompt and reinforce the other. The emergence, development, and maintenance of the organization and the affective sphere are interdependent.

(viii) As the affective sphere grows, there is the risk that it will become, conceptually, entirely distinct and separate from the organization, such that the social quality of the organization is no longer recognized, and instrumentalism (because of its potential threat to relationships) is taken to be synonymous with moral degeneration. Relationships and organizations, 'correctly' formed, are treated as symbols of moral purity; and there is increasing pressure to eradicate any symptom of instrumentalism. There is an attempt to prescribe not only correct action but also correct thought and, therefore, possible future action. Correct rules, roles, procedures, hierarchies, functions and objectives (in the professional sphere), and correct social relationships, constructs and emotions (in the affective sphere) are presented as facts; and a felt and intimate appreciation of their importance and meaning is lost.

(ix) Within the affective sphere there is now an unfelt acceptance of the importance of social relationships; while, in the professional sphere, the conceptual separation of the organization's rules, roles, procedures, hierarchies, functions and objectives from social relationships is so complete that their rigorous application in all circumstances becomes imperative. Instrumentalism and other expressions of self exhibited by non-conformists only prompt a further strengthening of this Puritanism.

(x) It is no longer enough to follow the rules or to choose to treat those rules *as if* absolute: rules within the organization, and relationships outside it, must be treated as absolutes; and behavior must be correctly motivated, and performed without discretion. The organization becomes less and less flexible; and self is marginalized by increasingly stringent orthopraxy. The repression of self generates intense frustration; at the same time it becomes possible, even laudable, to demand that others should endure misery simply in order to satisfy the Puritan's sense of the importance of absolutes. However, as a sense of rebellion mounts against repression, and as resentments build against the Puritan's growing callousness and officiousness, there are likely to be swings, possibly sudden and violent, towards personal interests and open instrumentalism. Sporadic at first, these swings become more and more frequent; relationships become more unstable as uncertainty over their significance and meaning deepens; organizations become weaker and less effective; and the affective sphere thins out and begins to fray. And, as instrumentalism becomes prevalent, conditions are now formed in which the affective may strengthen once again.

(xi) These swings from affective to puritanical, or to instrumental and authoritarian states, are neither preordained nor mutually exclusive. But they are mutually dependent. Thus, these conditions—disorder, instrumentalism and authoritarianism, settled affect, Puritanism, and liminality—come to fore at different scales and at different times and places, and take myriad forms.

(xii) The nature of relationships and emotion, and the changes that occur as they are re-shaped into organizations, has an important bearing on how people respond to the practical difficulties they face and, to some extent, on the kinds of difficulties they face. Of particular significance is an aspect of relationships—patronage.

(xiii) Each patron requires a growing band of followers: this increase in density of population supplies more labor to work the land more intensively, and to defend it more effectively. More followers also mean a greater demand for food, water, cloth, weapons, and shelter. Thus, with increasing density of population and keener competition, patrons are obliged to deliver to their clients perpetual improvements in the supply of materials and opportunities.

(xiv) At first, it is possible for patrons to meet these demands by leading their clients away onto greener pastures. When this is no longer possible, patrons and clients are confined to a given area (and this is especially true if environmental boundaries exist or if firm social borders have been established). Once territory has been delineated, and all available has been reclaimed and occupied, patrons are now faced with an intractable problem. When the productivity of land reaches its limits and, given that movement is no longer possible, a choice must be made. Either a patron must subject himself and his followers to a stronger community, or he must become 'the strong man' and take over other territories.

(xv) If conflicts are to be avoided, then competing patrons must find some way to share, limit and distribute power and resources. One other solution is to alter the group's basis of wealth from land to commerce. This releases the group from its dependency on the productivity and area of land; provides the wherewithal to support a growing band of followers; allows a far greater density of population; and has the potential to channel military conflict into commercial competition, at least in the first instance.

(xvi)   Trade is a practice and aspect of relationships which foreshadows this shift from land to commerce by a long way. Before the emergence of settled agriculture, itinerancy requires groups to put together mating networks, and to find places where they can meet other groups, victual, navigate, measure and shelter. Here, techniques that anticipate crop cultivation, animal husbandry, tool-making and the extraction of minerals, are experimented with for the first time and dispersed; and trade (and the sense of inequality and advantage is conveys) can be practiced more easily, precisely because outsiders are distant physically and conceptually from the relationships that comprise the group. These places have the potential (as population densities in a region increase) to be transformed from way stations (temporarily occupied by transient populations) into permanent settlements with constant populations.

(xvii)   The movement of larger groups around more complex circuits; the establishment of semi-permanent settlements and empty settlements; the rotation of related groups through those settlements; the challenges posed by permanent settlement and larger populations; and the need to avoid war and to share and amalgamate: all this demands larger and more complex organization.

(xviii) As population numbers and density continue to grow and intensify along with competition, commerce necessarily inveigles large tracts of the community. The use of machines in production soon follows, and industrialization becomes a strong possibility. Yet any relief for patrons is only temporary. Demands and expectations from clients continue to mount while the market they constitute is limited. One solution is to expand trade further and to become more closely integrated with other communities. Another is to create new, material products. A third is to trade in financial products tied only very loosely to a cash base: it then becomes possible to trade forward in time in a market that *seems* limitless until, in the absence of transfers to the bulk of society, crisis hits.

(xix)   The nature of relationships and emotional change may also influence the patterning of organization quite independently of these practical considerations. Emotional deepening outside and within organizations lends itself to the arts, music, and literature; to the provision of social necessities and welfare; to the study of the natural world; and to the creation of organizations with those ends in mind. In the longer term, formalism and sharpening distinctions between 'organization' and 'social relationships' may engender Puritanism. This in turn may nurture activities, representations and organizations that are more dogmatic and focused on control.

This understanding of development offers no prescriptions or policy advice. But it does offer a way to think about development; and, within those terms, it suggests *where* practical effort might be concentrated to facilitate development. It implies that development practice is about acceptance. It is, first, acceptance of population growth and high population densities, large towns and cities, and widespread infrastructure provision. Whatever direct economic stimulus this may provide, it encourages movement, the transmission of ideas and information, and makes life easier for organizations.

Development practice is, secondly, an acceptance that small businesses' have a vital role in fostering emotional change throughout the community, as does art, music, literature, and the study of the natural world (activities more usually treated as luxuries to be enjoyed only when a high standard of living is attained).

Thirdly, development practice is acceptance of organizational forms and patterns even if they offend more puritanical views of efficiency, rationality and probity. It means, for instance, acceptance of 'informal' business and practice, an acceptance of large enterprises with 'hidden' welfare functions, and tolerance of many forms of 'corruption'.

Fourthly, development practice is acceptance of political organizations and patterns even if they do not conform with explicitly democratic arrangements, systems, and processes. What matters is a willingness to serve the community and to distribute goods, materials and opportunities as widely and as evenly as necessary, even if this means providing in effect a universal income. Development practice, then, is also acceptance of maximum transfers from the financial sector to the real economy; public control of the financial sector; and control over the size and concentration of private businesses so that private monopolies and oligarchies are not established and do not become entrenched.

Is this simply an argument for a mixed economy? The answer is yes and no. Yes, in that it describes the presence of public and private ownership and control. No, in that a free market and a monolithic state-controlled economy are not alternatives forms (which a 'mixed' economy implies) but in fact one and the same in every significant respect. Both comprise relationships and organizations and their patterning. Both are faced with the problem of moving and distributing goods, services, materials, and opportunities. Both arrive at the same solutions from opposite directions. Free-marketeers imagine their world to be a borderless ocean where swells rise and fall, gather and dissipate, as naturally as breathing; where unevenness is only temporary, no matter how rough and mountainous its surface becomes. Yet they soon discover that in practice their 'ocean' turns out to be liquid cargo. When the ship turns, yaws, and pitches, buffeted by wind and wave, the cargo sloshes about; the vessel quickly becomes unstable and risks breaking up or rolling over. The statists, meanwhile, are content to view their world as a cargo but they imagine its behavior is predictable. They try to push and pull and transfer the liquid, only to find that the swirls and eddies they create either make no difference or aggravate the instabilities already set in motion by the sloshes. Thus, both free-marketeers and statists arrive at an arrangement of liquid and baffles to regulate and mitigate those movements.

The notion of development as an expression of being human, as rooted in social relationships, and as something best cultivated by acceptance of a world that is, from the Puritan's viewpoint, messy and imprecise, also offers a way of thinking through problems in the social sciences more generally. Just as there is no necessary choice to be made between market or state or some mixture of the two, so there is no necessary choice to be made between social phenomena as irreducible individuals with intentional states, or social phenomena as irreducible structures (or as reflections of those structures). Nor is there a need to position a study between these two ideals and to claim that individuals are to an extent shaped by structures just as structures are to an extent altered and influenced by individuals. 'Individual' and 'structure' and 'culture', like all ideas, emerge from interactions. Nor, then, is there any necessary choice to be made between deduction and induction. In the natural world, deduction certainly appears to be the only sure way to proceed from truth to truth especially when natural forces and processes are invisible and cannot be envisioned sensibly except as mathematical representations. But it fails in human affairs. If such forces are presumed to exist in the social world and yet do not in fact exist, then deduction offers no escape from the problem of induction. Free of the discipline imposed by their operation in fact, these imaginings provide the only light to interpret by. For this reason, abduction is essential. It begins with simple guesses and prototypes marked by an economy of ontology and, in particular, by the absence of law-like forces. These guesses are altered with experience. It is in this way that broader and more comprehensive accounts are built up.

Bibliography

Abrahamson, B. (1993). *Why organizations? How and why people organize.* Newbury Park, CA: Sage.

Adams, R. (1966). *The evolution of urban society.* Chicago: Aldine.

Adler, P. S. (2012). The sociological ambivalence of bureaucracy: From Weber via Gouldner to Marx. *Organization Science, 23,* 244–266.

Adolphs, R. (2012). Emotion. *Current Biology, 20,* R549–R552.

Agrylis, C. (1957). *Personality and organization: The conflict between system and individual.* New York: Harper.

Aimé, C., Laval, G., Patin, E., Verdu, P., Ségurel, L., Chaix, R., et al. (2013). Human genetic data reveal contrasting demographic patterns between sedentary and nomadic populations that predate the emergence of farming. *Molecular Biology and Evolution, 30*(12), 2629–2644. Advance Access, September 24, 2013.

Alchian, A., & Demsetz, H. (1972). Production, information costs, and economic organization. *American Economic Review, 62,* 777–795.

Aldrich, H., & Cliff, J. (2003). The pervasive effects of family on entrepreneurship: Toward a family embeddedness perspective. *Journal of Business Venturing, 18,* 573–596.

Ancona, D. (1992). *The classics and the contemporary: A new blend of small group theory.* Working paper 3445-92-BPS. Cambridge, MA: MIT Sloan School.

Anderson, B., & Harrison, P. (2006). Questioning affect and emotion. *Area, 38,* 333–335.

Ang, Y. Y., & Jia, N. (2013). Perverse complementarity: Political connections and the use of courts among private firms in China. *The Journal of Politics, 76,* 318–332.

Apicella, C., Marlowe, F., Fowler, J., & Christakis, N. (2012). Social networks and cooperation in hunter-gatherers. *Nature, 481,* 497–502.

App, B., McIntosh, D., Reed, C., & Hertenstein, M. (2011). Nonverbal channel use in communication of emotion: How may depend on why. *Emotion, 11,* 603–617.

Ashforth, B., & Kreiner, G. (2002). Normalizing emotion in organizations: Making the extraordinary seem ordinary. *Human Resource Management Review, 12,* 215–235.

Ashkenasy, N. (2003). Emotions in organizations: A multi-level perspective. In F. Dansereau & F. J. Yammarino (Eds.), *Multi-level issues in organizational behavior and strategy* (Vol. 2, pp. 9–54). Oxford, UK: Elsevier/JAI Press.

Au, K., & Kwan, H. K. (2009). Start-up capital and Chinese entrepreneurs: The role of the family. *Entrepreneurship: Theory and Practice, 33*(4), 889–908.

Aufrecht, S., & Bun, L. S. (1995). Reform with Chinese characteristics: The context of Chinese civil service reform. *Public Administration Review, 55,* 175–182.

Auyero, J. (1999). From the client's point of view: How poor people perceive and evaluate political clientelism. *Theory and Society, 28,* 297–334.

Bacon, C. (1922). The Anuak. *Sudan Notes and Records, 5,* 113–129.

Balogh, T. (1966). *The economics of poverty.* London: Weidenfeld and Nicolson.

Bardhan, P. (2002). Decentralisation of governance and development. *Journal of Economic Perspectives, 16,* 185–205.

Barker, H. (2017). *Family and business during the industrial revolution.* Oxford: OUP.

Barney, J. (1991). Firm resources and sustained competitive advantage. *Journal of Management, 17,* 99–120.

Barnhardt, B. (2015). The "epidemic" of cheating depends on its definition: A critique of inferring the moral quality of "cheating in any form". *Ethics and Behavior.* https://doi.org/10.1080/10508422.2015.1026595.

Bar-Yosef, O. (2002). The upper paleolithic revolution. *Annual Review of Anthropology, 31,* 363–393.

Barzel, Y. (1982). Measurement cost and the organization of markets. *Journal of Law and Economics, 25,* 27–48.

Bastress-Dukehart, E. (2001). Family, property and feeling in early modern German noble culture: The Zimmerns of Swabia. *Sixteenth Century Journal, 32,* 1–19.

Bauer, P. (1991). *The development frontier.* London: Harvester Wheatsheaf.

Bauer, P., & Yamey, B. (1963). *The economics of underdeveloped countries.* Cambridge: Cambridge University Press.

Bayley, D. H. (1966). The effects of corruption in a developing nation. *Western Political Quarterly, XIX,* 719–732.

Bearfield, D. A. (2009). What is patronage? A critical re-examination. *Public Administration Review, 69*(1), 64–76.

Bebbington, D. (2011). Christian higher education in Europe: A historical analysis. *Christian Higher Education, 10,* 10–24.

Bednarik, R. (1994). Art origins. *Anthropos, 89,* 169–180.

Belfer-Cohen, A., & Goring-Morris, A. (2011). Becoming farmers: The inside story. *Current Anthropology, 52,* s209–s220.

Belge, C. (2011). State building and the limits of legibility: Kinship networks and Kurdish resistance in Turkey. *International Journal of Middle East Studies, 43,* 95–114.

Bellamy, C. (2011). Alive and well? The 'surveillance society' and the coalition. *Public Policy and Administration, 26,* 149–155.

Benit-Gbaffou, C., & Piper, L. (2012). Party politics, the poor, and the city: Reflections from the South African case. *Geoforum, 43,* 173–177.

Bennett, R. J. (2014). *Entrepreneurship, small business and public policy.* New York: Routledge.

Berelowitz, S., Clifton, J., Firimin, C., Gulyurtlu, S., & Edwards, G. (2013). *If only someone had listened. Office of the Children's Commissioner's inquiry into child sexual exploitation in gangs and groups.* Final report. London: Office of the Children's Commissioner.

Berger, E. (1952). The relation between expressed acceptance of self and expressed acceptance of others. *Journal of Abnormal Social Psychology, 47,* 778–782.

Berger, P., & Luckmann, T. (1966). *The social construction of reality.* Garden City, NY: Anchor Books.

Berman, S. (2014). Paine and Burke now. *Democracy, 31,* 45–47 (Review of Levin, Y. (2013). *The great debate: Edmund Burke, Thomas Paine, and the birth of right and left.* New York: Basic Books).

Bevilacqua, L., & Goldman, D. (2011). Genetics of emotion. *Trends in Cognitive Sciences, 15,* 401–408.

Bies, R., & Tyler, T. (1993). The 'litigation mentality' in organizations: A test of alternative psychological explanations. *Organization Science, 4,* 352–366.

Bin Wong, R. (2002). The search for European differences and domination in the early modern world: A view from Asia. *The American Historical Review, 107,* 447–469.

Black, J. (2001). Warfare, crisis and absolutism. In E. Cameron (Ed.), *Early modern Europe* (pp. 206–230). Oxford: OUP.

Blaikie, P. (2000). Development, post-, anti-, and populist: A critical review. *Environment and Planning, 32,* 1033–1050.

Blair, T. (2006, January 10). *Respect agenda speech*. London.

Blau, P. (1973). *The dynamics of bureaucracy: A study of interpersonal relations in two government agencies* (Revised ed.). Chicago and London: University of Chicago Press.

Bloch, M. (1977). The past and the present in the present. *Man, 12*, 278–292.

Blowfield, M. (2005). Corporate social responsibility: Reinventing the meaning of development? *International Affairs, 81*, 515–524.

Blunt, P. (2009). The political economy of accountability in Timor-Leste: Implications for public policy. *Public Administration and Development, 29*, 89–100.

Boserup, E. (1987). Population and technology in preindustrial Europe. *Population and Development Review, 13*, 691–701.

Bourdieu, P. (1980). *The logic of practice*. Cambridge: Polity Press.

Bourdieu, P. (1990). *In other words*. Cambridge: Polity Press.

Bovil, E. (1922). Jega market. *Journal of the Royal African Society, 22*, 50–60.

Bovil, E. (1970). *The golden trade of the moors* (2nd ed.). London: OUP.

Brenner, R. (1976). Agrarian class structure and economic development in pre-industrial Europe. *Past Present, 70*, 30–75.

Brenner, R. (1977). The origins of capitalist development: A critique of neo-Smithian Marxism. *New Left Review, 104*, 25–92.

Brenner, R. (1982). The agrarian roots of European capitalism. *Past Present, 97*, 16–113.

Brentano, F. (1976). In O. Kraus (Ed.), *Psychology from an empirical standpoint* (Vol. 1) (L. McAlister et al., Trans.). London: Routledge.

Brief, A., & Weiss, H. (2002). Organizational behavior: Affect in the workplace. *Annual Review of Psychology, 53*, 279–307.

British Association for Early Childhood Education. (2012). *Development matters in the early years foundation stage*. London: British Association for Early Childhood Education.

Brockliss, L. (1996). Curricula. In H. de Ridder-Symoens (Ed.), *A history of the university in Europe, Universities in early modern Europe* (Vol. 2). Cambridge: CUP.

Brown, D. E. (1991). *Human universals*. Philadelphia: Temple University Press.

Brown, P. (1967). The later Roman empire. *The Economic History Review, 20*, 327–343.

Bryce, J. (1901). *The holy Roman empire*. Oxford: Macmillan.

Buck, A. D. (2006). Post-socialist patronage: Expressions of resistance and loyalty. *Studies in Comparative International Development, 41*, 3–24.

Budd, M. (1985). *Music and the emotions: The philosophical theories*. London: Routledge & Kegan Paul.

Bullock, A. (1990). *Hitler: A study in tyranny*. London: Penguin.

Bunyan, T. (2010). Just over the horizon—The surveillance society and the state in the EU. *Race and Class, 51*, 1–12.

Burrell, G., & Morgan, G. (1985). *Sociological paradigms and organizational analysis*. Portsmouth, NH: Heinemann.

Butt, A. (1952). *The Nilotes of the Sudan and Uganda*. London: International African Institute.

Caillie, R. (1968). *Travels through Central Africa to Timbuctoo*. London: Frank Cass and Co.

Callahan, J. (2002). Masking the need for cultural change. *Organization Studies, 23*, 281–297.

Calvo, E., & Murillo, M. V. (2004). Who delivers? Partisan clients in the Argentine electoral market. *American Journal of Political Science, 48*, 742–757.

Cannon, W. (1929). The James-Lange theory of emotions: A critical examination and an alternative theory. *American Journal of Psychology, 39*, 106–124.

Carneiro, R. (1970). A theory of the origin of the state. *Science, 169*, 733–738.

Casson, M., & Casson, C. (2014). The history of entrepreneurship: Medieval origins of a modern phenomenon. *Business History, 56*, 1223–1242.

Chabal, P., & Daloz, J. (1999). *Africa works: Disorder as political instrument*. Oxford: James Currey.

Chalklin, C. (2001). *The rise of the English Town, 1650–1850*. Cambridge: CUP.

Chambers, R. (1983). *Rural development: Putting the last first*. Harlow: Longman.

Chambers, R. (1997). *Whose reality counts? Putting the first last*. London: Intermediate Technology Publications.

Chambers, R. (2004). *Ideas for development: Reflecting forwards*. Brighton: IDS.

Childe, V. G. (1936). *Man makes himself*. London: Watts.

Childe, V. G. (1950). The urban revolution. *Town Planning Review, 21*, 3–17.

Chiodelli, F., & Moroni, S. (2014). The complex nexus between informality and the law: Reconsidering unauthorized settlements in the light of the concept of nomotropism. *Geoforum, 51*, 161–168.

Chirot, D. (1985). The rise of the West. *American Sociological Review, 50*, 181–195.

Christie, J. (1876). *Cholera epidemics in East Africa*. London: Macmillan.

Clark, K. (1970). *Civilization*. London: BBC and John Murray.

Coase, R. (1937). The nature of the firm. *Economica, 4*, 386–405.

Cohen, D. (2011). The beginnings of agriculture in China: A multiregional view. *Current Anthropology, 52*, s273–s293.

Cohen, R. (1978). Introduction. In R. Cohen & E. Service (Eds.), *Origins of the state*. Philadelphia: Institute for the Study of Human Issues.

Coleman, J. (1975). Review essay: Inequality, sociology, and moral philosophy. *American Journal of Sociology, 80*, 739–764.

Collins, R. (1981). On the micro-foundations of macro-sociology. *American Journal of Sociology, 86*, 984–1014.

Collins, R. (1986). *Weberian sociological theory*. Cambridge: CUP.

Collins, R. (1997). An Asian route to capitalism: Religious economy and the origins of self-transforming growth in Japan. *American Sociological Review, 62*, 843–865.

Communist Party (Tianjin). (1990). 天津市私营经济发展的现状与对策 [*The development of Tianjin's private economy—Current situation and policies*]. Tianjin.

Conard, N., Malina, M., & Munzel, S. (2009). New flutes document the earliest musical tradition in south western Germany. *Nature, 460*, 737–740.

Conner, K., & Prahalad, C. (1996). A resource-based theory of the firm: Knowledge versus opportunism. *Organization Science, 7*, 477–501.

Cooley, C. H. (1962). *Social organization*. New York: Schocken Books.

Cooley, C. H. (1964). *Human nature and the social order*. New York: Scribner and Sons.

Corbridge, S. (Ed.). (1995). *Development studies: A reader*. London: Arnold.

Creel, H. (1964). The beginnings of bureaucracy in China: The origin of the hsien. *Journal of Asian Studies, 23*, 155–184.

Crozier, M. (1964). *The bureaucratic phenomenon*. Chicago: University of Chicago Press.

Crush, J. (1993). Postcoloniality, decolonization and geography. In A. Godlewska & N. Smith (Eds.), *Geography and empire*. Oxford: Blackwell.

Crush, J. (1995). *Power of development*. London: Routledge.

Dahl, R. (1989). *Democracy and its critics*. New Haven: Yale University Press.

Damansio, A. (1994). *Descartes' error: Emotion, reason and the human brain*. New York: Gossett/Putnam.

Danforth, M. (1999). Nutrition and politics in prehistory. *Annual Review of Anthropology, 28*, 1–25.

Das, R. (2004). Social capital and poverty of the wage-labor class: Problems with social capital theory. *Transactions, Institute of British Geographers, 29*, 27–45.

Davis, R. H. C. (1988). *A history of medieval Europe*. London: Pearson.

de Jong, M. (2009). *The Penitential state: Authority and atonement in the age of Louis the Pious*. Cambridge: Cambridge University Press.

Deleuze, G. (1992). Postscript on the societies of control. *59*: 3–7.

De Leo, G., Rizzi, L., Caizzi, A., & Gatto, M. (2001). Evolution of prehistoric art. *Nature, 413*, 479.

De Soto, H. (1989). *The other path: The invisible revolution in the third world*. New York: Harper and Row.

De Soto, H. (2000). *The mystery of capital: Why capitalism triumphs in the west and fails everywhere else*. New York: Basic Books.

Department of Education (UK). (2014). *Statutory framework for the early years foundation stage: Setting the standards for learning, development and care for children from birth to five*. London: Department of Education.

Derrida, J. (1976). *Of grammatology*. Baltimore: Johns Hopkins University Press.

Derrida, J. (1978). *Writing and difference*. London: Routledge.

Dickens, A. (1982). Heresy and the origins of English protestantism. In A. Dickens (Ed.), *Reformation studies*. London: The Hambledon Press.

Diekhoff, G., LaBeff, E., Clark, R., Williams, L., Francis, B., & Haines, V. (1996). College cheating: Ten years later. *Research in Higher Education, 37*, 487–501.

Dillehay, T., Rossen, J., & Netherly, P. (1997). The Nanchoc tradition: The beginnings of Andean civilization. *American Scientist, 85*, 46–55.

Diner, D. (1999). Knowledge of expansion on the geopolitics of Karl Haushofer. *Geopolitics, 4*, 161–188.

Dittmer, L. (1995). Chinese informal politics. *China Journal, 34*, 1–39.

Dobb, M. (1947). *Studies in the development of capitalism*. New York: International Publishers.

Domagalski, T. (1999). Emotion in organizations: Main currents. *Human Relations, 52*, 833–852.

Downey, S., Boceage, E., Kerig, T., Edinborough, K., & Shennan, S. (2014). The Neolithic demographic transition in Europe: Correlation with juvenility index supports interpretation of the summed calibrated radiocarbon date probability distribution (SCDPD) as a valid demographic proxy. *PLOS One, 9*, 1–10.

Downs, A. (1967). *Inside bureaucracy*. Boston: Little, Brown and Company.

Dubetsky, A. (1979). Kinship, primordial ties, and factory organization in Turkey: An anthropological view. *International Journal of Middle East Studies, 7*, 433–451.

Dudley and Walsall Mental Health Partnership Trust NHS. (2013). *Winterbourne, Francis, Cavendish, Keogh and Berwick reports—Overview report*. London.

Dunleavy, P. (1991). *Democracy, bureaucracy and public choice: Economic explanations in political science*. London: Harvester Wheatsheaf.

Durkheim, E. (1984). *The division of labour in society*. Basingstoke: Macmillan.

Duveen, G., & Lloyd, B. (1993). An ethnographic approach to social representations. In G. M. Breakwell & D. V. Canter (Eds.), *Empirical approaches to social representations*. Oxford: Oxford University Press.

Dyball, M., Poullas, C., & Chua, W. F. (2007). Accounting and empire: Professionalization-as-resistance. The case of the Philippines. *Critical Perspectives on Accounting, 18*, 415–449.

Easterbrook, J. (1959). The effect of emotion on cue utilization and the organization of behavior. *Psychological Review, 66*, 183–201.

Einworgerer, T., Friesinger, H., Handel, M., Neugebauer-Maresch, C., Simon, U., & Teschler-Nicola, M. (2006). Upper palaeolithic infant burials. *Nature, 444*, 285.

Ekelund, R., & Tollison, R. (1980). Mercantilist origins of the corporation. *The Bell Journal of Economics, 11*, 715–720.

Ekman, P. (1972). Universals and cultural differences in facial expressions of emotion. In J. Cole (Ed.), *Nebraska symposium on motivation (1971)* (Vol. 19, pp. 207–282). Lincoln: University of Nebraska Press.

Eknoyan, G., & De Santo, N. (2012). The enlightenment kidney—Nephrology in and about the eighteenth century. *Seminars in Dialysis, 25*, 74–81.

Elahi, N., Nyborg, I., & Nawab, B. (2015). Participatory development practices: A critical analysis of gender empowerment and development in pre- and post-crises Swat, Pakistan. *Forum for Development Studies, 42*, 333–356.

Elfenbein, H. (2007). Emotion in organizations: A review and theoretical integration. *The Academy of Management Annals, 1*, 315–386.

Elvin, M. (1972). The high-level equilibrium trap: The causes of the decline of invention in the traditional Chinese textile industries. In W. Willmott (Ed.), *Economic organization in Chinese society* (pp. 137–172). Taipei: SMC Publishing.

Elvin, M. (1973). *Patterns of the Chinese past*. London: Methuen.

Engles, F. (1910). *The origin of the family, private property and the state*. Chicago: C.H. Kerr.

Epstein, S. (2000). *Freedom and growth: The rise of states and markets in Europe, 1300–1750*. London: Routledge.

Erdmann, G., & Engel, U. (2006). Neopatrimonialism revisited—Beyond a catch-all concept. *GIGA Research Program: Legitimacy and Efficiency of Political Systems*, No. 16. Hamburg.

Evans, P. (1989). Predatory, developmental and other apparatuses: A comparative political economy perspective on the third world state. *Sociological Forum, 4*, 233–246.

Evans, P. (1995). *Embedded autonomy: States and industrial transformation*. Princeton, NJ: Princeton University Press.

Evans-Pritchard, E. E. (1940a). *The political system of the Anuak of the Anglo-Egyptian Sudan. Monographs on Social Anthropology*, No. 4. London: London School of Economics.

Evans-Pritchard, E. E. (1940b). *The Nuer*. Oxford: Clarendon Press.

Faccion, M., Masulis, R. W., & McConnell, J. (2006). Political bailouts and corporate bailouts. *The Journal of Finance, 61*, 2597–2635.

Fama, E. (1980). Agency problems and the theory of the firm. *Journal of Political Economy, 88*, 288–307.

Fay, B. (1932). Learned societies in Europe and America in the eighteenth century. *The American Historical Review, 37*, 255–266.

Ferrazzi, G. (2008). *Exploring reform options in functional assignment (Indonesia)*. Deutsche Gesellschaft fur Technische Zusammenarbeit (GTZ).

Ferrazzi, G., & Rohdewohld, R. (2010a). *Functional assignment in multi-level government. Conceptual foundation of functional assignment* (Vol. I). Deutsche Gesellschaft fur Technische Zusammenarbeit (GTZ).

Ferrazzi, G., & Rohdewohld, R. (2010b). *Functional assignment in multi-level government. GTZ-supported application of functional assignment* (Vol. II). Deutsche Gesellschaft fur Technische Zusammenarbeit (GTZ).

Filani, M., & Richards, P. (1976). Periodic market systems and rural development: The Ibarapa case study, Nigeria. *Savanna, 5*, 149–162.

Fineman, S. (1993). Organizations as emotional arenas. In S. Fineman (Ed.), *Emotion in organizations*. London: Sage Publications.

Fineman, S. (1996). Emotion and organizing. In S. Clegg, C. Hardy, & W. Nord (Eds.), *Handbook of organization studies*. London: Sage Publications.

Firth, R. (1951). *The elements of social organisation*. London: Watts.

Flinders, M. (2009). The politics of patronage in the United Kingdom: Shrinking reach and diluted permeation. *Governance, 22*(547–570), 550.

Fluzin, P., Castel, G., & Tallet, P. (2011). Metallurgical sites of South Sinai (Egypt) in the Pharaonic era: New discoveries. *Paléorient, 37*, 79–89.

Fogg, W. A. (1938). A tribal market in the Spanish zone of Morocco. *Africa, 11*, 428–458.

Fogg, W. A. (1939). The importance of tribal markets in the commercial life of the countryside of northwest Morocco. *Africa, 12*, 445–449.

Fogg, W. A. (1940). Villages, tribal markets and towns: Some considerations concerning urban development in the Spanish and international zones of Morocco. *Sociological Review, 32*, 85–107.

Foucault, M. (1980). *Power-knowledge*. Brighton: Harvester.

Francis, R. (2010). *Independent enquiry into care provided by Mid Staffordshire NHS Foundation Trust* (Vol. I). London: The Stationary Office.

Fridja, N. (1986). *The emotions*. Cambridge: Cambridge University Press.

Fridja, N. (1988). The laws of emotion. *American Psychologist, 43*, 349–358.

Fukuyama, F. (1999). *The great disruption*. New York: Simon and Schuster.

Fulcher, J. (1988). The bureaucratization of the state and the rise of Japan. *The British Journal of Sociology, 39,* 228–254.

Funder, M., & Marani, M. (2015). Local bureaucrats as bricoleurs. The everyday implementation practices of county environment officers in rural Kenya. *International Journal of the Commons, 9,* 87–106.

Furniss, D. (1968). The monastic contribution to mediaeval medical care: Aspects of an earlier welfare state. *Journal of the Royal College of General Practitioners, 15,* 244–250.

Gaens, B. (2000). Family, enterprise, and corporation: The organization of Izumiya-Sumitomo in the Tokugawa period. *Japan Review, 12,* 205–229.

Galiani, S., & Weinschelbaum, F. (2012). Modeling informality formally: Households and firms. *Economic Inquiry, 50,* 821–838.

Gambetta, D. (1988). Mafia: The price of distrust. In D. Gambetta (Ed.), *Trust* (pp. 158–210). New York: Basil Blackwell.

Gamble, C. (1999). *The paleolithic societies of Europe.* Cambridge: Cambridge University Press.

Gao, N. (高 楠) (2002). 论 情 在 中国 古 代 文 学艺 术 中的 原 创 意 义 [Discussion on the original meaning of emotion in ancient Chinese art and literature]. 文学评论 [*Literary Commentary*], *1,* 126–133.

Gente, M. (2001). The expansion of the nuclear family unit in Great Britain between 1910 and 1920. *The History of the Family, 6,* 125–142.

Gerhart, K. (2001). Issues of talent and training in the seventeenth-century Kano workshop. *Ars Orientalis, 31,* 103–128.

Gernet, J. (1997). *A history of Chinese civilization* (2nd ed., J. Foster & C. Hartman, Trans.). Cambridge: CUP.

Giddens, A. (1984). *The constitution of society.* Cambridge: Polity Press.

Gignoux, C., Henn, B., & Mountain, J. (2011). Rapid, global demographic expansions after the origins of agriculture. *Proceedings of the National Academy of Sciences, 108,* 6044–6049.

Ginsburg, T., & Hoetkeer, G. (2006). The unreluctant litigant? An empirical analysis of Japan's turn to litigation. *Journal of Legal Studies, 35,* 31–59.

Gissing, G. (1884). A journey from Mombasa to Mounts Ndara and Kasigo. *Proceedings of the Royal Geographical Society, 6,* 551–556.

Goffman, E. (1983). The interaction order. *American Sociological Review, 48,* 1–17.

Goldstone, J. (1991). *Revolution and rebellion in the early modern world.* Berkeley: University of California Press.

Goldstone, J. (2002). Efflorescences and economic growth in world history: Rethinking the "rise of the West" and the industrial revolution. *Journal of World History, 13,* 323–399.

Gombrich, E. (1991). *The story of art.* Oxford: Phaidon.

Goodfriend, M., & McDermott, J. (1995). Early development. *The American Economic Review, 85,* 116–133.

Goody, J. (1996). *The east in the west.* Cambridge: CUP.

Gordin, J. (2002). The political and partisan determinants of patronage in Latin America, 1960–1994: A comparative perspective. *European Journal of Political Research, 41,* 513–549.

Goring-Morrris, A., & Belfer-Cohen, A. (2011). Neolithization processes in the Levant: The outer envelope. *Current Anthropology, 52,* s195–s208.

Gould, M. (1987). *Revolution in the development of capitalism.* Berkeley: University of California Press.

Granovetter, M. (1985). Economic action and social structure: The problem of embeddedness. *American Journal of Sociology, 91,* 481–510.

Gray, D., & Watt, P. (2013). *Giving victims a voice: A joint MPS and NSPCC report into allegations of sexual abuse made against Jimmy Savile under operation Yewtree.* London: MPS/NSPCC.

Gross, J. (2001). Emotion regulation in adulthood: Timing is everything. *Current Directions in Psychological Science, 10,* 214–219.

Guelke, L. (1974). An idealist alternative in human geography. *Annals of the Association of American Geographers, 61,* 193–202.

Gullick, J. (1958). *Indigenous political systems of Western Malaya. Monographs on Social Anthropology,* No. 17. London: London School of Economics, Athlone Press.

Gulyani, S., & Talukdar, D. (2010). Inside informality: The links between poverty, microenterprises, and living conditions in Nairobi's slums. *World Development, 38,* 1710–1726.

Gupta, A. (1995). Blurred boundaries: The discourses of corruption, the culture of politics, and the imagined state. *American Ethnologist, 22,* 375–402.

Gutiérrez, F. (1961). Sesshu and his masters. *Monumenta Nipponica, 16,* 221–262.

Ha, Y. C., & Kang, M. K. (2010). Creating a capable bureaucracy with loyalists: The internal dynamics of the South Korean developmental state, 1948–1979. *Comparative Political Studies, 44,* 78–108.

Haggard, S. (2000). *The political economy of the Asian economic crisis.* Washington, D.C.: Institute of International Economics.

Hall, J. (1961). Foundations of the modern Japanese daimyo. *The Journal of Asian Studies, 20,* 317–329.

Hall, J. (1962). Feudalism in Japan: A reassessment. *Comparative Studies in Society and History, 5,* 15–51.

Hall, J. (1985). *Powers and liberties.* Oxford: Blackwell.

Haller, D., & Shore, C. (2005). *Corruption: Anthropological perspectives.* London: Pluto.

Hallett, R. (1965). *The penetration of Africa.* New York: Praeger.

Hamilton, E. (1940). The growth of rigidity in business during the eighteenth century. *The American Economic Review, 30,* 298–305.

Hammer, M., Karafet, T., Park, H., Omoto, K., Harihara, S., Stoneking, M., et al. (2006). Dual origins of the Japanese: Common ground for hunter-gatherer and farmer Y chromosomes. *Journal of Human Genetics, 51,* 47–58.

Hareli, S., & Rafaeli, A. (2008). Emotion cycles: On the social influence of emotion in organizations. *Research in Organizational Behavior, 28,* 35–59.

Hart, K. (1973). Informal income opportunities and urban employment in Ghana. *The Journal of Modern African Studies, 11,* 61–89.

Hart, K. (2009). *On the informal economy: The political history of an ethnographic concept.* Centre Emile Bernheim Working Paper No.9/042. Solvay Brussels School of Economics and Management. Brussels: CEB.

Hartmann, C. (1996). La révolution verte du Siècle des lumières: les deux sociétés savantes orléanaises de la fin de l'Ancien Régime [The green revolution of the enlightenment: The two learned societies of Orléans at the end of the eighteenth century]. *Revue d'histoire des sciences, 49,* 5–22.

Hartwell, R. (1962). A revolution in the Chinese iron and coal industries during the Northern Sung, 960–1126 A.D. *Journal of Asian Studies, 21,* 153–162.

Hartwell, R. (1982). Demographic, political and social transformations of China, 750–1550. *Harvard Journal of Asiatic Studies, 42,* 365–442.

Haruko, W., & Phillips, D. (1993). Women and the creation of the *ie* in Japan: An overview from the medieval period to the present. *U.S.-Japan Women's Journal,* English Supplement 4, 83–105.

Haruko, W., & Rowley, G. (2010). The Japanese women in the premodern merchant household. *Women's History Review, 19,* 259–282.

Hayashi, K. (1980). *Xu* and *shi* in Guangdong province during the Ming and Qing periods. In *International Geographical Union Working Group on Market-Place Exchange Systems,* Nagoya, August 27-9.

Hein, L. (1963). The British business company: Its origins and its control. *The University of Toronto Law Journal, 15,* 134–154.

Herath, D. (2009). The discourse of development: Has it reached maturity? *Third World Quarterly, 30,* 1449–1464.

Hersey, R. (1932). Rates of production and emotional state. *Personnel Journal, 10,* 355–364.
Herwig, H. (1999). Geopolitik: Haushofer, Hitler and Lebensraum. *Journal of Strategic Studies,* *22,* 218–241.
Hill, C. (1972). *The world turned upside down.* Hammondsworth: Penguin.
Hill, C. (Ed.). (1988). *Collected essays of Christopher hill* (Vol. 2). *Religion and politics in* *seventeenth century England.* Brighton: Harvester.
Hilton, R. (1984). Women traders in medieval England. *Women's Studies: An Inter-Disciplinary* *Journal, 11,* 139–155.
HM Government. (2015). *Prevent duty guidance: Guidance for specified authorities in England* *and Wales on the duty in the Counter-Terrorism and Security Act 2015 to have due regard to* *the need to prevent people from being drawn into terrorism.* London: HM Government.
Hobsbawm, E. (1997). *On history.* London: Weidenfeld & Nicolson.
Hobsbawm, E. J. (1965). The crisis of the seventeenth century. In T. Aston (Ed.), *Crisis in Europe* *1560-1660* (pp. 5–58). London: Routledge and Kegan Paul.
Hodder, R. (2014). Merit versus kinship: A category mistake? The case of the Philippine civil service. *Public Administration and Development, 34,* 370–388.
Hodder, R. (2016). *High-level political appointments in the Philippines: Patronage, emotion and* *democracy.* New York: Springer.
Hodder, R. (2017). *Emotional bureaucracy.* New York: Routledge.
Hole, F. (1966). Investigating the origins of Mesopotamian civilization. *Science, 153,* 605–611.
Homans, G. (1950). *The human group.* New York: Harcourt.
Hoogvelt, A. (2001). *Globalization and the postcolonial world: The new political economy of* *development.* Baltimore: Johns Hopkins University Press.
Hoover, D., & den Dulk, K. (2004). Christian conservatives go to court: Religion and legal mobilization in the United States and Canada. *International Political Science Review, 25,* 9–34.
Horan, R., Bulte, E., & Shogren, J. (2008). Coevolution of human speech and trade. *Journal of* *Economic Growth, 13,* 293–313.
Horowitz, I.L., (2010). Legalism as a global strategy: foundations of Barak Obama's leadership. *New Global Studies 4*(1). Article 13: 1–2.
Houses of Parliament. (2015a). *Counter-terrorism and security act 2015, Chapter 6.* London: The Stationary Office.
Houses of Parliament. (2015b). *Explanatory notes: Counter-terrorism and security act 2015,* *Chapter 6.* London: The Stationary Office.
Huizinga, J. (1924). *The waning of the middle ages* (F. J. Hopman, Trans.). New York: Anchor Books.
Hull, E. (1939). Engineering—Ancient and modern. *The Scientific Monthly, 49,* 460–463.
Hulsheger, U., & Schewe, A. (2011). On the costs and benefits of emotional labor: A meta-analysis of three decades of research. *Journal of Occupational Health Psychology,* *16,* 361–389.
Hunt, L. (1992). *The family romance of the French revolution.* Berkeley, California: University of California Press.
Hunt, L., & Jacob, M. (2001). The affective revolution in 1790s. *Eighteenth-Century Studies, 34,* 491–521.
Hutchcroft, P. (1997). The politics of privilege: Assessing the impacts of rents, corruption and clientelism on third world development. *Political Studies, XLV,* 639–658.
Hutchcroft, P. (1998). *Booty capitalism: The politics of banking in the Philippines.* Ithaca, NY: Cornell University Press.
Hutchcroft, P. (2001). Centralisation and decentralisation in administration and politics: Assessing territorial dimensions of authority and power. *Governance, 14,* 23–53.
Hutchcroft, P., & Rocamora, J. (2003). Strong demands and weak institutions. *Journal of East* *Asian Studies, 3,* 259–284.
Isaac, G. (1983). Aspects of human evolution. In D. S. Bendall (Ed.), *Essays on evolution:* *A Darwin century volume.* Cambridge: Cambridge University Press.

Isbell, W., & Schreiber, K. (1978). Was Huari a state? *American Antiquity, 43*, 372–389.

Isen, A., & Baron, R. (1991). Poitive affect as a factor in organizational behavior. *Research in Organizational Behavior, 13*, 1–53.

James, W. (1894). The physical basis of emotion. *Psychological Review, 7*, 516–529.

Jarymowicz, M., & Imbir, K. (2015). Toward a human emotions taxonomy (based on their automatic vs. reflective origin). *Emotion Review, 7*, 183–188.

Jeffrey, C. (2002). Caste, class and clientelism: A political economy of everyday corruption in rural North India. *Economic Geography, 78*, 21–41.

Johnson, R. (1992). *Philosophy and human geography*. London: Edward Arnold.

Johnson, R. N., & Libecap, G. D. (1994). *The federal civil service system and the problem of bureaucracy*. Chicago: University of Chicago Press.

Join-Lambert, O., & Lochard, Y. (2011). Constructing merit in the civil service: The French Ministry of Culture (1880–1980). *Sociologie du travail, 53*, 38–56.

Jomo, K. S. (2000). Comment: Crisis and the developmental state in East Asia. In R. Robinson, M. Beeson, K. Jayasuriya, & H. Kim (Eds.), *Politics and markets in the wake of the Asian crisis*. London: Routledge.

Jones, D. (2011). Academic dishonesty: Are more students cheating? *Business Communication Quarterly, 74*, 141–150.

Junker, L. (1999). *Raiding, trading and feasting: The political economy of Philippine chiefdoms*. Honolulu: University of Hawaii Press.

Katz, D., & Kahn, R. L. (1967). *The social psychology of organizations*. New York: Wiley.

Katz, J., & Gartner, W. (1988). Properties of emerging organizations. *The Academy of Management Review, 13*, 429–441.

Kennedy, M. (1999). Fayol's principles and the rule of St Benedict: Is there anything new under the sun? *Journal of Management History, 5*, 269–276.

Kerkvliet, B. J. (1995). Toward a more comprehensive analysis of Philippine politics: Beyond the patron-client, factional framework. *Journal of Southeast Asian Studies, 26*, 401–419.

Keyser, P. (1993). The purpose of the parthian galvanic cells: A first-century A. D. electric battery used for analgesia. *Journal of Near Eastern Studies, 52*, 81–98.

Kierkegaard, S. (1957). *Concept of dread* (W. Lowrie, Trans.). Princeton, NJ: Princeton University Press.

Kieser, A. (1989). Organizational, institutional and societal evolution: Medieval craft guilds and the genesis of formal organizations. *Administrative Science Quarterly, 34*, 540–564.

Kilminster, R. (2008). Narcissism or informalization? Christopher Lasch, Norbert Elias and social diagnosis. *Theory, Culture and Society, 25*, 131–151.

Kim, A. (2012). Seeds of reform: Lessons from Vietnam about informality and institutional change. *International Economic Journal, 26*, 391–406.

King, B., Felin, T., & Whetten, D. (2010). Finding the organization in organizational theory: A meta-theory of the organization as a social actor. *Organization Science, 21*(290–305), 298.

Klein, H., Levenburg, N., McKendall, M., & William, M. (2007). Cheating during the college years: How do business school students compare? *Journal of Business Ethics, 72*, 197–206.

Klitgaard, R. (1991). *Controlling corruption*. London: University of California Press.

Knappen, M. (1939). *Tudor puritanism: A chapter in the history of idealism*. Chicago: University of Chicago Press.

Knight, C., Studdert-Kennedy, M., & Hurford, J. (2000). Language: A Darwinian adaptation? In C. Knight, M. Studdert-Kennedy, & J. Hurford (Eds.), *The evolutionary emergence of language: Social function and the origins of linguistic form*. Cambridge: Cambridge University Press.

Kondo, M. (2008). Merito-patronage management system. *Philippine Studies, 53*, 251–284.

Krause, D. (2012). Consequences of manipulation in organizations: Two studies on its effects on emotions and relationships. *Psychological Reports: Human Resources and Marketing, 111*, 199–218.

Kroes, R. (2015). Deficits don't matter: Abundance, indebtedness and American culture. *Society, 52*, 174–180.

Krugman, P. (1987). Is free trade passé? *Journal Economics Perspectives, 1*, 131–144.

Kunstler, B. (2006). The millennial university, then and now: From late medieval origins to radical transformation. *On the Horizon, 14*, 62–69.

Kuper, H. (1961). *An African aristocracy*. London: International African Institute, OUP.

La Prota, R., & Shleifer, A. (2014). Informality and development. *Journal of Economic Perspectives, 28*, 109–126.

Lachmann, R. (1989). Origins of capitalism in Western Europe: Economic and political aspects. *Annual Review of Sociology, 15*, 47–72.

Laguna, M. (2011). The challenges of implementing merit-based personnel policies in Latin America: Mexico's civil service reform experience. *Journal of Comparative Policy Analysis: Research and Practice, 13*, 51–73.

Lal, R. (2008). Macroeconomic policies to address informality: A two-pronged strategy to further dynamic transformations that reduce informality. *IDS Bulletin, 39*, 120–129.

Landé, C. H. (2002). Political clientelism, developmentalism and post-colonial theory. *Philippine Political Science Journal, 23*, 119–128.

Lane, F. (1979). *Profits from power*. Albany: Suny Press.

Lang, P. (1994). The varieties of emotional experience: A meditation on James-Lange theory. *Psychological Review, 101*(2), 211.

Lange, C. (1922). *The emotions* (I. A. Haupt, Trans.). Baltimore: Williams and Wilkins (Original work published 1885).

Larkin, P. (2014). The new Puritanism: The resurgence of contractarian citizenship in common law welfare states. *Journal of Law and Society, 41*, 227–256.

Lasch, C. (1980). *The culture of Narcissism: American life in an age of diminishing expectations*. London: Sphere Books.

Lasch, C. (1984). *The minimal self: Psychic survival in troubled times*. London: W.W. Norton.

Lasch, C. (1985). Historical sociology and the myth of maturity: Norbert Elias's "very simple formula". *Theory and Society, 14*, 705–720.

Lawler, A. (2006). North versus South, Mesopotamian style. *Science, 312*, 1458–1463.

Lawrence, P., & Lorsch, J. (1967). Differentiation and integration in complex organizations. *Administrative Science Quarterly, 12*, 1–30.

Leach, E. R. (1954). *Political systems of highland Burma*. London.

Leff, N. H. (1964). Economic development through bureaucratic corruption. *American Behavioral Scientist, VIII*, 8–14.

Levenson, R. W. (2011). Basic emotion questions. *Emotion Review, 3*, 1–8.

Levi, M. (1988). *Of rule and revenue*. Berkeley: University of California Press.

Lezine, M., Robert, C., Cleuziou, S., Inizan, M. L., Braemer, F., Saliège, J. F. (2010). Climate change and human occupation in the southern Arabian lowlands during the last deglaciation and the Holocene. *Global and Planetary Change, 72*, 412–428.

Li, L. (2009). State emergence in early China. *Annual Review of Anthropology, 38*, 217–232.

Lie, J. (1991). Embedding Polanyi's market society. *Sociological Perspectives, 34*, 219–235.

Lim, L., & Gosling, L. (Eds.). (1983). *The Chinese in Southeast Asia* (2 Vols.). Singapore: Marusen Asia.

Lipset, S. (1983). *Political man* (2nd ed.). London: Heineman.

Lofy, M. (1998). The impact of emotion on creativity in organizations. *Empowerment in Organizations, 6*, 5–12.

López-Ibor, J., & López-Ibor, M.-I. (2010). Anxiety and logos: Toward a linguistic analysis of the origins of human thinking. *Journal of Affective Disorders, 120*, 1–11.

MacFarlane, A. (1997). 'Japan' in an English mirror. *Modern Asian Studies, 31*, 763–806.

Mackinder, H. J. (1904). The geographical pivot of history. *The Geographical Journal, 23*, 421–437.

Madhok, A. (2002). Reassessing the fundamentals and beyond: Ronald Coase, the transaction cost and resource-based theories of the firm, and the institutional structure of production. *Strategic Management Journal, 23,* 535–550.

Maiti, D., & Mitra, A. (2011). Informality, vulnerability, and development. *Journal of Developmental Entrepreneurship, 16,* 199–211.

Malcolm, N. (1966). Knowledge of other minds. In G. Pitcher (Ed.), *Philosophical investigations: Critical essays* (pp. 371–383). Garden City, New York: Anchor.

Maloney, W. (2004). Informality revisited. *World Development, 32,* 1159–1178.

Mann, M. (1980). State and society, 1130–1815: An analysis of English state finances. In M. Zeitlin (Ed.), *Political power and social theory* (pp. 165–208). Greenwich, Connecticut: Jai Press.

Maranon, G. (1924). Contribution a Fetude de l'action emotive de l'adrenaline [Contribution to the study of the emotive action of adrenalin].*Revue Francaise d'Endocrinologie, 2,* 301–325.

Marlow, D., Taylor, S., & Thompson, A. (2010). Informality and formality in medium-sized companies: Contestation and synchronization. *British Journal of Management, 21,* 954–966.

Maroney, T., & Gross, J. (2014). The ideal of the dispassionate judge: An emotion regulation perspective. *Emotion Review, 6,* 142–151.

Martin, B. (2012). Are universities and university research under threat? Towards an evolutionary model of university speciation. *Cambridge Journal of Economics, 36,* 543–565.

McCabe, D. (2009). Academic dishonesty in nursing schools: An empirical investigation. *Journal of Nursing Education, 48,* 614–623.

McCabe, D., Treviño, L., & Butterfield, H. (2001). Cheating in academic institutions: A decade of research. *Ethics and Behavior, 11,* 219–232.

McCabe, D., Treviño, L., & Butterfield, H. (2006). Academic dishonesty in graduate business programs: Prevalence, causes, and proposed action. *Academy of Management Learning & Education, 5,* 294–305.

McCourt, W. (2003). Political commitment to reform: Civil service reform in Swaziland. *World Development, 31,* 1015–1031.

McGrath, J. (2006). Post-traumatic growth and the origins of early Christianity. *Mental Health, Religion and Culture, 9,* 291–306.

McMullan, M. (1961). A theory of corruption: Based on a consideration of corruption in the public services and governments of British colonies and ex-colonies in West Africa. *Sociological Review,* 181–201.

Mead, D., & Morrison, C. (1996). The informal sector elephant. *World Development, 24,* 1611–1619.

Meagher, K. (2006). Social capital, social liabilities, and political capital: Social networks and informal manufacturing in Nigeria. *African Affairs, 105,* 553–582.

Meagher, K. (2007). Manufacturing disorder: Liberalization, informal enterprise and economic 'ungovernance' in African small-firm clusters. *Development and Change, 38,* 473–503.

Melé, D. (2012). The firm as a "community of persons": A pillar of humanistic business ethos. *Journal of Business Ethics, 106,* 89–101.

Meramveliotakis, G., & Milonakis, D. (2010). Surveying the transaction cost foundations of new institutional economics: A critical inquiry. *Journal of Economic Issues, 44,* 1045–1071.

Merrington, J. (1978). Town and country in the transition to capitalism. In R. Hilton (Ed.), *The transition from feudalism to capitalism* (pp. 170–195). London: Verso.

Meyer, T., & Van Audenhove, L. (2010). Graduated response and the emergence of a European surveillance society. *Info, 12:* 68–79.

Meyer, J., & Bromley, P. (2013). The worldwide expansion of "organization". *Sociological Theory, 31,* 366–389.

Michels, R. (1962). *Political parties.* New York: Collier Books.

Middleton, J., & Tait, D. (1958). *Tribes without rulers: Studies in African segmentary systems.* London: Routledge and Kegan Paul.

Milgrom, P., & Roberts, J. (1988). Economic theories of the firm: Past, present and future. *The Canadian Journal of Economics, 21*, 444–458.

Miquel, G. P. I. (2007). The control of politicians in divided societies: The politics of fear. *Reveiw of Economic Studies, 74*, 1259–1274.

Mitchell, B. (1998). *International historical statistics: Europe 1750–1993*. London: Macmillan.

Mizubayashi, T. (1987). *Hokensei no saihen to Nihonteki shakai no kakuristu*. Tokyo: Yamakawa shuppan.

Mohamed, J. (2007). Kinship and contract in Somali politics. *Africa, 77*, 226–249.

Monroe, J. (2013). Power and agency in precolonial African states. *Annual Review Anthropology, 42*, 17–35.

Moore, B. (1966). *Social origins of dictatorship and democracy: Lord and peasant in the making of the modern world*. London: Penguin Books.

Morand, D. (1995). The role of behavioral formality and informality in the enactment of bureaucratic versus organic organizations. *Academy of Management Review, 20*, 831–872.

Morrise, M., & Keltner, D. (2000). How emotions work: The social functions of emotional expression in negotiations. *Research in Organizational Behavior, 22*, 1–50.

Mosca, G. (1939). *The ruling class*. New York: McGraw-Hill.

Moscovici, S. (1981). On social representations. In J. P. Forgas (Ed.), *Social cognition: Perspectives on everyday understanding*. London: Academic Press.

Moscovici, S. (1982). The coming era of representations. In J. P. Codol & J. J. Leyens (Eds.), *Cognitive approaches to social behaviour*. The Hague: Nijhoff.

Moscovici, S. (1984). The phenomenon of social representations. In R. Farr & S. Moscovici (Eds.), *Social representations*. Cambridge: Cambridge University Press.

Mumford, L. (1952). *Art and technics*. New York: Colombia University Press.

Mundt, P., Förster, N., Alfarano, S., & Milaković, M. (2014). The real versus the financial economy: A global tale of stability versus volatility. *Economics: The Open-Access, Open Assessment E-Journal, 8*, 1–16.

Needham, J. (1969). *The grand titration: Science and society in east and west*. London: Allen and Unwin.

Nicholson, H. (2013). Emotion. *Contemporary Theatre Review, 23*, 21–22.

Niskasen, W. (1971). *Bureaucracy and representative government*. Chicago: Aldine-Atherton.

Noble, T. F. X. (1980). Louis the Pious and his piety re-considered. *Reveue belge de philogie et d'histoire*. Tome 58 fasc2. Histoire (depuis l'Antiquite) – Geschiedenis (sedert de Oudheid) pp. 297–316.

Nobukio, N., & McClain, J. (1991). Commercial change and urban growth in early modern Japan. In W. Hall (Ed.), *The Cambridge history of Japan* (Vol. 4, pp. 519–595). New York: CUP.

North, D. (1990). *Institutions, Institutional Change and Economic Performance*. Cambridge: CUP.

North, D. (2004). *Institutions, institutional change and economic performance*. Cambridge: CUP.

North, D., & Thomas, R. (1973). *The rise of the western world: A new economic theory*. Cambridge: Cambridge University Press.

Nunberg, R., & Taliercio, R. (2012). Sabotaging civil service reform in aid-dependent countries: Are donors to blame? *World Development, 40*, 1970–1981.

Nye, J. S. (1967). Corruption and political development: A cost benefit analysis. *American Political Science Review, LXI*, 417–427.

Ofek, H. (2001). *Second nature: Economic origins of human evolution*. Cambridge: Cambridge University Press.

Ogilvie, S. (1992). Germany and the seventeenth-century crisis. *The Historical Journal, 35*, 417–441.

Olson, M. (1982). *The rise and decline of nations*. New Haven: Yale University Press.

Omobowale, A. O., & Olutayo, A. O. (2010). Political clientelism and rural development in South-Western Nigeria. *Africa, 80*(3), 453–472.

Oppenheimer, F. (1926). *The state* (J. Gitterman, Trans.). New York: Vanguard.

Overbeck, J., Neale, M., & Govan, C. (2010). I feel, therefore you act: Intrapersonal and interpersonal effects of emotion on negotiation as a function of social power. *Organizational Behavior and Human Decision Processes, 112,* 126–139.

Paine, R., & Soper, A. (1974). *The art and architecture of Japan.* Harmondsworth: Penguin.

Parsons, T. (1949). *The structure of social action.* New York: Free Press.

Parsons, T. (1951). *The social system.* New York: Free Press.

Parsons, T., & Shils, E. A. (1951). *Toward a general theory of action.* Cambridge, Mass: Harvard University Press.

Parsons, T., & Smelser, N. (1956). *Economy and society.* New York: Free Press.

Pasinetti, L. (1962). Rate of profit and income distribution in relation to the rate of economic growth. *The Review of Economic Studies, 29,* 267–279.

Pearce, J., Branyiczki, I., & Bigley, G. (2000). Insufficient bureaucracy: Trust and commitment in particularistic organizations. *Organization Science, 11,* 148–162.

Pepinsky, T. (2007). Autocracy, elections, and fiscal policy: Evidence from Malaysia. *Studies in Comparative International Development, 42,* 136–163.

Perinbanayagam, R. (1985). *Signifying acts.* Carbondale: Southern Illinois University Press.

Perrow, C. (2000). An organizational analysis of organizational theory. *Contemporary Sociology, 29,* 469–476.

Peteraf, M. (1993). The cornerstones of competitive advantage: A resource-based view. *Strategic Management Journal, 14,* 179–191.

Petroski, H. (1996). Engineering: Harnessing steam. *American Scientist, 84,* 15–19.

Phillips, A. (2010). The protestant ethic and the spirit of Jihadism—Transnational religious insurgencies and the transformation of international orders. *Review of International Studies, 36* (257), 280.

Pieke, F. (1995). Bureaucracy, friends, and money: The growth of capital socialism in China. *Society for Comparative Study of Society and History, 37,* 494–518.

Pile, S. (2010). Emotions and affect in recent human geography. *Transactions, Institute of British Geographers, 35,* 5–20.

Pinker, S. (2010). The cognitive niche: Coevolution of intelligence, sociality and language. *PNAS, 107,* 8993–8999.

Plymouth University. (2015a). *Programme specification, BSc (Hons) Nursing, Year 1.* Plymouth, UK: Plymouth University.

Plymouth University. (2015b). *Programme specification, BSc (Hons) Geography.* Plymouth, UK: Plymouth University.

Polanyi, K. (1944). *The great transformation.* New York: Farrar & Rinehart.

Portes, A., & Sassen-Koob, S. (1987). Making it underground: Comparative material on the informal sector in western market economies. *American Journal of Sociology, 93,* 30–61.

Postan, M. M. (1976). *The medieval economy and society.* Aylesbury: Penguin.

Price, T., & Bar-Yosef, O. (2011). The origins of agriculture: New data, new ideas. *Current Anthropology, 52,* s163–s174.

Putnam, R. (1995). Bowling alone: America's declining social capital. *Journal of Democracy, 6,* 65–78.

Putnam, R. D. (1993). *Making democracy work.* New Jersey: Princeton University Press.

Putnam, R. D. (2000). *Bowling alone: The collapse and revival of American community.* New York: Simon and Schuster.

Radcliffe-Brown, A. R. (1930). *Applied anthropology.* Australian and New Zealand Association for the Advancement of Science. Brisbane Meeting.

Radcliffe-Brown, A. R. (1952). *Structure and function in primitive society.* London: Cohen & West.

Radford, L., Corral, S., Bradley, C., et al. (2011). *Child abuse and neglect in the UK today.* London: NSPCC.

Rafaeli, A. (2013). Emotion in organizations: Considerations for family firms. *Entrepreneurship Research Journal, 3,* 295–300.

Rafaeli, A., & Sutton, R. (1987). Expression of emotion as part of the work role. *Academy of Management Review, 12,* 23–37.

Rafaeli, A., & Vilnai-Yavetz, I. (2004). Emotion as a connection in physical artifacts and organizations. *Organization Science, 15,* 671–686.

Rajan, R., & Zingales, L. (1998). Which capitalism? Lessons from the East Asian crisis. *Journal of Applied Corporate Finance, 11,* 40–48.

Ramseyer, J. (1979). Thrift and diligence. House codes of Tokugawa merchant families. *Monumenta Nipponica, 34,* 209–230.

Ravine, M. (1995). State-building and political economy in early-modern Japan. *The Journal of Asian Studies, 54,* 997–1022.

Reade, J. (2001). Assyrian King-Lists, the royal tombs of Ur, and Indus origins. *Journal of Near Eastern Studies,* No. 60, 1–29.

Redding, S. (1990). *The spirit of Chinese capitalism.* Berlin: Walter de Gruyter.

Reno, W. (2002). The politics of insurgency in collapsing states. *Development and Change, 33,* 837–858.

Rocheleau, D., & Roth, R. (2007). Rooted networks, relationships webs and powers of connection: Rethinking human and political ecologies. *Geoforum, 38,* 433–437.

Romanelli, E. (1991). The evolution of new organizational forms. *Annual Review of Sociology, 17,* 79–103.

Rose, J. (2004). New evidence for the expansion of Upper Pleistocene population out of East Africa, from the site of Station One, Northern Sudan. *Camrbidge Archaeological Journal, 14,* 205–216.

Rosenberg, J. (1992). Secret origins of the state: The structural basis of raison d'état. *Review of International Studies, 18,* 131–159.

Rosenwein, B. (2002). Worrying about emotions in history. *The American Historical Review, 107,* 821–845.

Roxas, B., Chadee, D., & Pacoy, E. (2013). Effects of formal institutions on business performance in the Philippines: An exploratory study. *South East Asia Research, 21,* 27–40.

Ruef, M. (2005). Origins of organizations: The entrepreneurial process. *Entrepreneurship, 15,* 63–100.

Runciman, W. (1982). Origins of states: The case of archaic Greece. *Comparative Studies in Society and History, 24,* 351–377.

Rustow, D. (1970). Transitions to democracy. *Comparative Politics, 2,* 337–363.

Sachs, J., & Warner, A. (1995). Economic reform and the process of global economic integration. *Brooking Papers on Economic Activity, 1,* 1–118.

Sahlins, M. (1974). *Stone age economics.* London: Tavistock Publications.

Santos, F., & Eisenhardt, K. (2005). Organizational boundaries and theories of organization. *Organizational Science, 16,* 491–508.

Saxonhouse, G. (1995). The stability of megaorganizations: The Tokugawa state. *Journal of Institutional and Theoretical Economics, 151,* 741–747.

Sayles, L. (1958). *Behavior of industrial work groups: Prediction and control.* New York: Wiley.

Scally, K. (2011). Beware Greeks bearing steam engines: A response to the Kastelle and Steen proposition. *Prometheus: Critical Studies in Innovation, 29,* 207–217.

Schachter, S., & Singer, J. (1962). Cognitive, social and physiological determinants of emotional states. *Psychological Review, 69,* 379–399.

Schachter, S., & Wheeler, L. (1962). Epinephrine, chlorpromazine, and amusement. *Journal of Abnormal Social Psychology, 65,* 121–128.

Schiele, J. (1990). Organizational theory from an afrocentric perspective. *Journal of Black Studies, 21,* 145–161.

Schoenberger, E. (2008). The origins of the market economy: State power, territorial control, and modes of war fighting. *Comparative Studies in Society and History, 50,* 663–691.

Schollhammer, H. (1971). Organization structures of multinational corporations. *The Academy of Management Journal, 14,* 345–365.

Schott, R. (2000). The origins of bureaucracy: An anthropological perspective. *International Journal of Public Administration, 23,* 53–78.

Schutz, A. (1932) [1967]. *Phenomenology of the social world* (G. Walsh & F. Lehnert, Trans.). Evanston, IL: Northwestern University Press.

Scott, J. (1976). *The moral economy of the peasant.* New Haven: Yale University Press.

Scruton, R. (1971). Attitudes, beliefs and reasons. In J. Casey (Ed.), *Morality and moral reasoning* (pp. 25–100). London: Methuen.

Seed, J. (2005). The spectre of puritanism: Forgetting the seventeenth century in David Hume's history of England. *Social History, 30,* 444–462.

Seers, D. (1969). The meaning of development. *IDS Communication, 44,* 1–26.

Sen, J. (1983). Development: Which way now? *The Economic Journal, 93,* 745–762.

Sheehan, J. (2006). The problem of sovereignty in European history. *American Historical Review, 111*(1–15), 4.

Shiba, Y. (1970). *Commerce and society in Sung China* (M. Elvin, Trans.). Center for Chinese Studies, Michigan Abstracts of Chinese and Japanese Works on Chinese History, No. 2, Ann Arbor.

Siddiqui, K. (2016). International trade, WTO and economic development. *World Review of Political Economy, 7,* 424–450.

Sidel, J. (1997). Philippines politics in town, district and province: Bossism in Cavite and Cebu. *Journal of Asian Studies, 56,* 947–966.

Sidel, J. (1998). The underside of progress: Land, labor and violence in two Philippine growth zones, 1985–95. *Bulletin of Concerned Asian Scholars, 30,* 3–12.

Sidel, J. (1999). *Capital, coercion and crime: Bossism in the Philippines.* Stanford: Stanford University Press.

Sidel, J. (2008). Social origins of dictatorship and democracy re-visited: Colonial state and Chinese immigration the making of modern Southeast Asia. *Comparative Politics, 40,* 127–147.

Sidel, J. T. (2002). Response to Ileto. Or, why I am not an orientalist. *Philippine Political Science Journal, 23,* 129–138.

Siebert, S., Haser, J., Nagieb, M., Korn, L., & Buerkert, A. (2005). Agricultural, architectural and archaeological adaptation of a scattered mountain oasis in Oman. *Journal of Arid Environment, 62,* 177–197.

Silverman, D. (1971). *The theory of organizations.* New York: Basic Books.

Siwach, G. (2016). Trade liberalization and income convergence: Evidence from developing countries. *Economic and Political Weekly, 51,* 115–120.

Sleigh-Johnson, N. (2007). The merchant Taylors' company of London under Elizabeth I: Tailors' guild or company of merchants? *Costume, 41,* 45–52.

Sobel, J. (2002). Can we trust social capital? *Journal of Economic Literature, 40,* 139–154.

Solinger, D.J. (1984). *Chinese business under socialism.* University of California Press: London.

Sorokin, P. (1937). *Social and cultural dynamics.* New York: American Book Company.

Southall, A. (1957). *Alur society.* Cambridge: CUP.

Spencer, C., & Redmond, E. (2004). Primary state formation in Mesoamerica. *Annual Review Anthropology, 33,* 173–199.

Spencer, H. (1898). *The principles of sociology (in Three Volumes).* D. Appleton and Company: New York.

Spencer, J. (1940). The Szechwan village fair. *Economic Geography, 16,* 48–58.

Stanish, C. (2001). The origin of state societies in South America. *Annual Review Anthropology, 30,* 41–64.

Stanley, L. (2010, November). Emotions and family business creation: An extension and implications. *Entrepreneurship: Theory and Practice, 34*(6), 1085–1092.

Starbuck, W. (2007). The construction of organization theory. In C. Knudsen & H. Tsoukas (Eds.), *The oxford handbook of organization theory* (pp. 143–182). London: OUP.

Stiner, M., Munro, N., Surovell, T., Tchernov, E., & Bar-Yosef, O. (1999). Paleolithic population growth pulses evidenced by small animal exploitation. *Science, 283,* 190–194.

Stobart, J. (2004). Personal and commercial networks in an English port: Chester in the early eighteenth century. *Journal of Historical Geography, 30,* 277–293.

Stoelhorst, J., & Richerson, P. (2013). A naturalistic theory of economic organization. *Journal of Economic Behavior and Organization, 90S,* S45–S56.

Stone, L. (1977). *The family, sex and marriage in England, 1500–1800.* London: Weidenfeld and Nicolson.

Streeten, P., & Burki, S. (1978). Basic needs: Some issues. *World Development, 6,* 412–421.

Sui, X. (Ed.). (1988). 商业地理学概论 [An introduction to commercial geography] 黑龙江人民出版社 黑龙江.

Sultana, F. (2009). Community and participation in water resources management: Gendering and naturing development debates from Bangladesh. *Transactions, Institute of British Geographers, 34,* 346–363.

Sutherland, G. (1973). Social policy in the inter-war years. *The Historical Journal, 16,* 420–431.

Sweezy, P. (1976). A critique. In R. Hilton (Ed.), *The transition from feudalism to capitalism* (pp. 33–56). London: Verso.

Sydow, J., Schreyögg, G., & Koch, J. (2009). Organizational path dependence: Opening the black box. *The Academy of Management Review, 34,* 689–709.

Tadashi Wakabayashi, B. (1991). In name only: Imperial sovereignty in early modern Japan. *Journal of Japanese Studies, 17,* 25–57.

Tawney, R. H. (1963). *Religion and the rise of capitalism.* New York: Mentor.

Teece, D. J., Pisano, G., & Shuen, A. (1997). Dynamic capabilities and strategic management. *Strategic Management Journal, 18,* 509–534.

Tilley, C., & Ardant, G. (Eds.). (1975). *The formation of national states in Western Europe* (Vol. 8). *Studies in political development.* Princeton: Princeton University Press.

Tocqueville, A. (1968). In J. P. Mayer (Ed.), *Journeys to England and Ireland.* New York: Doubleday.

Todaro, M. (1997). *Economic development* (6th ed.). London: Longman.

Tooby, J., & Devore, I. (1987). The reconstruction of hominid evolution through strategic modeling. In W. G. Kinzey (Ed.), *The evolution of human behavior: Primate models.* Albany, NY: Suny Press.

Toshio, F. (1991). The village and agriculture during the Edo period. In W. Hall (Ed.), *The Cambridge history of Japan* (Vol. 4, pp. 478–518). New York: CUP.

Townsend, C., & Rheingold, A. A. (2013). *Estimating a child sexual abuse prevalence rate for practitioners: A review of child sexual abuse prevalence studies.* Darkness to Light: Charleston, S.C.

Trachtenberg, A. (2003). The incorporation of America today. *American Literary History, 15,* 759–764.

Tredget, D. (2002). The rule of benedict and its relevance to the world of work. *Journal of Managerial Psychology, 17,* 219–229.

Trevelynan, G. M. (1980). *English social history.* London: Penguin.

Trinterud, L. (1951). The origins of Puritanism. *Church History, 20,* 37–57.

Trost, K. (2009). Psst, have you ever cheated? A study of academic dishonesty in Sweden. *Assessment and Evaluation in Higher Education, 34,* 367–376.

Tucker, V. (Ed.). (1997). *Cultural perspectives on development.* London: Frank Cass.

Turner, V. (1969). *The ritual process: Structure and anti-structure.* New York: Aldine de Gruyter.

Vince, R. (2004). Action learning and organizational learning: Power, politics and emotion in organizations. *Action Learning: Research and Practice, 1,* 63–78.

Vivanathan, S., & Sethi, H. (1998). By way of a beginning. In S. Vivanathan & H. Sethi (Eds.), *Foul play: Chronicles of corruption 1947–97.* New Delhi: Banyan Books.

von Mises, L. (1944). *Bureaucracy.* New Haven: Yale University Press.

Wade, R. (1990). *Governing the market: Economic theory and the role of government in East Asian industrialization.* New Jersey: Princeton University Press.

Waldo, D. (1956). *Perspectives on administration.* Alabama: University of Alabama Press.

Walker, C. (1931). The history of the joint stock company. *The Accounting Review, 6,* 97–105.

Wallerstein, I. (1974/1980). *The modern world-system* (Vols. 1 and 2). New York: Academic Press.

Wang, G. W. (1995). *The Chinese way: China's position in international relations. Nobel Institute Lecture Series.* Oslo: Scandinavian University Press.

Weber, M. (1997). Bureaucracy. In H. H. Gerth & C. Wright Mills (Eds. & Trans.), *From Max Weber: Essays in sociology* (pp. 196–244). London: Routledge.

Weber, M. (2003). *General economic history* (F. Knight, Trans). New York: Dover.

Weiss, L. (2000). Developmental states in transition: Adapting, dismantling, innovating, not normalizing. *Pacific Review, 13,* 21–55.

Wenke, R. (1989). Egypt: Origins of complex societies. *Annual Review of Anthropology, 18,* 129–155.

White, K. D. (1967). Gallo-Roman harvesting machines. *Latomus, 26,* 634–647.

Whyte, W. (1948). *Human relations in the restaurant industry.* New York: McGraw-Hill.

Wieck, K. (1995). *Sensemaking in organizations.* Thousand Oaks: Sage.

Williams, C., & Nadin, S. (2013). Harnessing the hidden enterprise culture: Supporting the formalization of off-the-books business start-ups. *Journal of Small Business and Enterprise Development, 20,* 434–447.

Williamson, O. (1975). *Markets and hierarchies: Analysis and antitrust implications.* New York: Free Press.

Williamson, O. (1985). *The economic institutions of capitalism.* New York: Free Press.

Wilson, D. (1981). Of maize and men: A critique of the maritime hypothesis of state origins on the coast of Peru. *American Anthropologist, 83,* 93–120.

Wilson, G., & Wilson, M. (1945). *The analysis of social change.* Cambridge: Cambridge University Press.

Wittfogel, K. (1957). *Oriental despotism.* New Haven: Yale University Press.

Wolkersdorfer, G. (1999). Karl Haushofer and geopolitics—The history of a German mythos. *Geopolitics, 4,* 145–160.

Wood, P. (2014). Teacher professionalism: Subverting the society of control. *Forum, 56,* 223–234.

Woodcroft, B. (1854). *Titles of patents of invention chronologically arranged.* London: Queen's Printing Office.

Worsley, P. (1978). *The third world.* London: Weidenfeld and Nicolson.

Wright, F. (1917). Roman factories. *The Classical Weekly, 11,* 17–19.

Wright, H. (1977). Origin of the state. *Annual Review Anthropology, 6,* 379–397.

Wright, H. (2006). Early state dynamics as political experiment. *Journal of Anthropological Research, 62,* 305–319.

Wright, H., & Johnson, G. (1975). Population, exchange, and early state formation in southwestern Iran. *American Anthropologist, 77,* 267–289.

Wurtele, S., Simons, D., & Moreno, T. (2014). Sexual interest in children among an online sample of men and women: Prevalence and correlates. *Sexual Abuse: A Journal of Research and Treatment, 26,* 546–568.

Yamamura, K. (1973). The development of *za* in medieval Japan. *Business History Review, 47,* 438–465.

Yang, M. (1994). *Gifts, favors and banquets: The art of social relationships in China.* Ithaca: Cornell University Press.

Yang, M. (2000). Putting global capitalism in its place: Economic hybridism, bataille and ritual expenditure. *Current Anthropology, 41,* 477–509.

Yang, M. (2002). The resilience of *guanxi* and its new deployments: A critique of some new *guanxi'* scholarship. *China Quarterly, 170,* 459–476.

Yao, S. C. (2002). *Confucian capitalism: Discourse, practice and the myth of Chinese enterprise.* London and New York: Routledge-Curzon.

Yao, Y., & Yueh, L. (2009). Law, finance and economic growth in China: An introduction. *World Development, 37,* 753–762.

Yates, J., Davis, J., & Glick, H. (2001). The politics of torts: Explaining litigation rates in the American states. *State Politics and Policy Quarterly, 1,* 127–143.

Yates, J., Tanklersley, H., & Brace, P. (2010). Assessing the impact of state judicial structures on citizen litigiousness. *Political Research Quarterly, 63,* 796–810.

Zapf, D., & Holz, M. (2006). On the positive and negative effects of emotion work in organizations. *European Journal of Work and Organizational Psychology, 15,* 1–28.

Zheng, H. X., Yan, S., Qin, Z. D., & Jin, L. (2012). MtDNA analysis of global populations support that major population expansions began before Neolithic time. *Scientific Reports.* https://doi.org/10.1038/srep00745.

Zinn, D. (2001). *La Racconandazzione: clientelismo vecchio e nouvo.* Roma: Donzelli.

Zucker, L. (1987). Institutional theories of organization. *Annual Review of Sociology, 13,* 443–464.

Printed by Printforce, the Netherlands